Education Reform

Confronting the Secular Ideal

Education Reform

Confronting the Secular Ideal

Craig S. Engelhardt

*Society for the Advancement of Christian Education
(SACE)*

INFORMATION AGE PUBLISHING, INC.
Charlotte, NC • www.infoagepub.com

Library of Congress Cataloging-in-Publication Data

A CIP record for this book is available from the Library of Congress
http://www.loc.gov

ISBN: 978-1-62396-322-4 (Paperback)
         978-1-62396-323-1 (Hardcover)
         978-1-62396-324-8 (ebook)

I dedicate this book to all those who have labored to preserve religious schooling against the tide of secularism and also to those who will invest to recover America's public education efforts from the hollowness of the "secular ideal."

Craig S. Engelhardt

Contents

Preface

America seeks to reform public education to address deepening human, social, and intellectual needs, but *Education Reform* argues that current pursuits are inadequate. Charting new territory, this book looks deeply into the philosophical nature of education to challenge traditional distinctions between private and public education models. It reveals "secular education" as a failed ideal and certain versions of school choice as uncertainties. While many propose reform within the secular paradigm, few identify the paradigm itself as the source of our nation's educational woes. *Education Reform* shows how the "secular ideal" strips education of needed meaning, morality, and intellectual depth. The remedy? Dr. Engelhardt proposes a radical shift from a "secular" to a "plural" public education paradigm, which allows for the reconnection of education with meaningful ideological roots in a manner that addresses the concerns of individual families and the public.

The argument of this book is developed in three parts: an analysis of education history to discern the relationship between ideological beliefs and the public's education goals, a critical discussion of the fears and concerns associated with religious schooling, and an exploration of the public benefits associated with ideologically based education. *Education Reform* ends by proposing a philosophical and structural model of an American plural public education system that allows the public to draw from the strengths of religious schools while insuring the public's education interests. *Education Reform* is a pivotal book that aims not only to strengthen public education but also to further the American democratic experiment. This is a pivotal read for education scholars, reformers, and concerned citizens alike.

Foreword

Craig S. Engelhardt's book, *Education Reform: Confronting the Secular Ideal*, is a powerful and timely book that will cause any person with an open mind to reconsider a faith-based rubric of public education. Dr. Engelhardt makes an excellent argument supporting the notion that America's public schools have become "myopic." He asserts that the major problem with public schools is that they are "secular" and that as long as that is so, these "common schools" are ill-equipped to prepare children to be civic-minded and moral individuals. One of the most remarkable aspects of his book is the way he frames his argument. He does not merely assert that the option is between choice and no choice, but instead presents a contrast between common versus plural visions of education. Moreover, Dr. Engelhardt declares, "The secular education paradigm not only limits the moral nurture of students, but it limits the academic program as well." Dr. Engelhardt avers that the secular system lacks the moral compass and fortitude that is needed to spawn an ethic of character and discipline that is necessary for public health. Academically, he affirms that learning is inspired when it is presented within a meaningful worldview, and reason is sharpened when grounded upon coherent conceptions of truth—neither of which can be satisfactorily accomplished within secular educational paradigms.

Dr. Engelhardt rightly claims that a plethora of the problems that America's children and adults face today originates with the fact that public educators have eschewed the more plural model on which this nation was founded and instead have chosen a narrow secular model that claims to be neutral. However, in reality, this secular model overlooks most of the claims

Education Reform, pages xv–xiii
Copyright © 2013 by Information Age Publishing
All rights of reproduction in any form reserved.

that religious groups place upon the education day. He notes that, "Public education's diminished concern regarding the holistic nurture of the child betrays both the public's moral and academic concerns." Dr. Engelhardt then launches a historical analysis of the role of religion in public education followed by a critique of contemporary concerns opposing religious schooling. In the second half of the book, Dr. Engelhardt seeks to allay the concerns of some who believe that an inclusion of religious schools within a plural system of public education would oppose the best interests of the public.

As the reader peruses this book, that person will discover that Dr. Engelhardt not only gives a thoughtful overview of the secular versus plural perspectives of education but also periodically presents some profound statements that warrant remembrance. For example, Dr. Engelhardt states, "Both the culture and the paradigm of the common public school tends to hear or consider only concerns that pass the filter of 'secular.'" Dr. Engelhardt offers a compelling argument via both direct and subtler means that, to the detriment of liberal society, government throughout much of the 19th and 20th centuries has sought to replace the authority of parents with the mandates and even the oppression of the state.

Beyond Dr. Engelhardt's historical and philosophical overview, he presents answers that indicate that religious schools can do a far better job of accomplishing the goals of teaching tolerance, instilling morality, and enhancing achievement than secular public schools can. For example, Dr. Engelhardt presents Abraham Kuyper, Prime Minister of the Netherlands from 1901 to 1905, as an example of a successful leader who affirmed the saliency of a plural approach to education that emphasized diverse religious schools funded with public money.

Dr. Engelhardt does a wonderful job of tracing how this tainted evolution from a religious to a secular educational orientation took place in a nation that was largely very Judeo-Christian based. He reviews a gamut of issues along these lines involving historic prejudices, public philosophies, judicial interpretations, religious beliefs, and academic presumptions. Dr. Engelhardt addresses the philosophies of John Dewey, Mortimer Adler, and secular textbooks. He also persuasively argues that schools with religious orientations can be a better support to the public's educational interests and asserts that allowing a more plural perspective is not only a rubric that needs to be encouraged but is really the only viable alternative to the present monolithic secular system. Whatever one's perspective, Dr. Engelhardt's perspectives are worthy of one's attention and explicate well the views of a growing number of Americans who believe that the nation is paying a price for its emphasis on secular education, its ostentatious embracing of relativism, and its aversion to truth. Dr. Engelhardt makes an academically passionate plea for reform that is really a call for the American educational community to again enter the realm of true religious tolerance, values, intellectual foundations, the development of the whole child, and yes, sanity.

—William H. Jeynes
Senior Fellow, Witherspoon Institute, Princeton, New Jersey
Professor, California State University, Long Beach

Introduction

Common Education's Systemic Flaw

The success of America's public education system is less than stellar. It is failing to meet its obligations to the public. Whereas our schools were at one time shaped by high human and civic ideals, under the shaping force of the common education paradigm, public education is now molded merely by test scores and the most basic civic concerns. In response, scholars, politicians, and the public propose solutions in the form of testing, accountability, pedagogy, school climate, and school choice. However, most of these solutions merely rearrange, revise, or reemphasize accepted public education practices. Only the latter challenges some of the basic assumptions of public education. If we are looking for fundamental improvement, perhaps the potentially radical restructuring of school choice holds our best hope for change.

I support the school choice movement, but challenge it to more deeply engage questions related to the public's educational interests and the nature of a good education (see Null, 2011, pp. 53–56). School choice proponents believe that parents will "know a good education when they see it." However, without revisiting the premises of a "good education," without deeper philosophic analysis, it is possible that the school choice movement will produce schools that look little different from familiar "successful" public schools in suburban America. Most parents and education leaders would likely consider this a positive outcome, but I believe "choice" has more to offer. I believe our nation's educational vision is myopic. We strive for aca-

Education Reform, pages xix–xxiii
Copyright © 2013 by Information Age Publishing

demic proficiency while our public schools fail to nurture young men and women with the wisdom, insight, personal inspiration, creativity, compassion, and character required for a flourishing democratic society—qualities difficult to address meaningfully even in today's best public schools.

The school choice movement currently offers insight regarding the weaknesses of bureaucratic control, the possible misuse of unionized power, the questionable value of standardization, and the motivational spark that is lit when families make their own educational choices. However, too many in the movement seem satisfied with a choice among secular schools when, as this book argues, the benefits of choice will be most apparent when publicly supportive religious schools are equally included as "choice" options. A recent article by Cooper, McSween, and Murphy (2012) documents how school choice is blurring the lines between private and public schooling. Though school choice is moving education in a positive direction, America's public education system reflects a systemic flaw that tends to limit the vision of the school choice movement as well as proposals of virtually all other public education leaders.

If correction of the flaw promised few positive outcomes, the educational restructuring associated with the correction would be too great to consider. However, the individual and social ramifications associated with a public education system revised to correct this flaw are many and promise to reinvigorate our schools and society.

So, what is this systemic flaw? The flaw is that public education is "common" or "secular." Reflecting the philosophic mindset that shaped America's public schools in the early 20th century, public schools attempt to nurture children toward good American and global citizenship without helping to build the primary philosophic foundations of beliefs and values upon which humans learn and grow. If public education is about nurturing good people as well as good test scores, a secular system is ill-equipped.

In noncommon or "religious" settings, parents and teachers not only have greater freedoms to nurture specific religious beliefs and traditions, but to shape the entire course of education to reflect the highest values, beliefs, and aspirations of their home and community. Could the ideological "commonness" of public schooling be working *against* public education efforts to nurture good Americans? Though public schools are well intentioned, a recent review "of social studies curricula found that they...had little effect on students' civic commitments, either in terms of attitudes or behaviors" (Kunzman, 2006, p. 141). If religious school settings provide greater opportunities to transmit the high ideals of humanity, could it be both possible and beneficial to the nation to reshape public education to draw from the strengths of religious schooling?

━━━
Common vs. Plural Public Education

Since the landmark case *Pierce v. Society of Sisters* (1925), the U.S. Supreme Court has supported the right of parents to select the educational philosophy of the schools their children attend. However, America's current public education funding systems, which generally exclude religious schools, discourage this choice. Yet it was not always so. Historically, American public education has followed two basic paradigms: either one of "plural education" or one of "common education." Plural public education systems, widespread in Europe, Canada, and Australia, fund schools of varying religious perspectives and regulate them to accommodate the public's educational goals. Common public education systems, on the other hand, attempt to address education goals from "noncontroversial" or "secular" perspectives. As one might expect, the wedge that separates the two paradigms is the role and place of foundational philosophic beliefs—"religion"—in the classroom.

Early American families and education leaders supported the educational relevance of religion, so they founded diverse religious schools in which the core beliefs and values of attending families shaped the educational philosophy and curriculum. They held that an education deeply contextualized in the beliefs and values of most American homes was not only the best nurture of the individual for life, but also the best nurture for a reasonable, reflective, and moral citizenry. Later, 20th-century supporters of the common paradigm of education believed that moral and civic identity were better shaped by reason than by religion, and that "common" classrooms would promote harmony between the diverse philosophic threads of the social fabric.

Proponents of both plural and common education paradigms must address the relevance of religion to educational goals, particularly the *public's* educational goals. Is religion merely a private matter, a subject for possible classroom study, or does it have broader educational relevance? Should religious motivations, perspectives, and values shape the school day, or do they weaken a good education and ultimately the nation? Can a secular state legitimately involve itself with religious schools, or is the entanglement inevitably too great? Whereas proponents of common education must defend the irrelevance or harm of religious schools to public education interests in a manner that recognizes individual religious liberties, proponents of plural systems of public education must defend the general value of religious schools to the public and provide a regulatory system that avoids entanglement.

American colonists, founders, and first-generation citizens considered little beyond the plural education model. However, once the contentious move to common education was settled in all states, relatively few Americans considered little beyond the common public education model that endures to the present.

Weaknesses of the Secular Education Paradigm

Though enshrouded with hope, the common education model has been a pauper dressed in fine clothes; while making promises that come and go with the decades, it lacks the resources to deliver upon its obligations to the public. For over half a century, parents, politicians, and scholars alike have recognized public education's shortcomings. Although many parents have found satisfaction by moving their children to religious schools, most scholars and politicians continue to attempt to strengthen public education with remedies drawn merely from within the secular education paradigm. Though school choice proposals occasionally include religious schools, these proposals generally gain their strength from the recognized failure of *particular* public schools rather than from the general public benefit associated with greater religious school attendance.

Some may argue that we already have a plural public education system because families have long been free to attend religious schools at their own expense. This may be true, but the "religious" choice is discouraged by our education funding system. A plural *public* education system would make the choice of secular vs. religious schools more one of family philosophy rather than family finances or public preference. If religious educational settings can be shown to strengthen the public's educational goals, then America holds a virtually untapped resource. With perhaps the richest and most vibrant religious traditions of any nation, an American version of a plural public education system would open entirely new ground for educational research, accountability, and evaluation. This new paradigm would not eliminate education problems, and it would surely create new ones, but within religious settings, educators could bring needed meaning, understanding, and motivation to the school day by drawing with conviction from the philosophic roots of knowledge, morality, motivation, civilization, and progress—roots that secular schools generally avoid.

Some may argue that religious schools have been studied, and there is no evidence that mixing religion and education will revitalize public education. However, this conclusion is premature based upon the fact that these studies (many of which have been conducted to test the efficacy of school choice initiatives) have generally evaluated religious schools using a secular education paradigm. In other words, these studies generally looked only at school qualities (like test scores) that fit under the secular education umbrella. I argue that the paradigm is too narrow and therefore these studies (most of which find little to criticize regarding religious schools academically or otherwise) give us little insight into the relationship between religion and education. This is the goal of this book.

The Public's Educational Interests

Carl Kaestle (1983) argues that public schools have been considered the "pillars" of our nation. They were entrusted with the mission of nurturing children not only with academic knowledge, but also with the moral and intellectual qualities considered necessary for the peace and prosperity of society. Contemporary discussions associated with such things as health care, lifestyle, corporate investment policy, marriage, environmental responsibility, poverty, and foreign policy provide examples of the moral and philosophic nature of civic life. Academic knowledge that enables one to participate and "succeed" in American life is not enough; good citizens must have informed moral and philosophic understandings that engage the many aspects of society. However, understanding and knowledge alone are also insufficient; the well-being of society also relies upon the character strength of its members to act in accordance with their understanding.

The public interests associated with the moral and philosophic nurture of children to engage these and other civic issues of everyday life may be considered to reflect both academic and "human" concerns. Fortunately, in addition to desiring to administer an academic curriculum, many teachers are drawn to the field of education with a desire to deeply nurture growing children and young adults. Unfortunately, the depth of the nurture these teachers may offer is severely limited by policy and law that prevent public employees, while on the job, from advocating beliefs, actions, perspectives, or values that strongly reflect a religious perspective. Teachers can tell children they are valuable, but they cannot address the "Truths" that they believe underlie that value; they can advocate for peace and forgiveness between feuding teens, but they cannot draw motivating power from religious beliefs that might provide the strength to "turn the other cheek."

Most parents are likely glad that church/state separation prevents their children's teachers from using their public positions to pass on their religious beliefs, but this satisfaction is linked to the inability of public school parents to choose the worldview of their child's teacher. If this choice were provided, most parents would likely prefer to send their children to schools in which the teachers reinforced the beliefs and values of the home rather than ignoring them. Thus, parental choice must be a part of a plural public education system that naturally draws from the religious perspectives attending families.

The secular education paradigm not only limits the moral nurture of students, but it limits the academic program as well. Without a deeper context of meaning and relevance, subject matter is more apt to become dull and uninspiring. Since much of one's overall vision for learning draws strength from one's understanding regarding the "religious" questions of life, secular classrooms are forced to draw out student motivation merely through immediate rewards and punishments or the distant goal of "getting a good job." When classrooms actively engage questions such as "Who am I?" "What is my purpose?" "What is valuable as a life pursuit?" and "What are the foundational principles and purposes of life, society, and my coursework?" they not only unlock the possibility of inspiring children at a deeper level, but they place subject matter in a meaningful context. Surely, parents are the primary ones to address these questions, but to ignore them in the educational setting removes much of the substance of both the academic and the human preparation of our nation's citizens.

Thus, although the public is *very* interested in citizens who are compassionate, philosophically astute, productive, honest, law abiding, relationally stable, civically involved, and environmentally aware, academic and human nurture are so laden with "religious" beliefs and grounds, that public common schools can address these concerns utilizing only common (rather than the most compelling) moral precepts and reasoning. While our public stability and prosperity remain indebted to the nurture of a wise and moral citizenry, our secular model of public education hampers schools from deeply addressing these concerns. Thus, public schools are rarely evaluated by the human qualities or depth of philosophic reflection they advance; rather, standardized academic test scores are utilized as virtually the sole criteria of public school success.

American public education began with primary concerns toward the nurture of the moral and intellectual qualities associated with good people and good citizens; these concerns were greater than concerns toward the teaching of academics and job skills. Though these concerns overlap, the first are more holistic and enshrouded in religious perspective. While the explosion of knowledge that began in the latter quarter of the 19th century raised the priority of academic knowledge and market skills, it did not diminish concerns related to the former. Parents and the civically minded called for schools that would nurture young people to be good as well as knowledgeable and skilled. Public education's diminished concern regarding the holistic nurture of the child betrays both the public's moral and academic concerns. As a nation, we did not merely choose to weaken public education by selecting a narrow academic focus; we arrived here incrementally by following the common education paradigm. As with the proverbial frog in a pot made to boil, gradual change over the passage of time deadened our national senses and memories as to the holistic concerns that a good education traditionally addressed.

Public education leaders may also dismiss religious education by insisting that America's "separation of church and state" prohibits common public schools from promoting a religious perspective and thereby addressing the human concerns I speak of. However, this is a conditional truth. It is true that public employees cannot advocate a religious perspective, and public money cannot *directly* support or discriminate between religious perspectives, but religious schools may constitutionally receive *indirect* public money through certain voucher or tax-credit programs, and public school personnel need not be employees of the state (more on this later). The will to improve public education exists at local, state, and national levels, but "will" alone is insufficient if the goals of public education require "tools of nurture" that reside beyond the legal boundaries that constrain the secular education paradigm.

As a priority, public schools should be structured to serve the public's educational interests. If laws obstruct these interests, no tradition, structure, interest group, or temporary inefficiency associated with change should be allowed to impede the reformulation of public education to achieve the broad goals for which it was founded. This book will demonstrate, in short, that child and youth education is, by nature, a "religious" endeavor that socially diverse democratic societies can address adequately only within a plural public educational paradigm.

Overview of Chapters

The following pages contain an investigation into the philosophies, claims, and relative successes of plural and common educational paradigms from the American experience. Though no one has yet provided an effective challenge to our current educational paradigm, this book will attempt to do so. It will offer evidence that, while public education is intrinsically religious, the secular education model has become a pillar of American society. And it became this pillar less because of its successful nurture of the American citizenry than because of religious ignorance, unforeseen developments in church/state legal understanding, the philosophic climate of modernity, and finally, because of the entrenchments of bureaucracy, unionization, and tradition.

I will present this argument through a historical analysis of the role of religion in public education followed by a critique of contemporary concerns opposing religious schooling. The historical analysis will show that the civic nurture of students is most effective when it engages their worldviews and shapes the education day around a meaningful religious perspective. The analysis of the second half of the book will address the concerns of those who seem to believe that the inclusion of religious schools within a system of public funding would oppose the best interests of the public. I will conclude with a discussion of the strengths of religious education and a description of a proposed plural public education system that recognizes and protects the interests of attending families and the public.

In greater detail, Chapter 1 provides a historical and philosophic setting, defines the nature and power of "religion" as it will be addressed throughout this book, and presents an overview of concerns regarding religious schooling. Chapter 2 defines the historic philosophy and vision of the public common school model, its eventual acceptance by some and rejection by others, and an analysis of the effectiveness of its moral, civic, and academic programs in relationship to its secularizing trajectory. These serve to illustrate that public education's civic success is not only dependent upon its degree of acceptance by religious people, but also upon the degree to which it is empowered by accepted religious themes. Additionally, the chapter demonstrates that those viewed as most in need of Americanization frequently reject public common education on religious grounds. Summarily, the common education model is the cause of many education problems as growing diversity forces educators to avoid utilizing the religious themes that public education once meaningfully engaged.

Chapters 3 and 4 will analyze the results associated with the implementation of "scientifically based" or "reason-based" moral and civic education programs within the context of modernity's and postmodernity's increased disengagement with traditional religious views. To conduct this analysis, I show that most citizens accepted the scientific paradigm of education because it found general accommodation within their faiths, fit the needs of a diversifying society, and became the only option allowed by law for public schools. However, I will show that religion still played a role in schools. Believers rejected "false" claims, disconnected from many public education efforts, or left the public schools, while education theorists often drew from religious views for their ideas. Despite its broad acceptance, the secular paradigm did not demonstrate particular success as a foundation for moral and civic nurture.

The history section concludes by noting that contemporary public schools (separated from comprehensive conceptions of truth) maintain the mission to unify, academically prepare, and morally nurture the next generation; but they have little evidential support for their success while remaining sources of civic division for many individuals and groups. Summarily, the study of 20th-century education will show that secularized moral and civic curricula were often controversial and unsatisfactory as they less directly engaged religious frames of reference as sources of meaning, value, and motivation.

Moving from a historical analysis of the role of religion in public education, Chapters 5 and 6 engage and refute the concerns of those who might oppose a plural public education system. The concerns addressed include liberal autonomy, democratic autonomy, deliberative democracy, educational equity, religious social division, and the adequacy of common education to engage religious beliefs. While these discussions serve to weaken arguments opposing a plural public education system, Chapter 7 provides compelling reasons for the acceptance of religious schooling in spite of the uncertainties of change. These reasons will build upon the evidence and rationales of the history chapters. They show that religious schools represent a public educational asset because they provide superior settings for "traditional" education, superior sources of grounded moral education, means to nurture strong civic character, resources to close the achievement gap and revitalize impoverished communities, resources to build social capital and restore public meaning, secure ideological foundations for the state, and resources to advance public unity. Finally, Chapter 8 concludes with a presentation and defense of a plural public education model to end our nation's singular support for—and failed experiment with—the paradigm of secular public education.

In the pages to come, I hope to illuminate and untangle the American educational journey as an experiment regarding the religious nature of both education and the public's educational interests. I will confront the public's secular education ideal and propose the ideal of plural public education. As the journey proceeds, it will reveal that the grounds upon which the secular model of public education stands are not as solid as our enduring commitment to it seems to reflect. Let us begin by attempting to understand the religious nature of education—yes, even public education.

1

Public Education's Perspectives and Concerns

If the United States accepts my assertion that public education would be stronger built upon a plural rather than a common education model, a vast reconstruction of the system would follow. The move implies foundational revisions regarding education authority, reflective redefinition of the goals of public education, review of state and local school organizations, and modification of the educational relationship between religious groups and the state. It implies a broadening of educational research, the rewriting of curriculum from multiple worldview perspectives, and new public regulatory structures. Since the issue is weighty and has far-reaching ramifications, it should not be considered lightly.

So much of my discussion uses the language of religion, morality, and civic development; I fear that readers might presume this book to be relevant only to those in curricular fields of civics or social studies. This is not so. A religious paradigm of education has philosophic and procedural implications for every facet of education from administration to art. Evaluat-

Education Reform, pages 1–23
Copyright © 2013 by Information Age Publishing
All rights of reproduction in any form reserved.

ing the common (or secular) model of public education in contrast with a plural (or religious) model of public education is an extensive undertaking that requires broad academic evaluation even when the specific topics of discussions become narrow. Not only is the civics teacher interested in the nature of "civic education," but so also is the political philosopher, the sociologist, the priest, the parent, and the public. Also, since the nature, goals, structure, and representative interests of public education extend beyond the academic, so must also the discussion.

This first chapter will provide an overview of some of the central perspectives and representative concerns that inform the educational paradigms that I challenge and propose. Each of these perspectives will speak to the widely recognized tenet that the liberal state has valid concerns related to the education of children associated with the civic health of the polity and the personal well-being of each individual. With little surprise, attempts to define the character, knowledge, and moral needs of the state vary widely and imply differing educational paradigms for their support. Broadly, the discussions I will include focus on (a) the needs of the democratic state to have an educated citizenry, (b) differing views of education based on the nature of the student, and (c) democratic concerns that every child receive an equal, quality education.

As I proceed, I emphasize that these discussions *should* reflect the limited interests of the state. Parents and children also have valid interests related to education that are obviously not set aside merely because their school is funded by the state. The public education endeavor within the liberal state is truly a conscientious and reasoned blending of concerns for the good of all.

Public and Scholarly Discussions

An Educated Citizenry

Public education grew largely out of the concern that the freedom under America's representative democracy required an educated citizenry. Expressed succinctly by Thomas Jefferson in 1816, "If a nation expects to be ignorant and free, in a state of civilization, it expects what never was and never will be." Thus, scholars from a perspective of political philosophy speak into the discussion of how the public should be educated. Today, though the content of the academic curriculum generates intermittent discussions regarding the "truths" public schools can/should espouse (especially in the sciences), the moral perspective of public education draws the greatest focus because morality is so deeply linked with diverse religious perspectives. Agreeing that our political structure is indebted to public education for both academic and moral instruction, scholars address the conflicts over the religious nature of morals and truth in several ways. Some begin within the secular education paradigm and discuss the ideological limits of what the state can espouse, while others argue as to which education model they perceive to provide the best philosophical nurture for the nations peoples.

Just Schools and Civil Discourse

John Rawls (1971, 1996, 1999, 2001) spoke to the issue of what the state, and thus state schools, can advocate. In the name of justice, he argued that public schools should not represent or condone particular comprehensive views. Those who take this position believe that public schools may only utilize secular grounds for the moral and civic nurture of students. However, from a different perspective, some claim that the act of avoiding religious grounds can pose its own injustice. Scholars such as Michael McConnell (2002) argue that secular curricula can inadvertently advocate their own comprehensive views. He notes that when secular schools avoid discussions of a religious nature, they tacitly imply that religious teachings are either not "true" or they are irrelevant to learning and public life. In other words, secular education seems to run the danger of *opposing* religion regardless of well-intended attempts at neutrality. Overlooking this latter concern, there is general agreement that public common schools should not teach from a particular religious perspective.

Though I believe McConnell's concern is worthy of greater attention, my particular concern regards the best role for religion in public education. There is little argument as to the value of teaching *about* religion from a secular academic perspective, but there is strong disagreement as to whether teaching *from* a religious perspective supports or opposes the health of our polity. Stephen Macedo (1991, 1995, 2000, 2005; Macedo & Tamir, 2002), Robert Audi (1997, 2000, 2001; Audi & Wolterstorff, 1997), Will Kymlicka (2001; Kymlicka & Norman, 2000), and Amy Gutmann (1999; Gutmann & Thompson, 1996, 2004) seem generally opposed to a move from a common to a plural public education system. They're writings seem to affirm that public education *should not* be built upon comprehensive views because this would largely separate students into schools according to family beliefs. This in turn would undermine public education's vital efforts to bring the diverse sectors of society together and to teach democratic values and skills. They argue that the common education paradigm uniquely enables citizens of differing values and beliefs to learn to reason respectfully with others in civil discourse. Religious schools, on the other hand, are feared to be sources of public division wherein children are indoctrinated to view things rigidly from only one perspective of truth. They believe secular public schools have a positive civic influence upon children unavailable in religious school settings. In particular, Amy Gutmann and Dennis Thompson (2004), leading proponents of what they term *Democratic Education*, define their concerns toward a polity built upon discursive resolution rather than the politics of majoritarian rule favored by proceduralists. They fear that without greater philosophical resolution born of deliberation, the growing diversity of our society will undermine its stability.

Central to Gutmann and Thompson's conception of public deliberation is that grounds of reason must be accessible to all. They write, "Most fundamentally, deliberative democracy affirms the need to justify decisions made by citizens and their representatives.... Its first and most important characteristic, then is its *reason-giving* requirement" (2004, p. 3, emphasis in the original). They argue that public deliberation requires the exchange of reasons that

> appeal to principles that individuals who are trying to find fair terms of cooperation cannot reasonably reject... reasons that should be accepted by free and equal persons seeking fair terms of cooperation.... It would not be acceptable, for example, to appeal only to the authority of revelation. (2004, p. 3)

As a vital support to national unity, Gutmann and Thompson argue that public justice and peace are indebted to the formative growth that comes from deliberation within common school settings.

Gutmann and Thompson's (2004) concern regarding the secular nature of public deliberation and justifications is not unique. Political scholars Stephen Macedo, Robert Audi, and others also maintain that political discussion in the public sphere should be free of religious grounding. Robert Audi argues that within a pluralistic society, legal coercion should be based upon publicly accessible reasons (2000, p. 30). Society's laws should coerce only in areas in which the rational person would act if properly informed. Thus, children should be taught to use public secular reasoning and to advance coercive measures on the public only when one's secular motivations are high enough to move other citizens (Audi, 1993, p. 691). Scholars who hold these views tend to oppose schools with religious orientations because they are likely to be ill-equipped to nurture these skills of civic discourse or to reject them outright.

Other scholars do not agree. While this manner of reasoning seems to support the current secular nature of public education, it is not evident that secular public reasoning is necessary or even humanly possible. Gerald Gaus argues that this kind of speech is difficult both to define and to achieve (2003, p. 210). It requires that one presume to know what is acceptable to others and seems to limit society from aspiring to higher-than-common ideals. Education scholar Elmer Thiessen also rejects secular concepts of public reason because of how they constrain the individual. Not only do some scholars question that these universal reasons exist, but he writes, "Civic education based only on public reasonableness further requires a kind of intellectual schizophrenia from students and teachers. It forces them to leave behind their most cherished beliefs in public discussions" (1995, p. 5).

The idea of secular reason is built upon the presumption that we can readily identify "generic human beliefs and values." Perhaps this is a holdover from modernity's overzealous dismissal of religious thought and overconfident trust in human reason. Postmodern scholarship points to the ideological nature of reason. No one enters a discussion without a set of preconceived beliefs about the world that they are often unaware of. Individuals within a culture are shaped to some degree by the religious foundations of the culture—even the "unbelievers." Thus, it is only marginally possible to discern secular reasons from religious ones. In fact, the effort may lead a nonreligious person to support an idea as secular while a religious person holds back that same idea because they understand its religious roots.

Scholar Christopher Eberle (2002) also rejects the claim that good citizens should sensor their religious reasons in public discussions. The doctrine not only assumes that people can reach neutral public decisions that are empirical and free from "irrational beliefs," but it also arbitrarily assumes secular reasons are more "right" than religious ones. Scholar Paul Weithman (2002) notes that the requirement of public reason is a point of division for those who do not accept the tenet, and scholar Kent Greenawalt (1995) argues that liberalism allows for different viewpoints, and only individuals can weigh the value of their reasons (religious or otherwise) regarding their public concerns.

Finding the overlap of secular public perspectives to be narrower and shallower than many suppose, political scientist William Galston advocates that neutral government has greater limits than previously presumed and that liberal society should provide a wider place for ideological views. He argues that "a liberal polity guided by a commitment to moral and political pluralism ... will be cautious in interfering with civil associations" (2002, p. 20). He develops the insight that the diversity and autonomy often linked to liberalism may be opposed to the current common education vision. State-enforced diversity within the public schools tends to create an amalgam that in effect destroys diversity. Thus, a true respect for diversity allows distinct groups to flourish apart from state manipulation. Summarily, Galston writes, a "liberal pluralist society will organize itself around principles of maximum feasible accommodation of diverse legitimate ways of life, limited only by the minimum requirements of civic unity" (2002, p. 119). Whereas Gutmann and Thompson's (2004) concerns would standardize all education according to a democratically chosen model, Galston argues that democracy should not be used to oppose our diversity.

Though Galston (1991, 2002, 2004) says little directly concerning plural public education, his writings provide a productive and conscientious model for addressing the conflicting ideological issues associated with education within the liberal democratic tradition. Galston not only views many of the conflicts of pluralism as being too deep for resolution, but he maintains that liberalism supports a wide sphere of individual liberty into which many public educational concerns can fit. He says,

> The state must be parsimonious in defining the realm in which uniformity must be secured through coercion. An educational program based on an expansive and contestable definition of good citizenship or civic unity will not ordinarily justify the forcible suppression of expressive liberty. (2004, p. 109)

Addressing the issue of national unity, scholars such as Peter Berkowitz (2003), Michael Sandel (2002), and Kent Greenawalt (1995) claim that individual and societal wholeness is dependent upon the transmission of cultural understanding from one generation to the next. Some of these supporters advocate that religious beliefs provide a resource for the advance and the critique of the liberal tradition. They question whether the curriculum that remains after passing through common education filters of justice is substantive enough to provide a foundation for public life. Without the formative understanding that religious schools provide, public schools are less likely to reproduce the civic qualities America needs. Like Galston (2002) above, their concerns support the idea that philosophically diverse religious schools may be vital to the health of liberal polity.

Other scholars find other substantive reasons as to why our current paradigm of public education fails to adequately address our nation's civic concerns. Charles L. Glenn (1989, 2005, 2011; Glenn & Cook, 2004; Glenn & de Groof, 2002) has written widely regarding not only the successes of plural public education systems but on what he considers false claims regarding the "commonness" or neutrality of public schools and their effectiveness as a source of public unity. Also, James Carper and Thomas Hunt

(2007; Hunt & Carper, 1997) articulate the histories of many groups who have been marginalized by the common school system. Together, their works help to raise awareness that common education has its "victims" and that articulating a "state interest" should not be done lightly in an arena that touches deeply on the conscientious concerns of America's citizens.

The Nature of the Student

Moving from perspectives associated with justice, public discourse, and public unity, scholars debate the nature and role of autonomy and authority in the classroom. Whereas some scholars argue both the dignity of the individual as well as the good of the public rely on treating children as morally and intellectually autonomous, others disagree. Whereas the former believe teachers should *minimally* influence the moral and ideological perspectives of children, the latter argue that children are born *to a future* state of autonomy as they mature in knowledge, reason, and experience. Both the good of the child and the good of society are advanced when adults consciously attempt to pass on the wisdom gained from their generation's learning and experience to the next. Thus religious schools, taught by caring adults, help students to mature morally and ideologically in ways that secular schools cannot.

Reflecting the concerns of the first group, many contemporary scholars address the role of religion in public education from a liberal philosophic perspective that grew out of the writings of Immanuel Kant (1724–1804) and similarly expressed by others. Though Kant (1785) argued for a universal moral law based upon the value of others, he also argued that individuals should reason autonomously and reflect on their moral commitments apart from the authority of others. He believed that one recognized the dignity of others by granting them the freedom to think and act according to their view of what is good. Similarly, in his influential work *Émile,* Rousseau (1762) argued that the authoritarian nature of traditional education corrupted children and society by transmitting the errors of one generation to the next. His solution was to conceive of education as more of an autonomous endeavor.

Meira Levinson (1999, 2002, 2003, 2004), Rob Reich (2002, 2003), Harry Brighouse (2004a, 2004b, 2006), and James Dwyer (1998) represent this liberal perspective. They view autonomy not only as a value that contributes to the health of our democratic system, but as a liberal right of every citizen. With regard to education, this right places limits upon what both the state and parents should teach as "true." For example, in *The Demands of Liberal Education,* Levinson (1999) claims that individual autonomy is a central tenet of liberalism. Thus, the nurture and protection of autonomy becomes a public duty. Since their perspectives tend to oppose even the moral education common to secular schools, their opposition to a plural public education system is assured.

What is common to these past and present educational philosophers? They are grounded in a distrust of the conclusions of parents and society in general. Foundationally, the distrust is not merely toward a presupposed ill will of parents and teachers, but toward the unintended ill effects of the well-intentioned ignorance of all members of society. Building upon a respect for the individual dignity and a confidence in nature of the individual child, these philosophers trust that both individuals and society will be better off when freed from the authoritative influence of teachers, parents, and communities. When brought into public education as an ideological framework, school systems should act to limit communication of the moral and ideological perspective of both the state and the home. Thus, these education philosophers not only oppose the plural public education model, but they may also challenge the common school model on the rightness of the presumptive teaching of "common" values and beliefs. Though most educators do not advance this concern for student autonomy to an extreme end, there is much evidence that a moderate liberal perspective pervades the public schools. From my own experience, I find that most public school teachers reflexively and energetically respond that they strive to let students make up their own minds on issues discussed in class.

But not all agree that the interests of public education are deeply linked with a robust view of childhood autonomy. In contrast, some scholars believe that the nature of children permits and even obligates adults to guide them toward moral and ideological maturity throughout the school day.

The writings of these scholars tend to support the move toward a plural public education system wherein the broader ideological concerns of parents and teachers could be addressed more freely. These supporters not only address the nature of children, but also the civic concerns of the state. They argue that schools with religious foundations have greater resources to nurture the future citizens needed for a healthy society. Among others, these scholars include Elmer Thiessen (1995, 2001), Brian Crittenden (1988), Stephen Gilles (1996), Michael McConnell (2002; McConnell, Cochran, & Carmella, 2001), Mary Ann Glendon (2006; Glendon & Blankenhorn, 1995), William Jeynes (2005, 2007a, 2008), and David Blankenhorn (Glendon & Blankenhorn, 1995). These apparent supporters of plural public education focus on the strengths that religious education brings to education goals associated with moral and human nurture.

Equal Education

The concerns that undergird discussions regarding our model of public education also delve into questions of educational equity. These concerns draw academics to provide support for both sides of the common versus plural public education discussion that have recently grown out of concern for those trapped by the districting requirements of failing (generally urban) schools. Birthing the language and the rationale of the school choice movement, these scholars argued that many of the structures and presumptions that have materialized around the common education paradigm serve to *obstruct* the public's concerns regarding equal educational opportunity. Once school choice became a reality in some districts, it drew the attention of other scholars to argue that the interests of parents *could not* be relied upon to uphold the equal education interests of the state. Both perspectives inform the common versus plural public education discussion. Whereas school choice proponents do not specifically address plural public education as a necessity, their rationale supports educational diversity and the competence of parents who choose religious schools, both of which are central to a plural public education system. The concern for educational equity tends to oppose a plural public education system, because parental choice reduces the power of the state to control "who" attends "which" schools.

The school choice movement forms around the argument that educational competition between schools will increase the quality of the education provided by both private and public school sectors. Free-market theory, applied to education by Milton Friedman (1955, 1962), provided the early rationale for this argument through the claim that free competition raises quality and consumer satisfaction. The idea of competition, further developed by scholars such as John Chubb and Terry Moe (1990, 1991), remains the central argument for school choice, and studies have verified its positive effects in the educational realm (see Brandon, 2006; Cain, 2006; Chakrabarti, 2004; Forster & Thompson, 2011). Though the idea of free-market competition appeals to many, it has failed to substantially sway the opinions of educators who hold that public education must serve the interests of the public rather than the interests of individual citizens.

If parents are allowed to choose the schools their children attend, especially if they are ideologically dissimilar to secular schools, will the state be able to insure that children are protected from educational abuse? Many education leaders claim religious schools do not provide an equal education nor do they follow the democratic spirit with openness to all. This group maintains that the inclusion of religious schools within a system of public funding would not only hurt the public schools that remain but that the lack of diversity found in religious schools would undermine much of the public mission of education leading to factions and social fractures built around growing prejudices and unequal educations.

A Constitutional Education System

The nature of public school ideology and the public funding of religious schools have been perhaps the two most enduring and contentious church-state issues in American history. Scholar Stephen Macedo (2000, p. 151) remarks that since their inception, public schools have continually been the arena for the clash between families and the state. The source of the various conflicts stems not only from different understandings of liberal democracy and interpretations of the First Amendment's religion clauses but also from deeper philosophical questions regarding the means and ends of childhood education. Though our nation's courts rightly give little advice on best educational practices, state and federal courts have played a central role in defining the philosophy of America's educational paradigm. Their historic efforts to protect the religious rights of students unequivocally silenced all plural public education discussions for nearly a century and dictated that public education could *only* be secular. Though recent rulings have opened the door for discussion to advance, few scholars have challenged the secular public education paradigm.

There are four key ways in which court decisions shaped the public's education paradigm. The first is associated with the *Pierce v Society of Sisters of the Holy Names of Jesus and Mary* Supreme Court case of 1925. In this decision, the Court ruled that families could fulfill their educational obligations to the state by sending their children to private schools. This case firmly supported an "escape valve" that allowed those with alternate educational interests to leave the public school system to attend private schools. Though these schools are popularly associated with elitism, they have overwhelmingly been the educational residence of those who see the value of religious schooling. Further, in terms of research and schooling, the ruling strengthened the association of public with "secular" and private with "religious." This complemented the secular assumptions of modernity and likely influenced public education scholars to overlook the possibility that religious schools could advance the public's education interests.

A second way court decisions shaped our paradigm of public education came through the 1947 case of *Everson v. Board of Education*. Here, the Supreme Court ruled that not only *federal* statutes, but henceforth all *state* statutes, would have to comply with the Establishment Clause of the First

Amendment. This ruling framed the discussion for later rulings that associated the receipt of public money by religious organizations with a constitutionally prohibited state establishment of religion. Though later cases qualified ways in which religious schools could legally use public money, this case ensconced the "high wall of separation" as the metaphor of church-state relations for most of the 20th century. A third way court decisions shaped the public education paradigm is associated with a series of cases beginning in the 1960s. These cases attempted to remove the vestiges of religious perspective that remained in the public common schools. Common faith tenets and practices were no longer acceptable; public schools were mandated to advocate only secular perspectives of truth, value, and practice.

Finally, a fourth shaping influence of the courts occurred early in 2003. Here, the Supreme Court ruled that public money *could* go to religious schools *without* violating the First Amendment's Establishment Clause. The legality of this use of public money relied upon the concern of the state being upon the education of the children, the choice that the money was to be used in a religious school had to be made by a private citizen, and the choice of a religious school had to be only one of other options. The 2002 *Zelman v. Simmons-Harris* decision inadvertently constructed the necessary constitutional groundwork for the nation to consider the claims and possibilities of a plural public education system.

It may appear that these court decisions have done little to actively shape the American public education system; after all one might rightly note that the common education paradigm was popularly chosen before these laws took effect, and a central tenet of common education was a respect for conscience. Rather than shaping public education, one might reasonably argue that the courts merely kept public schools honest to their conscientious commitments to diversity, and increasing diversity naturally transforms *common* schools into *secular* schools. This may be true, and it also may be true that court decisions consistently upheld the value of conscience.

However, to argue that court actions within the schools merely paralleled public commitments overlooks a central reality; the courts were focused on the concerns of law rather than the concerns of education; though there is some overlap, *the courts were more concerned with human rights rather than with a consideration of religion's role in public education.* The legal decisions that prevented government from advocating a religious perspective while concurrently prohibiting government money from reaching religious schools left secular education as the *only* educational option for the public, regardless of its efficacy. Thus, at pivotal times when the public was more aware of religion's role in education, court decisions preempted public philosophic discussion associated with religion and education.

Plural public education systems may likely have taken root across the nation in the 1970s as a result of widespread opposition to school secularization. Since leaving the public education system was the only alternative left for conscientious objectors of this and other generations, the Christian private school movement came to life. However, this movement did not include all objectors; those financially unable to pay tuition expenses had little option save to remain in the public school.

Some scholars have argued that the some of the cases cited above were wrongly—even improperly—decided. They use their conclusions to support local religious discretion within public schools; if some schools want to start the day with a teacher-led prayer, then let them. However, though I might support their readings of the cases, I do not find their arguments for local discretion compelling because it leaves discretion about religious matters in either majoritarian control or the hands of government employees. Though I do not support all the particulars of these court decisions, I do support their efforts to protect the rights of conscience. Though early court decisions bound public education to a secular model, I blame the majoritarian public's choice of the common school model for foreordaining this result. If a plural model of public education had been established early in our nation's history, the courts would likely have been presented with few cases associated with religion and the public schools.

Concerns of the People

Scholars are people too, and their concerns have been listed above; but often the concerns of families are unheard or discarded in discussions of public education. From a parent whose children attend a public school, it is likely that our principal would find this comment surprising: opportunities to help within the school never end! Teachers always need help, the PTA always needs volunteers, and the school even solicits parent input once or twice a year. As if this local school input were not enough, family representatives may run for state and local school boards. However, I still maintain that although parents can freely "speak," both the culture and the paradigm of the common public school tends to "hear" or consider only concerns that pass the filter of "secular." Perhaps this filter is necessary under the current paradigm, but as with the discussion of court rulings above, the decision to "recognize" secular educational voices reflects the constraints of the common school paradigm, not necessarily the good of students or the public's educational concerns. Though not all of the voices below attempt to "speak to the public" (most are focused and invested heavily on educating their own children), their educational concerns tend to broaden the discussion coming from the conventional academic quarter. Their commitments and successful achievements speak loudly, and their concerns are relevant to our discussion of common versus plural public education models.

School Choice Community

Families across the nation have called for greater authority over the education of their children than what local "educational establishments" have permitted them. Though each family is free to leave public schools, not all can afford the expenses and commitments associated with home and private schooling. With greater concern for their individual children than for public education traditions, many parents have called for at least a choice of schools. Representing many concerns, this movement has gained greatest traction in low-performing districts where the obvious needs of students have risen to challenge the philosophically based districting commitments associated with the common public education model.

Though the school choice movement primarily rides on arguments associated with educational competition, the concerns that it represents are broader. These concerns are reflected by the kinds of schools that parents are choosing as the movement has expanded across the country. Some of these schools reflect religious foundations, some provide particular academic focuses, and some offer nontraditional teaching methods. Regarding the discussion of education models, those in the school choice movement broadly argue that parents of all financial resources should have greater individual authority over their children's *public* education and that educational diversity is more desirable than standardization.

Homeschool Voice

Homeschooling parents reflect the most philosophically dynamic and successful education movement in the nation today. An academic study found that the mean score of homeschooled students on standardized tests was above 80 in all subject areas. Further, their high achievement remained consistent regardless of the student's household income, gender, parent education level, the amount spent on education supplies, or their degree of public regulation (Ray, 2011). Though the number of homeschooling proponents is growing, their voice is virtually inaudible within the public education discussion. One might argue that they are not involved in "public education," but perhaps this is largely a matter of semantics and in need of reassessment.

Homeschooling parents have much to say regarding education, but since their concerns find little-to-no room within the public education "box," their voices generally go unheard. However, if I draw them into a discussion about public education models, I believe they would say that they are providing superior educations in line with the best interests of the child as well as the public; their children are moral, disciplined, socially mature, academically prepared, and civically aware. Their educational priorities demonstrate that they view the current model of public education to be not only an academic failure but also a human failure. And they would likely say that the leading causes of these failures are standardization, depersonalization, and lack of religious context. Since these attributes are intrinsically linked with the common education model, I believe homeschool families would overwhelmingly recommend a plural public education model able to accommodate personalized education ideals within a meaningful philosophic context.

Religious/Ideological School Voices

According to the 2009–2010 Private School Universe Survey, religious/parochial schools make up 80% of all private schools. The concerns of these attending families are infrequently given attention in public school discussions as are the concerns of homeschool families, and for many of the same reasons. However, they too are citizens with valid perspectives on the public's educational concerns. Catholics have supported the idea of a plural public education system for over a century, while many other religious groups are more distrustful of state control. They fear that involvement with public regulatory systems could cause a watering down of their distinctive ideological expressions, which are their *raison d'être*.

Though private religious schools appear more similar to common public schools than homeschools, this similarity may be deceptive. Although the classroom model and many teaching methods of religious schools often follow that of public schools, their ideological concerns are more closely allied with homeschoolers. Both groups heavily invest time and money to give their children an education that is grounded in the moral, philosophical, and ideological ideals of the home. If asked whether a common or plural public education system would be better for the nation, they would surely respond that a plural system is superior. It would allow parents more authority over their children's education and better reflect the nation's human diversity.

If you asked whether they fear that the schools they currently attend promote disunity and social division, religious school supporters would likely laugh and ask if you were serious. If informed about some of the academic concerns above, they would likely view concerns associating religious schools with intolerance and public fracture to be exaggerated in light of the historical record associated with religious schools. My presumption of their opinion is supported by research on the civic outcomes of religious schools (Campbell, 2008).

Conflicts Illuminate Nature

Reflecting these and other interests, public schools have been a focal point of concern and conflict throughout their history. It would be unreasonable to expect that any institution intended to serve the diverse interests of both the public and America's diverse families to be universally accepted, but to ignore these conflicts is unreasonable as well. The history chapters that follow attempt to explore the nature of education by, in part, utilizing these conflicts to illumine the religious nature of education. I will focus on two general types of conflict: ideological and legal. Ideological conflicts serve to alienate some families from the public schools even as attempts to avoid these conflicts shape the curriculum and climate of each school. Caring parents naturally have both a concern and an obligation to monitor what their children learn from their peers, the media, and other adults. Thus, the teachers and the school setting are rightly and frequently scrutinized for what they teach. Similarly, though with less frequency, schools are scrutinized for what they *do not* teach. Though dissatisfied parents have the right to leave the public school system, their criticisms generally point to ideals and insights that may serve to strengthen the entire project of public education.

The second type of conflict that illumines the nature of education relates to law. Historically, public schools have been shaped not only by the concerns of parents, education professionals, and public leaders, but they have been shaped by the courts whose focus is to insure that schools comply with the law and constitution of each state and the nation. However, though some court decisions have fundamentally shaped public education, these decisions (as mentioned above) do not reflect a recognized educational expertise or even a particular concern for public education itself; the courts are primarily concerned with the adherence to law. I will illuminate some of the legal conflicts and analyze court decisions in light of their effect on public education.

My analysis of both ideological and legal conflicts will focus on the ways in which these conflicts not only serve to shape public education, but more substantively serve to illuminate the religious nature of public education.

Centrally, these conflicts will be used to evaluate the common education model as to its viability: Does the common education model have the resources necessary to provide the public education Americans need?

Public Interests and Viability

While the previous discussions inform our choice of public education's structure, there is an overarching realistic concern that also must be discussed—that of viability. *Public schools do not exist merely to illuminate the nation's educational ideals, but to accomplish them!* The public's education model must demonstrably have the pedagogical resources to realize its goals. Many schools of today are officially rated as failing, but even "exemplary" schools are rated on such a narrow scale that they likely fail to advance many of the concerns that gave rise to public education. These failures come in spite of the efforts of compassionate teachers, increased teacher training, increased educational funding, and over a century of research and experimentation *from within the common education paradigm.* Perhaps it is time for public educators to consider the pedagogical tools that are a common part of life—and education—outside the secular restraints.

A great many rational, concrete, and effective resources exist that are only accessible from within a religious paradigm of education. Since my goal is to convince the reader of the greater viability of the plural public education model that accesses these resources, I will illuminate the religious nature of many of the public's educational interests, describe the broader resources of religious schools, and show how the common education model is less viable in these areas without providing other redeeming qualities.

Viability Expanded

It is easier to have a goal than it is to achieve it. Some goals are difficult to achieve because the resources they require exceed what is available, or their technological requirements are beyond current levels of development. Other goals are difficult to reach because they require the committed participation of large numbers of people. Though the private sector, through personal drive, organization, ingenuity, and amassed resources, has achieved remarkable personal and corporate goals, the public sector, with its ability to draw on broader intellectual, financial, and human resources seems able to achieve the loftiest goals. Public efforts have protected nations from tyrants, put men on the moon, and conquered once-deadly diseases.

Public education reflects some of the loftiest of America's ideological goals. It encompasses goals associated not only with future workplace achievement but also with public unity, human identity, public morality, human awareness, and personal motivation. By means of a public education, it is hoped that all children, as individuals of equal value, will be able to achieve their human potential; that public schools will be a channel through which the intellectual, cultural, moral, and social capital of the nation will flow into all demographic locations. These goals for the individual reflect goals for the public, which invests in childhood education not only for the good of the child but to insure the good of the nation.

However, without the necessary tools and resources, goals may more accurately be termed public *wishes*, and efforts to achieve them will fall short. Though many presume that given the will, the public can achieve any of its current "goals," its efforts are often more limited than many of its grand programs suggest, especially in cases in which human change is required. Here, the public's greatest limitations are not merely material or intellectual, but they often involve issues of the human will or constitutionally protected human rights that establish barricades to prevent, limit, or redirect governmental efforts.

Under a common education paradigm and the First Amendment's religious restrictions on government, America is relying on an education system that structurally lacks many of the educational tools and resources *necessary* to the success of its human-shaping educational goals. Under this paradigm, it may be merely chasing after wishes. The nurture of moral, intellectual, and civic qualities, conceived as a religious endeavor by the colonial generations (McClellan, 1999), has been disassociated from the ethical frameworks that inform their development. In particular, morality must be nurtured apart from religious roots, curricula may alienate citizens over issues of truth and conscience, secular curricula serve to disengage the values of society from foundational beliefs resulting in shallow civic identities, and apart from "first truths," the moral and intellectual reasoning of students tends to remain shallow and inconsistent.

Further, over a century of our nation's secular scholarship has not come up with alternative educational resources that adequately address our broad array of educational concerns. Currently, many of our best strategies to improve public education are merely variations of "big stick motivations" such as high-stakes testing, accountability, and campus police. Motivations and inducements of this kind are not without their place and are often demonstrably effective, but they tend to motivate students, teachers, and administrators superficially through external rewards and punishments rather than internal beliefs and values. The public's goal should be to help

children develop internal motivations and integrated patterns of reasoning that shape their lives toward ideological "goods" without the need for
rewards and punishments.

Generally speaking, most of the failures associated with public schooling are not due to student inability, poor curricular strategies, inadequate
teacher training, low pay, or the need for more accountability; rather educational failures stem largely from a lack of internal student motivation.
Herein lies the strength of religious schooling. Religious schools provide
the opportunity to inspire students positively and deeply from within. Students can be nurtured with a broad vision for life, a framework of meaning
and value for curricular knowledge, a school climate of deeper community,
and greater parental support as school concerns align more deeply with
family concerns. Plural public education makes available the tools and resources of religious schooling toward the achievement of the public's education goals and calls for our consideration.

Why Religion?

Every public educator is thoroughly trained that they should not promote
religious views at school. They not only know that church-state law forbids
this, but also they were taught some general philosophic ideals that associate the dignity of the child, the development of independent thought, and
the public good with neutral or nonreligious teaching. On the other hand,
our popular culture, if not our education colleges, tends to associate religious instruction with dogmatism, indoctrination, and shallow thinking—
qualities unfitting for any child and incompatible with the ideals of public
education. Thus, how can I advocate that buy-in to the religious education
project is in the public's educational interest?

I cannot enter lengthy discussions on law, human dignity, the nature of
reason, and the public's interest here, but religious schools do not necessarily oppose these concerns. First, I remind readers that the court rulings that
separated public schools from religious perspectives were imposed upon
the common education model. Then, in 2003, in *Zelman v. Simmons-Harris*
(2002), the Supreme Court ruled that under an alternate education structure, public money *could* reach religious schools. The earlier separation did
not reflect an education ideal but a necessary condition to prevent a government establishment of religion under the existing educational paradigm.

Second, religious schools can support the dignity of the child. Though
some claim that this dignity is diminished when authorities teach religious
views, this is a controversial perspective held by a minority. The classroom is
an extension of the parenting role (teachers act *in loco parentis*), and most

parents believe they are responsibly loving their child by teaching them the ideals they have found to be true and valuable. Teachers already prepare their children for life by teaching them what is true and valuable in limited areas, and religious schools holistically expand these concerns. Thus, religious schoolteachers can support the dignity of the child by teaching not only common facts and skills but also by teaching the ideals and principles that they have discovered to be the foundations of life.

Third, bumbling, narrow-minded pastors with their dutiful flocks (made popular by the media) have and will exist. However, this caricature is obviously far from the norm because most people are religious, and they do not denigrate themselves as authoritarian or sheepish. Becoming a teacher in a religious school does not transform the average believer into an authoritarian ideologue nor does entering a religious school prevent a child from thinking independently. Rather, religious schools are environments that provide the opportunity for deeper levels of communication and community expression around topics of life-defining importance. Within them, children get to discuss and reflect upon the mature beliefs and rationales of trusted individuals rather than merely on the superficial opinions of classroom peers.

The fact that most religions are associated with a set of beliefs and practices does not imply that religious people are merely thoughtless followers. History, sociological study, and religious infighting provide abundant evidence that religious people are intellectually engaged, form their own opinions, and disagree with one another. Democratic society needs citizens who think independently, and there is little evidence that religious schools are averse to (or incapable of) teaching independent reflective thought.

Finally, sociological research further supports the connection between religion, morality, and the public good. Esteemed scholar Rodney Stark concludes, "Images of Gods as conscious, powerful, morally concerned beings function to sustain the moral order" (2004, p. 162). In other words, the moral fabric of a society is closely linked with the nature of the gods of the people and the degree of commitment they show to them. Healthy religious foundations can provide societies with a source of moral stability that secular ideologies have been unable to parallel. Stark notes that the statement, "*Religions function to sustain the moral order* . . . is regarded by many as the closest thing to a law that the social scientific study of religion possesses" (2004, p. 136, emphasis in the original). From these assertions, one may conclude that nations imperil their stability by favoring secular schools that fail to nurture a socially supportive view of God among families that would prefer religiously based schools.

Though this previous discussion defends schools that are religious in the traditional sense, my rationale for including religious schools relies on a broader definition of religion that marks nearly every individual as religious. The definition I use comes from sociology and defines as a religion *any* set of beliefs and values that "function" in a similar manner to a traditional religion in a person's life. Thus, using this functional definition, a school that integrates an atheistic worldview would be considered a religious school alongside the Baptist and Jewish dayschools.

Choosing to follow this definition not only broadens the scope of religious school possibilities, but more importantly, it provides a definition that serves to illuminate the role and power of religion in a manner that traditional definitions do not. Sociologist Stanley Kurtz defines religion as "an encompassing world-view that answers the big questions about life, dignifies daily exertions with higher significance, and provides a rationale for meaningful collective action" (as cited in Berkowitz, 2003, p. 31). Sociologist Edward Bailey provides this definition: "'Religion' and 'religiosity' then ... describe voluntary yet compelling 'commitments.'. . . Religion is, in a word, what is 'most valued'—in intent and/or in practice" (as cited in Greil & Bromley, 2003, p. 65). Anthropologist Clifford Geertz defines religion as

> (1) A system of symbols which acts to (2) establish powerful, pervasive and long-lasting moods and motivations in men by (3) formulating conceptions of general order of existence and (4) clothing these conceptions with such an aura of factuality that (5) the moods and motivations seem uniquely realistic. (1973, p. 90)

Summarily, these definitions describe religion as any set of ideas that act as a source of meaning, understanding, motivation, and order. Research supports this role of religion (Spilka, Hood, Hunsberger, & Gorsuch, 2003), and Chang-Ho Ji confirms its positive effect in the academic realm (2010). Thus, they serve to provide motivating foundations upon which moral, intellectual, and ideological growth can take place.

Though a functional definition of religion allows individuals to have their own individual "faiths," those sets of beliefs and values that endure and are found to be compelling by others become the hubs around which communities form. At this level, others can more holistically discern the nature, claims, and social value of the religion as it is transposed from individual theory to social practice. The great religions of today's world have not only survived the questions of countless skeptics, but they have demonstrated the ability to provide stable and meaningful foundations for both individual and social life. Whereas no civilization of the past endured without a core of ideological community, the challenge of pluralistic democratic society is to maintain the health of its communities while concurrently nurturing a sense of wider community built on "overlapping values" or mutual concerns.

Utilizing a functional definition and the insight, the benefit of religious schooling to the public education project becomes more clear; education efforts that build upon existing foundations of meaning, motivation, and understanding are more likely to succeed than efforts that avoid or even appear opposed to those foundations. Whereas secular public schools present the interests of the public in nonreligious environments, a plural public education system brings the interests of the public *and* the religious beliefs of attending families together in the classroom. If religions are a shaping force, the goal of public education should not be to ignore or oppose them but rather to see a confluence grow between them and the public's educational interests. When successful, this confluence is likely to produce more knowledgeable, moral, motivated, and intellectually engaged citizens.

Expanding these ideas, religions reflect the mental frameworks that people utilize to help make sense of everything they encounter. Educational scholar Robert Kunzman draws upon a functional definition of religion when noting, "We all have an underlying structure or framework to our lives that reflects our sense of what we value and pursue in life. This ethical framework helps orient and guide our lives, as well as shapes our sense of identity" (2006, p. 35). He too argues for the public significance of these frameworks. "The civic and political realms have necessary and important boundaries, but must be informed by the private realm's deep ethical frameworks if they are to have any purchase and power in our lives together" (2006, p. 35). Thus, American society needs the support of religion, but the human rights of conscience forbid the state from actively supporting or opposing any view. While the common education paradigm separates church and state interests, a plural public education system provides the opportunity to conscientiously allow the concerns of the state to become empowered by and integrated into the religious views of the people.

My Concerns, Rationale, and Purpose

Before articulating an argument that claims that over a century of educational research and tradition have (in spite of many successes) held a systemic flaw, allow me to describe the sources of my perspective and offer an explanation of how this flaw could have received so little recognition by other scholars. I write as a Christian who has traveled in nations reflecting the world's primary religious (and nonreligious) heritages; worked as a Christian-school teacher and administrator; informally studied a variety of Christian, religious, and public schools; and trained as a church-state scholar.

The argument I will present is complex. It draws from broad historic, philosophic, legal, and educational sources as well as my own experience. However, I do not believe complexity is the reason our nation has over-looked the vital and intrinsic connections between religion and educa-tion. Rather, I attribute the lack of clarity on the subject to be remnants of modernity's fears and philosophy. Whereas citizens of the 19th century relied upon a broad place for religion, I find that most people today have difficulty recognizing the "faith roots" of not only public life and human expression, but also of their own reason, values, and beliefs. Under the lin-gering influence of modernity's confidence in human reason, fears regard-ing religion and a relative blindness to presuppositions, education leaders overlook the foundational roles that philosophic and religious influences play in the educational nurture of healthy individuals and citizens.

Further, I do not write to disparage the public's interests regarding education, nor do I question the general tenets of the liberal democratic tradition that have molded our public education system. I do not write to revive the preferential establishment of a Protestant Christian worldview in the public schools that was declared unconstitutional in the 1960s. To the contrary, I will argue that both public interests and liberal democratic traditions require support for a public system of moral, civic, and academic education that avoids linking government with any particular worldview. I hope to show that the public's educational goals cannot be adequately addressed under the common model of public education—a situation in which the model cannot be "fixed" but may only be replaced. Though the ends of public education may be noble, the current model is ill-equipped to address these ends effectively.

The superior replacement I propose (described in Chapter 8) is a plural public education system made up of an array of traditional secular schools and privately operated "religious" schools. Without mandating that all private schools join this plural public system, all that choose to would be (a) considered public schools, (b) broadly aligned with the public's educa-tional interests, and (c) accessible to families with the use of public funds. Following this new education model, public schools could divert from the philosophic and structural constraints required of secular bodies and re-shape education to reflect more holistic human concerns in ideologically rich environments.

Again, I note that few have investigated the claim that the comprehensive nature of religious schools enables them to address more fully the civic concerns of the state. As I review varying education models, the nature of education, and the nature of the public's educational interests, my findings will hopefully shed light on why America's current public education model has failed both the public's educational interests and the liberal democratic tradition, and I will show how a plural system would likely do better.

The discussions that surround the structural and philosophic nature of America's model of public education are as broad as the ramifications of change. I could continue to theorize about these ramifications, but I believe it is more valuable to illuminate the religious nature of the public's educational interests by first analyzing our public education history. Thus, through the following three chapters, I will tease from America's educational history the role of religion in public education as schools transitioned from being denominational to nonsectarian to secular. This analysis will serve to clarify ways religion supports the public education project, clarify the effects of school secularization, and provide a framework to understand education weaknesses that have failed to respond to the best efforts of secular scholars, public leaders, and skilled teachers. This history will leave academic concerns opposed to plural public education for Chapters 5 and 6, while Chapter 7 (my favorite chapter) will illuminate ways religious schools can provide superior support for the public's educational goals. While in the final chapter, I propose a philosophic and structural model for a healthy plural public education system, I also revisit the perplexing question of why it has taken so long for Americans to confront public education's secular ideal.

2

Unity, Diversity, and Religious
Public Education

> From the origin of the American public school . . . to the present day, educa-
> tors have tried to state what values should govern the school in its effort to
> form character and to inculcate value judgments. These attempts at a phi-
> losophy of values have been complicated by the shifting and highly dynamic
> religious pluralism of American Society. Often enough discussions of values
> in public education fail to touch the central problem: the limitations inher-
> ent in the ideal of a *common* school serving a pluralistic society. . . . For in the
> final analysis values are rooted in what men hold as ultimate or supreme in
> life—in what may be taken in a broad sense as "religion."
>
> —McCluskey, 1958, p. 1 (emphasis in the original)

The 1800s were a transitional century for education in America. It began
with most families educating their children at home or in church-run
schools, and it ended with a well-established public school system operated
by the state. The century also began with a firm conviction that childhood
education should be deeply informed by the religious beliefs of the family,
but it ended with schools that, under the state, increasingly separated religion from the curriculum. A philosophic battle drove this transition. At the
heart of this battle was religion, which, in addition to holding deep family

Education Reform, pages 25–52
Copyright © 2013 by Information Age Publishing
All rights of reproduction in any form reserved.

significance, was also understood to inform the public philosophy of the new nation.

The ethics of this battle—perhaps it could rightly be called an experiment—were of particular concern. Under the totalitarian regimes of predemocratic Europe, governments facing philosophic invasions had attempted to dictate the religious beliefs of families for the sake of God and society. But a new idea, born from within the American (overwhelmingly Protestant) psyche, was shaping the culture and the institutions of the new nation. Growing public conviction regarding "liberty of conscience," the first human liberty, forbade the state from interfering with the religious beliefs of the individual. Following massive waves of Catholic immigrants, perceived to be a moral and ideological threat favoring totalitarian control, American leaders were challenged with never-before-answered moral, cultural, and ideological questions. Foremost, if papal control of the Church was a tenet of Catholic faith, would/could committed Catholics express the independent thought considered indispensable to democratic society? Or would Catholics undermine the democratic experiment by "mindlessly" voting as a bloc according to the dictates of the pope (as the popular characterization implied)?

While the public and its leaders wrestled with the ethics of this educational battle, it unintentionally initiated an experiment regarding the religious nature of personal and civic life. To what degree was the "American identity" indebted to Protestant beliefs, and to what degree were the public's educational goals linked to religious beliefs at all? What would be the educational effects of progressively separating religion from the curriculum? Would both Protestants and Catholics willingly dilute the educational role of faith for broader public concerns? Who would resist this dilution and why? Who would accept it and why? Though 19th-century Americans would hand this battle/experiment to those of the 20th century, their recorded perceptions, responses, actions, and the public effects of these actions provide illuminating data to discern the interactive role of religion in education. The following record and analysis will help us understand the religious nature of public education to answer these questions.

Religion and Public Education Prior to the Common School

Early colonial education in America reflected the priority of religious and moral training, and this focus included a concern for the community. The concern for the healthy religious faith of others was virtually indivisible from a concern for a healthy society; the community *was* a conscious expression of their religious beliefs. Educationally speaking, "The Puritans viewed schools as having a stabilizing influence on society via drawing children closer to God" (Jeynes, 2007b, p. 6). Their religious traditions provided both the knowledge of what was good and the moral motivation to accomplish that good. Religious schoolings supported home nurture through teaching and discipline to build strong individual faith, which in turn supported a stable society.

Other Protestant communities with similar concerns toward public morality formed the ethical and philosophical fabric of America (McClellan, 1992). The relatively seamless relationship between the Protestant faiths and the public's moral and political conceptions was so strong that civic leaders viewed Protestant religious perspectives to be particularly capable of supporting the American democratic experiment.

Sectarian Public Schools and Religious Foundations

From its colonial roots in America, education slowly moved from the home to the schoolhouse. As individual concerns became public, education increasingly came under governmental regulation. The first evidence of this occurred in Massachusetts in 1642 when "a law was passed asserting [the] right to force apprenticeship training upon children in all towns and villages" (Anthony & Benson, 2003, p. 292). Later, this same state enacted what became known as the "Old Deluder Satan" law of 1647. It required that towns of more than 50 families appoint a schoolmaster to teach the children to read and write, and that towns of more than 100 families establish grammar schools. Moral education historian B. Edward McClellan says that concerns supporting general education were moral. He writes, "The primary aim of these Massachusetts laws and of similar enactments in other colonies was not to create schools but rather to ensure that moral education be accomplished by whatever institutional means were available" (1992, p. 6). As secondary schools and colleges developed, "moral education suffused... [them] as it did elementary education" (McClellan, 1992, p. 9).

The agrarian base of the Southern colonies was less favorable to the formation of tax-supported community schools. Kaestle writes that, commonly, either itinerant schoolmasters started their own tuition-funded schools, or parents engaged a schoolmaster to teach their children or a group of local children. In either case, these schools often looked little different from the district schools in the North (Kaestle, 1983, p. 13). Thus, education in both the North and the South had a strong religious base that supported the concerns of parents. "The terms 'public' and 'private' did not have their present connotations, and most schools did not fit neatly into either of our modern categories" (Kaestle, 1983, p. 13).

Colonial New England schools have often been seen as the precursors of the common school, but the former embodied a central difference. Though they were under town control and not Church control, they were more deeply concerned with inculcating the Puritan worldview. The public nature of control did not lesson this concern because "ministers played the leading roles on local school committees, and instruction was permeated with the themes and content of Puritan theology" (Glenn, 1988, p. 147).

This educational concern for the development of faith integrated with the development of skills and knowledge continued into the early republican period. Public leaders viewed the development of religious faith as critically important to the development of moral character and good citizenship. President George Washington's *Farewell Address* powerfully reflected this prevalent link between faith and citizenship. He said,

> Of all the dispositions and habits which lead to political prosperity, religion and morality are indispensable supports. In vain would that man claim the tribute of patriotism, who should labor to subvert these great pillars of human happiness, these firmest props of the duties of men and citizens. (2008)

Thus, religion traditionally held a central place within school curricula for individual as well as civic reasons. However, the public interest in an educated citizenry and in the promotion of a distinctive American civic identity would test the degree to which religious citizens were willing to dilute their faith for the sake of common public school education.

▬▬▬▬
Jefferson's Unacceptable Public Education Proposals

Throughout his public life, Thomas Jefferson asserted that the key to continuing liberty resided in individual citizens. Political figures, he believed, would advance the powers of government to encroach upon the citizenry, thus, citizens should receive adequate education to enable them to participate in community affairs and control the advances of government (Healey, 1962, p. 169). With this in mind, Jefferson's greatest concern was for the universal basic education of all children. He said, "It is safer to have a whole people respectably enlightened, than a few in a high state of science, and the many in ignorance. This last is the most dangerous state in which a nation can be" (as cited in Healey, 1962, p. 186).

According to historian Robert Healey, Jefferson believed that the two priorities of a democracy were local control and "general education to enable every man to judge for himself what would secure or endanger his freedom" (1962, p. 178). Jefferson said, "I consider the continuance of republican government as absolutely hanging on these two hooks" (as cited in Healey, 1962, p. 178). Thus, in Virginia, Jefferson proposed systems of public education in 1779, through the 1790s, and again in 1817, but his proposals failed to gain broad public support (Kaestle, 1983, p. 9). Analysts could blame the failure of early attempts on economic struggles, but after the last failed attempt, Jefferson blamed the resistance on, "ignorance, malice, egoism, fanaticism, religious, political and local perversities" (as cited in Kaestle, 1983, p. 9). Education historian S. Alexander Rippa attributes the rejection of Jefferson's public school plans to "the refusal of well-to-do citizens to pay taxes for the education of the poor" (1992, p. 56). More broadly, Kaestle attributes rejection to the fear of a transfer of educational power to the state and to a satisfaction with contemporary systems that allowed for local control and parental choice (1983, p. 9).

But Jefferson's personal evaluation of the failure of his proposals reveals his own religious biases against sectarian religion for which he was well known. His biases not only molded his education plans, but they hindered their public acceptance. His first proposal, the *Bill for the More General Diffusion of Knowledge* (1779), was a comprehensive plan for public education at the primary and secondary levels. Though Jefferson believed that religion supported morality, religious instruction was completely absent from the proposed curriculum at a time when it was a prominent feature in schools everywhere else.

The omission was deliberate. Jefferson wrote in his *Notes on the State of Virginia,*

> Instead therefore of putting the Bible and Testament into the hands of the children, at an age when their judgments are not sufficiently matured for religious enquiries, their memories may here be stored with the most useful facts from Grecian, Roman, European, and American history. (Levy, 1963, p. 8)

Religion was also conspicuous by its absence from Jefferson's plan of 1817; his *Bill for Establishing a System of Public Education* enumerated only secular subjects. He sought to eliminate possible sectarian religious influence by specifying that "no religious reading, instruction, or exercise, shall be prescribed or practiced inconsistent with the tenets of any religious sect or denomination" (as cited in Healey, 1962, p. 186) and that ministers should not serve as visitors or supervisors.

Jefferson's plans would separate civic education from the core religious beliefs of a significant portion of the population. He believed that schools should not teach theologies because this created divisions and corrupted rulers, but whether true or not, his convictions made for an education system disagreeable to many religious believers.

With the failure of the first nonsectarian education proposals, parents and local traditions drove the development of education. "By 1830 schools were available to most white Americans in the North" (Kaestle, 1983, p. 62). The South had lower enrollment rates, but in the North, "rural district school enrollment became almost universal, and throughout the nation, charity schooling for the urban poor was advocated with little opposition and with increasing organizational vigor" (Kaestle, 1983, p. 62).

A more faith-centered "nonsectarian" public education system would later find acceptance. However, it would require the zealous promotion of a "full-bodied" nonsectarian religion by Horace Mann, coupled with the perceived threat of an invading civic ideology, to convince the majority population to surrender its choice of sectarian religious schooling for common education. Neither the public nor education leaders fully surrendered their concerns regarding faith. Though nonsectarian education avoided religious particulars, common components of faith were necessary to bring meaning, motivation, and individual buy-in to the public curriculum.

America's Choice of the Common School Model

Horace Mann and the Religious Nature of the Common School

Horace Mann was the first Secretary of the Massachusetts Board of Education (1837–1848), and he began the nation's first schools to train teachers, which became known as "normal" schools. According to educational historian James Fraser, during his 12 years as secretary of Massachusetts Board of Education, Mann "did more to define the role and purpose of public schools... in the new nation than any other American" (1999, p. 25). Thus, many scholars consider Mann the "father" of American public education.

Reflecting the view that civic beliefs and behaviors were conceived and motivated by personally held religious beliefs, Horace Mann "chose to ignore" the "more militantly secular" educational option implemented in France (Fraser, 1999, p. 25; see also Glenn, 1988, p. 18). Mann and his educational allies "presented the mission of the common school in essentially religious, salvific terms to a Protestant majority that was quite prepared to identify the institutions of American society with the Kingdom of God" (Glenn, 1987, p. 205). This presentation would aid the acceptance and effectiveness of "nonsectarian" education.

Mann passionately supported the common school as the key instrument of national advance. European countries had relied upon state churches to define their identity and to propagate their unifying beliefs, but America's First Amendment forbade a federal establishment, and the individual states had recently disestablished, with Mann's own state being the last in 1833. Fraser reflects that Mann saw the common school as the civic replacement for the church:

> In an era of increasing diversity, when no one religion could claim such loyalty, the church could no longer serve as a unifying force. But the school, reaching all citizens, could replace the church as the carrier of culture and creator of national unity. (2001, p. 48)

Confidence was high in the 1830s that the common school would alleviate many social problems and "secure the nation's destiny" (Kaestle, 1983, p. 75).

> Because the public school brought children of all social stations into a common classroom, many saw it as a powerful democratizing force—a logical extension of democratic tendencies in politics and culture. Others expected it to ease social tensions by increasing opportunities and promoting a common culture. (McClellan, 1992, p. 24)

The controversies surrounding its slow acceptance did not diminish Mann's vision for the school's future. In his last (1848) *Annual Report*, he said, "Without undervaluing any other human agency, it may be safely affirmed that the Common School, improved and energized, as it can easily be, may become the most effective and benignant of all the forces of civilization" (as cited in Fraser, 2001, p. 179).

Central to the common school and this study is the relationship between religious views and public civic interests. Glenn notes,

> For Horace Mann and his fellow reformers of the common school, both religious and moral instruction were essential elements of sound education. It was beyond questioning that schools should seek to educate the heart and the will as well as to fill the mind with facts and skills. (1988, p. 146)

Mann labored to broaden civic propagation utilizing state power, and he argued that the state could accomplish its goals without intruding too deeply upon representative faiths to create a state religious establishment. Thus, he declared, "Religious instruction in our schools, to the extent which the constitution and the laws of the State allowed and prescribed, was indispensable to [the student's] highest welfare, and essential to the vitality of moral education" (1848).

Though he did not consider it a state religious establishment, Mann affirmed that the common school was deeply religious.

> Our system earnestly inculcates all Christian morals; it founds its morals on the basis of religion; it welcomes the religion of the Bible; and, in receiving the Bible, it allows it to do what it is allowed to do in no other system—*to speak for itself.*" (1848, emphasis in original)

The use of Scripture stopped short of doctrinal advocacy, which, according to Mann's beliefs, increased the moral purity and the inclusiveness of common schools. He said that

> government should do all that it can to facilitate the acquisition of religious truth, but shall leave the decision of the question, what religious truth is, to the arbitrament, without human appeal, of each man's reason and conscience. [The common schools] bear upon their face that they are schools which the children of the entire community may attend. Every man not on the pauper-list is taxed for their support; but he is not taxed to support them as special religious institutions; if he were, it would satisfy at once the largest definition of a religious establishment. (1848)

Mann conceived that successful common education was to call upon deeply held and influential beliefs, and he was convinced the state could do it in a conscientious, legal, and nondivisive manner.

Attempting to Recognize Protestant Civic Ideals and Conscience

In spite of attempts to be nonoffensive, nonsectarian education took on Protestant hues that were offensive to Catholics. The required public reading of the Bible without comments, the reading of Protestant versions of the Bible, and the Protestant interpretation of history created tensions (Carper & Hunt, 2007, pp. 30–34). But poignant to this study, civic leaders viewed the Protestant slant as a civic necessity. Supporters of the common school, such as Horace Mann, George Emerson, and Samuel F. B. Morse (see Glenn, 1988, p. 66; McCluskey, 1958, p. 48) argued that Roman Catholicism lacked the resources to propagate the values and beliefs believed to be vital to American liberty. The values and beliefs of Enlightened Protestantism had birthed and undergirded the prosperity of the young nation.

Yet, while Mann believed the formation of American civic identity was a philosophic or moral proposition, he was also concerned about the rights of conscience. He wrote, "Our own government is almost a solitary example among the nations of the earth, where freedom of opinion and the inviolability of conscience, have been even theoretically recognized by the law" (as cited in Milson, Bohan, Glanzer, & Null, 2004, p. 187). In spite of early conflicts, common school proponents believed the common school model was suitable for the American situation; it claimed the ability to propagate a civic identity shaped by the deep Protestant beliefs of the majority of the population while accommodating conscientious differences.

Public concerns regarding the moral and civic nurture of American children justified the need for public education. Other states adopted Mann's common school model because they doubted whether other private or plural public education models would satisfy the public's educational interests. Disestablishment had already ruled out state-favored religious schooling as a violation of conscience, but other public education models were available. New York City, for example, provided public money for the operation of Catholic schools, a variety of Protestant schools, and schools of various other organizations (Fraser, 1999, p. 51). However, political scientist Stephen Macedo writes, "Rome furnished ample ground to question whether one could be a good Catholic and a good republican" (2000, p. 69). To expand this model would allow the civic teachings of Catholicism to advance at public expense.

Alternatively, states could have preferred all Protestant schools for public funding while rejecting Catholic schools. But this too directly discriminated against one faith. Thus, removing the state from education would lead to an uncertain civic future, state support of all schools equally likewise seemed contrary to the civic health of democracy, and state support for "preferred faith" schools would violate the public's developing attempts to protect the rights of conscience. Again, the common education model seemed to provide the public with both the means to propagate its civic ideals and a means to reasonably accommodate diverse religious beliefs. However, concerns for broad public approval and moral/civic effectiveness were destined to conflict surrounding religion.

Pressured Acceptance of the Common School Model

The arguments of Jefferson in support of secular education found only measured acceptance when placed in competition with traditional denominational schooling. Later, Mann's common school had little appeal to all save a limited elite in the 1830s who viewed civic nurture apart from the particularities of religious traditions in accord with their individual faiths. However, Glenn argues that the waves of poor Catholic immigrants who came in the following decades provided circumstances around which education leaders advanced successful arguments for common schooling. According to Glenn, the common school project became understood

> as an urgent necessity by virtually all Americans of social and political influence, including orthodox Protestants who otherwise might well have insisted upon more direct doctrinal content in the schools. Anxiety about the assimilation of the immigrant prevented the development of a religiously differentiated educational system. (1988, p. 84)

Common education was not the preferred ideal for most families or educators. Rather it appears to have been perceived as the best of bad choices and was compelled by what appears to have been an exaggerated fear of Catholicism. It required nearly three decades for the public to accept the common school model and to link it exclusively with the American civic vision. Once Protestant buy-in was virtually universal, all other education systems would be denied public funding in most states and territories by law. What follows are the four key arguments (often presented in idealized form by Mann) that moved the public to accept common education.

The Moral Argument

First, the civic relevance of moral formation was widely recognized since before the American Revolution. The public believed that morality contributed toward the stability of society, and it relied upon religion for its maintenance (Hauerwas, 1991, p. 79). Legal scholar Steven Smith notes that "received wisdom and tradition" informed the founding generation that stable social orders depended upon healthy moral formation, which they attributed to religion (1995, p. 19). Limited government necessitated high moral character, and "the growing absence of external, institutional restraints required the development of strong internal controls. In the minds of nineteenth-century Americans, the price of liberty was rigorous self-discipline and upright personal conduct" (McClellan, 1992, p. 17).

The nation's founders frequently articulated this concern for morality in their writings. Clinton Rossiter, a historian of the American Revolution, summarized *The Federalist* in these words: "No happiness without liberty; no liberty without self government; no self government without constitutionalism; no constitutionalism without morality—and none of these great goods without order and stability" (cited in Neuhaus, 1995, p. 159). Similarly, in a 1788 speech before the Virginia Convention, James Madison stated, "To suppose that any form of government will secure liberty or happiness without any virtue in the people is a chimerical idea" (2012); and President

John Adams said, "We have no government armed with power...to rule a people unbridled by religion and morality" (as cited in Adams, 1854, p. 229). Thus, in the words of historian James Turner, "The founding ideology of the republic, forged in the Revolution, proclaimed liberty to depend on a virtuous people.... The conviction remained vital in the nineteenth-century" (1985, p. 83).

Neither families nor public leaders believed that the moral nurture of children should be merely a concern of the home and church. McClellan writes that although

> Protestant Americans of the nineteenth-century valued the Sunday school, they never believed that it could serve as more than an adjunct in the task of moral education. One day a week was simply too little time to give to a process that required constant and intensive effort. (1992, p. 23)

Some were concerned that poor and immigrant communities that lacked access to schooling would not nurture sufficient morality. Kaestle found that education leaders such as Horace Mann and Henry Barnard responded to the 1830s call for "free common schooling dedicated to moral education and good citizenship" (1983, p. 75). "Thus, it was the common daily school that Americans called upon to provide primary support for the early educational efforts of the family" (McClellan, 1992, p. 23).

The public schools were viewed as "God's machinery of assimilation" (Handy, 1991, pp. 37–38) for moral as well as civic education. As Catholic immigration created a sense of urgency to Americanize immigrant citizens, Mann proclaimed, "The germs of morality must be planted in the moral nature of children, at an early period of their life" (1838, p. 14). Further, he questioned the moral training of nonpublic settings while offering the common school as the means to insure appropriate moral instruction (Barnard, 1846, p. 98).

> Do they [parents] cultivate the higher faculties in the nature of childhood—its conscience, its benevolence, a reverence for whatever is true and sacred; or are they only developing, upon a grander scale, the lower instincts and selfish tendencies of the race? (Mann, 1891, p. 3)

Many viewed religion as the primary source of civic motivation and the nation's transcendent ideals, thus Mann drew from general religious principles to empower the common school's moral mission. Central to this concern was Mann's strategy (noted above) of daily Bible reading without comment. Teachers would read from the Bible to draw from religious truths and cultivate motivation, but they would give no commentary to avoid sectarian alignments and the conflicts it promoted. He supported this method of moral education, thus he reflected, "If this Bible is in the schools, how can it be said that Christianity is excluded from the schools; or how can it be said that the school system, which adopts and uses the Bible, is an anti-Christian, or an un-Christian system?" (as cited in Fraser, 1999, p. 27). But this rhetorical question did not represent mainstream Christianity; it was asked by a Unitarian whose faith aligned with common school religious philosophy (see Fraser, 1999, p. 27; Glenn, 1988, p. 131). Later, I will show that traditional Christians believed that nonsectarian education failed to fulfill their conceptions of Christian education.

Supporters of the common school held that children of other faiths were teachable. Though they did not believe that all faiths sufficiently promoted the moral qualities necessary for American citizenship, they believed common school curricula could do so. Within a presumptuously inoffensive nonsectarian religious framework, civic education held the potential either to support the formative beliefs of the majority population or to modify the comprehensive beliefs of children of unsupportive religious beliefs. Thus, following the conviction that moral identities drew from religious beliefs, common school proponents sought to achieve coherence between faith and the moral values of the public. Toward this end, common school leaders pressed conscientious limits to impart what they considered the American view of civic morality and truth. Meanwhile, educational dissenters generally argued that the common school education model surpassed the limits of state interference with their liberty of conscience.

The Civic Unity Argument

A second argument that supported common school acceptance was based upon the fear of public disunion. Fearing factional divisions, education reformers argued the need for public schools to mold citizens into a unifying American identity. They advanced the common school's vision of unity by a "deliberate effort to create in the entire youth of a nation common attitudes, loyalties, and values, and to do so under the central direction of the state" (Glenn, 1988, p. 4). Education reformers were concerned about increasing diversity, "but their overriding preoccupation was with spiritual disunity, the growing gap between their own 'enlightened' values and stubborn vestiges of what they regarded as superstition and fanaticism" (Glenn, 1988, p. 8). Thus, reflecting the religious nature of the common school's philosophy, Stephen Carter concludes that public education's goal, in part, was to wean immigrants from aspects of their native faiths (2000, p. 180).

Concerns over unity not only supported the adoption of the common school, but acceptance of the common paradigm of education compounded and redefined these concerns. Under the common school, diversity was viewed as a problem, and schools not accountable to public authority were considered a threat to social stability. Most people viewed public schools as a force for social unity. According to Glenn,

> The liberal elite developed a program for a certain type of popular education as a reaction against the perceived threat of emerging class interests and of the "irrationality" of revivalistic religion. Through the common school, they believed, class antagonism would be overcome and sectarian divisions reconciled. (1988, p. 87)

Whether or not the diversity of the 19th century was a real threat to civic unity, with the acceptance of the common school, "those who demanded the right to provide or obtain schooling marked by traditional religion were seen as divisive of national and social unity" (Glenn, 1988, p. 262). Hence, for common school supporters, national unity was at the heart of their argument as much as was civic moral formation.

The Catholic Threat Argument

A third argument that supported common school acceptance was empowered by the perception of an invasive civic threat. In an atmosphere already charged by the common school debate, the influential Evangelical minister Lyman Beecher is largely known for writing *Plea for the West* in 1835. In this plea, he contrasted his millennialistic concerns that destined America to spread its God-glorifying institutions into the western parts of the continent with the consequences he perceived to follow the spread of Catholic ideology. He promoted fears that Catholics would unite church and state in an antirepublican despotism (Marsden, 1994). "Much of *Plea* was a fervid effort to document a conspiracy of the alliance of Catholic ecclesiastical power and Romanist European despots to capture the American West through massive Catholic immigration" (Marsden, 1994, p. 84). However, Beecher also argued that the common school was a vital tool to Americanize the immigrants. Articulating his confidence in the state's ability to propagate an American civic philosophy among those of undemocratic ideologies, he said, "Let the Catholics mingle with us as Americans, and come with their children under the fell action of our common schools and republican institutions, and we are prepared cheerfully to abide the consequences" (as cited in Marsden, 1994, p. 84).

Claims as to the nonsectarian nature of public policies often belied the anti-Catholic biases that continued from the nation's founding. According to Elson,

> It is . . . clear that the many Catholic immigrants arriving in America in this period [1776 to the Civil War] would face strong hostility for their religion as well as for their foreign birth. The school child in this period would associate Catholicism only with unpleasant behavior and subversive beliefs. He would imbibe not only the idea that its theology is false, but that it is inimical to industry, prosperity, knowledge, and freedom—concepts considered basic to all civilization. According to those schoolbooks published before 1870, Catholicism has no place in the American past or future, nor in the economic and political climate of the United States. (1964, p. 53)

It was this uncertainty regarding the civic values of some faiths "that led them to see rural Calvinists and immigrant Catholics as a profound threat to the emerging national society" (Glenn, 1988, p. 8).

Though Catholics in particular opposed the common school, Mann's vision of social unity motivated him to try to accommodate their faith in the public school. McClellan describes the rationale behind this effort:

> To exclude Catholic . . . workers and immigrants was to weaken the school's power to serve as a cohesive force in society and to increase the prospect that the children of the "dangerous classes" would grow up undisciplined, illiterate, and a threat to the stability of the society. (1992, p. 39)

Thus, it required a substantial motivation to overcome the public's resistance to nonsectarian state education. Glenn surmises that if not for the specter that linked Roman Catholic immigrants with immorality and authoritarianism, perhaps two of the greatest threats to society and democratic liberty, the common school ideas may never have won acceptance (1988, pp. 205–206).

The American Faith Argument

A fourth argument that supported common school acceptance was empowered by the close tie that Protestantism shared with American public ideology. Common education would propagate a distinctively American identity that reflected the values of most homes. Supporting the common school movement seemed to complement the mission of the church and helped to win over supporters. With the linkage of the Protestant mission with that of Americanization, Marsden writes,

> The public schools... became part of the united Protestant mission to the
> nation. Catharine Beecher... envisioned an army of single women teach-
> ers... civilizing the nation.... Conversion was less of an issue, and growth
> in Christian morality and American civility were more central concerns.
> (1994, p. 89)

Though the common school held that the nonsectarian faith of the
schools supported the national vision, this faith was actually an extension
of the Protestant faiths that many conceived as the source of civic ideals.

National interests were grounded in a transcendent good; civic ideals
were not just functional, they were in accord with transcendent views of
reality that held their place for the conscientious public in the form a civil
religion if not in full-bodied faith. Historian James Turner notes, "Civil religion made traditional religious concerns, chiefly morality, critical in the
secular arena, where they naturally lost their transcendent reference. Not
man's eternal fate, but the nation's political future, was at stake" (1985,
pp. 83–84). But the lack of transcendent reference did not negate its understood reality. Religious and public sectors alike shared moral and character concerns that fueled the growth of public school systems in which
self-restraint, diligence, and duty were much more important than reading,
writing, and arithmetic.

Extensive surveys of 19th-century common school textbooks reveal the
flavor of what education leaders considered nonsectarian and supportive of
the public civic philosophy. Although the religious emphasis changed over
time, Elson writes,

> None of these books is secular; a sense of God permeates all books.... All
> of the early Readers and Spellers devote the greater part of their space to
> the subject of God's relationship to the universe, to man, and to the child
> himself. (1964, p. 41)

Clearly, public textbooks, driven by a mission to advance public morality, avoided strict neutrality toward the comprehensive views of the day.
Moral propagation required the motivating force of a concern for God,
thus, in textbooks "deism and atheism are assumed to be illogical as well
as sinful. They are also believed to be a fertile source of immorality and
depravity" (Elson, 1964, p. 44).

The close alignment of civic education philosophy with general Protestant religious beliefs provided a means to broaden the spiritual mission of
many believers. Thus, the argument that common schools represented the
"American faith" rather than just denominational faith convinced Mann

to support common schooling. Unfortunately for traditional believers, this strategy to spread faith undermined its religious resources. Glenn writes, "The historic role of schools in transmitting religious traditions was attenuated [by the common school] into perfunctory observances and moralizing" (1988, p. 115). Thus, the model chosen to propagate a deep civic identity was increasingly unable to propagate the faith to which that identity was considered indebted.

Did Nonsectarian Schooling Imply Less Concern for Religion?

If a grounding of knowledge and value in Christian revelation was important to America's Protestant majority, why did it choose a shallower, nonsectarian educational system under the state rather than church authority? Francis Curran, a Jesuit Catholic scholar, expressed the concern that "if . . . a Christian church relinquished its claims on any one of the divisions of formal education, it implicitly admits that it has no part in education" (1954, p. 5). But one cannot read the Protestant response so simply. Many Protestants perceived the dangers associated with large-scale Catholic immigration to be greater than the dangers posed by the displacement of *some* religious interests from school to home. Additionally, the path of secularization was uncharted; common school supporters did not expect that the philosophy of the public school would increasingly diverge from the religious beliefs of their homes.

Protestant church members were not immune to the promises of the common school, which expanded beyond the more compelling rationales discussed above. As the pressures of operating private schools forced religious leaders to entertain common school possibilities, lay members moved *beyond* the cautions of their pastors. Curran analyzed the typical mid-19th-century American's swing from parochial to public school commitment as follows:

> When the leaders of his church unanimously called for parochial schools, it would appear that he was ready to follow their guidance. When that leadership wavered, he hesitated. Dutifully, as an American and as a Protestant, he had rallied to the defense of the common school, "godless" as it might be, against alien Catholicism. His denominational organs of opinion began to tell him that the state school was not "godless," but Christian and even Protestant, and above all "American." He was urged to see to it that the common school remained Protestant by retaining the Protestant Bible. The primary education controlled by the state was Protestant. Why should he expend labor and money to create other Protestant schools under the control of the church? (1954, p. 128)

Glenn notes that Orthodox Protestants were the first to object to common schooling based on how it dealt with religious differences (1987, p. 179). However, once they came to view Catholicism as a civic threat, most Protestants began to support public common schooling. Glenn writes, "The immigrant threat created near unanimity among Protestant leaders, by the early 1850s, in support of the common school" (1987, p. 235). Though the acceptance of nonsectarian education seems to imply a diminished concern for religious truth, one better interprets its acceptance as a move to align public power with the preservation of a broad view of the Protestant faith and the Protestant nature of America's civic identity. Philosophically, little seemed to be lost and much seemed to be gained, and most churches came to see the public school as their ally.

Curran (1954) writes that the acceptance of the common school led to the closure of most Protestant parochial schools and produced the side effect of an increased animosity toward Catholics who criticized or shunned what had become a thoroughly American institution. In a series of 1870 issues, the Baptist quarterly, *Watchman*, condemned the use of public money for sectarian education, demanded that Biblical truth be taught in common schools, and justified the potential closing of Catholic schools for the "safety" of Catholic children (Curran, 1954, p. 106). Thus, for most Protestants, the eventual acceptance of the common school did not represent a decreased concern regarding the place of religion in education. To the contrary, they accepted the common school as an acceptable means by which to promote their religiously based conceptions of morality, unity, and American identity against the real and perceived threats associated with ignorance and Catholicism.

Offenses Associated With the Common School

Horace Mann advocated nonsectarian religious schooling. But nonsectarian education created opponents who claimed that it was either too sectarian or not sectarian enough. The general and eventual acceptance of the common school by the Protestant majority may hide the concerns of its opponents and the evidence they offer regarding its shortcomings. Kaestle (1983) emphasizes that there was much greater opposition to the common school than has survived in popular history. "Opponents of state school systems began as a majority in many states, and in 1860 they remained a strong minority, even in the Northeast" (Kaestle, 1983, p. 136).

Common School Curricula Alienated Catholics

Common schooling became a powerful source of civic alienation for Catholics as it opposed or neglected their faith. They saw the link between common school ideology and the Protestant civic identity. Thus, the "common school" could not be truly common and was, as to be expected, most acceptable to those who already embodied traditional American ideals. The imposition of common education upon one's conscience was relative to one's distance from the philosophically "common" mean. This mean "centered on republicanism, Protestantism, and capitalism, three sources of social belief that were intertwined and mutually supporting" (Kaestle, 1983, p. 76). Most Americans came to accept this mean as the nation viewed its identity in Protestant conceptions of truth and value. Fraser notes the effect on outsiders: "Catholics were tolerated, even welcomed, but only on Protestant terms. It was not an arrangement designed to make the new immigrants or their religious leaders happy" (1999, p. 51).

Within the common schools, Protestant ideals were associated with progress and enlightened thinking, while Catholicism was linked to absolutism, suppression of the individual, and the suppression of inquiry. From her research, Elson found

> Only books designed for use in Catholic parochial schools deal favorably with the Catholic religion and Catholics. In the others, stories of individual Catholics in a favorable context do occur, but they are rare, and they are lost in the vehemence and reiteration of condemnations that are stated and implied in the rest of the same schoolbook. (1964, p. 52)

It is no wonder that Catholics in particular rejected what the public accepted as common.

Some common school dissenters ran parochial schools at their own expense. These costly endeavors generally reflected opposition to the common school's philosophy by those who held that their children's education should more faithfully reflect their particular religious beliefs. Catholics were more likely to argue that the common school opposed their faith, while both Catholics and dissenting Protestants were likely to argue that the common school unacceptably minimized the place of their religious beliefs in their children's educations.

While religious diversification forced a thinning of the philosophical base of the common school model, Catholic parochial schools maintained their sectarian and truth-centered perspectives. McClellan writes that Catholics were

> reluctant to confine the authority of the church to narrow spheres, to separate the sacred from the civil, to draw lines between public and private domains, or to make sharp distinctions between universally acceptable truths and the doctrinal beliefs of particular denominations.... They found it dif-

ficult to imagine a schooling devoid of elementary doctrinal instruction. (1999, p. 37)

Elson's textbook study concludes, "Catholic schoolbooks retain throughout the century the same kind of sectarian religious zeal exhibited by Protestant books in the first part of the century, but it is Catholicism rather than Protestantism that is the foundation of civilization and American independence" (1964, p. 55). For example, one 1878 Catholic school text implied that American successes were indebted to the Catholic faith; it said, "'there can be but one true religion,' whose benign influence is the basis of civilization" (Elson, 1964, p. 55). The reattribution of many American successes demonstrates that Catholics were buying into American society even though the school system often alienated them from the mainstream. Further, since this buy-in largely occurred *outside* the common schools, it appears that perhaps the fear of Catholic education was as exaggerated as public confidence in common education.

Selective Public Funding as a Source of Offense and Alienation

Based upon its public mission to advance civic concerns, public education was not to be just an equal educational alternative but to be a publicly favored one. This preferential funding not only demarked civic values, but also it provided a source of civic alienation. During the 1840s, immigration to America tripled the number of Catholic citizens who were an already marginalized group. The Protestantism of the common schools became a point of contention. In New York, when the Catholics asked for public money to run their own schools, heated debates arose that reflected a general anti-Catholic sentiment. Michael McConnell writes that it was "insisted that public funds should not be used to teach superstition and disloyalty" (2002, p. 111). Religious historian Mark Noll notes that 19th-century Protestants "almost universally suspected Roman Catholics of undermining Christian as well as American values" (1992, p. 300). From this beginning, public funding would increasingly serve to exclude sectarian schools.

Through the mid-19th century, local control determined the spending of public education dollars, but a new national trend began in the century's fourth quarter. In 1876, President Ulysses S. Grant warned a veteran's organization against the regressive influences of sectarian schools:

If we are to have another contest in the near future of our national existence, I predict that the dividing line will not be Mason and Dixon's, but it will be between patriotism and intelligence on one side, and superstition, ambition, and ignorance on the other. . . . Encourage free schools, and resolve that not one dollar appropriated to them shall be applied to the support of any sectarian school; resolve that any child in the land can get a common school education, unmixed with atheistic, pagan, or sectarian teachings. (1898, p. 788)

The specific meaning of Grant's comment is lost unless one understands that "common" schools reflected the Protestant culture and that "sectarian schools" was a direct reference to *Catholic* parochial schools and clearly understood by the citizens of his day. Grant did not oppose the public funding of religious schooling; he opposed the funding of the "wrong" religious schooling.

Inflamed by fear of un-Americanized Catholicism, the nativist climate of 1875 inspired James G. Blaine (1830–1893) to lead a federal campaign to further establish common public schools and to prohibit the public funding of sectarian schools. After the failure of this attempt, many states adopted constitutional amendments largely intended to prohibit state support of Catholic schools. A typical version of these *Blaine Amendments* prohibited state money and land from being given to a religious sect or denomination (Jorgenson, 1987). The Blaine Amendments remain a part of the constitutions of 37 states, and they are often used to oppose school choice measures that include religious schools.

However, religious prejudice alone does not explain the choice of Protestant conceptions of truth to support civic education. If national unity required common convictions regarding the deeper and transcendent qualities of democratic liberty, and if historical evidence linked Protestant ideas and values with the success of the polity, then a civic education grounded in the soil of these beliefs seemed vital to the public interest. It would require the greater detachment of later generations to realize that other faiths could deeply support democratic liberty as well. Thus, state laws came to reflect, with virtual unanimity, that the educational interests of the state required the public support of a view of civic truth and value grounded in nonsectarian Protestant beliefs.

This was possible because, until the latter part of the 19th century, most of the population subscribed to many common values. Most worshiped God and shaped their moral and philosophic outlook upon their Judeo-Christian heritage. Marsden writes that most Americans

believed people should control their passions and desires, not commit murder or adultery, steal, lie, or succumb to envy and greed. . . . Individual character was seen as the chief force in history, and virtue of the individual was seen as the key to a healthy society. (1990, p. 75)

The Catholic Church reacted to the increased pressure to attend common schools by expanding its own school system. In 1884, after much controversy regarding the alienating effects of the common schools, the Third Plenary Council of the Catholic Church met in Baltimore and decreed "that near every church a parish school, where one does not yet exist, is to be built and maintained in perpetuum within two years. . . . All Catholic parents are bound to send their children to the parish school" (as cited in Fraser, 1999, p. 60).

Thus, the exclusive linking of the common school's version of moral and civic nurture with public funding, meant to advance concerns for morality and unity, became a source of offense and alienation. Catholics set about the project of nurturing their children to be good American citizens according to their religious beliefs and their perceptions of societal needs. However, the negative labeling and the added burden of funding both common schools and their parochial schools did little to help their social buy-in.

Other Groups Alienated by Common Schooling

Although some Jews opposed the common school system for religious reasons, having been publicly alienated in other lands, most Jews were grateful for the freedoms they found in America and valued the opportunity to blend with American culture in the schools (Handy, 1991). With most Jews, Protestants, and other Americans growing to support the common school system, the Lutheran Synodical Conference, the Old School Presbyterians, and the Catholics remained philosophically opposed to the system and maintained their own schools. While in the latter half of the 19th century Lutheran schools diminished from their peak of 2,500 schools (Curran, 1954, p. 120), Catholic schools continued to multiply, and by 1920, they operated 5,852 schools (Carper & Hunt, 2007, p. 66).

Other Protestant schools found it difficult to survive financially against the competition of tax-funded schools. Old-school Presbyterians were in this group. They mounted the greatest Protestant opposition to the common school movement over concerns that common schools would not teach distinct doctrines. Influential theologian Charles Hodge argued that common schools focused on secular subjects, would promote religious infidelity, and were discriminatory to those wanting a more comprehensive Christian education for their children. In 1854, the Old-school Presbyterians had 264 schools, but support for their movement soon dwindled as concerns regarding national influence, sectarianism, and social progress prevailed.

Efforts Toward Inclusion

Though common schooling was an offense to many, this was not the intent of education leaders. Common school supporters encouraged Catholic families to support the "American school" through concessions for instructional language, use of the Douay Bible, and the removal of offensive texts, but these efforts were not wholly effective. As discussed above, common school support often represented a blend of nativist and democratic motivations. Thus, concessions were not uniform, and struggles to meet the concerns of the growing pluralism met with various responses in different locations. With the denial of public funding for private denominational schools, the expense of private education pressured outsider schools to look for ways to work conscientiously with public school systems. However, efforts to compromise with the concerns of common school dissenters met with only mixed success.

Education leaders experimented in some locations with the incorporation of Catholic schools into the public system. This experimentation produced a relatively successful example of accommodation in Poughkeepsie, New York, in 1873. The parish relinquished most of the control over several of its schools to the public school board. The board then used public money to operate the schools while it selected teachers and curricula that met the approval of the local priest. The church provided religious instruction before and after school and controlled the facilities when they were not in use by the school board.

Though these efforts met with relative success, they were rare against the backdrop of separated public and private school systems. They provided evidence that public educational concerns could advance through efforts to accommodate, rather than to alienate, religious groups who held a broader educational place for their religion than common schooling allowed. However, these efforts also point to the dangerous effects of *too great* a subordination of religious concerns to the secular state, for in the ensuing years, these formerly parochial schools all lost their Catholic flavor.

The Decline of Religious Instruction and Its Civic Effects

As noted above, the common school's particular mission focused on the moral and civic nurture of young children; though other schools might provide academic preparation, only the "public" schools were trusted to nurture the necessary qualities of American citizenship. Moral instruction was not isolated to a particular course but "moral lessons suffused nineteenth-century textbooks—not just readers, but spellers and arithmetic books as well" (McClellan, 1992, p. 25). However, this early instruction relied upon religious foundations that were to be removed slowly. Early curricula often called upon religious beliefs to define or reinforce these concerns, but as common school leaders attempted to accommodate diverse religious perspectives, the overt place of religion decreased. Religion had not been dismissed as an insufficient moral foundation, it just fit poorly into the common education paradigm. Textbook scholar William Kailer Dunn concluded, "The struggle over sectarianism . . . and not hostility or indifference to religion as such mainly caused the decline of religious teaching" (1958, p. 309).

Elson's studies also confirm that textbooks reflected the decreased place of religion. She found that

> religion in the schoolbooks lost its earlier doctrinal content in the second part of the century. Man and his civilization are just as dependent on God as they were in the earlier books, but God is now shown to be the creator of the world and the founder and executor of the ethical system on which our civilization rests—although religion is still basic to life, religious institutions are less prominent. Whose interpretation of Scripture as authoritative becomes less important. (1964, p. 54)

As the common school tried to remain nonsectarian, its moral advocacy became less reliant upon specific religious teaching. As McClellan writes, "Despite the presence of religion, most moral education focused on values that required little theological sanction, values such as honesty, industry, thrift, and kindness" (1992, p. 38).

Dunn's (1958) research also affirms that under the common education model, religious themes were displaced by moral themes even as both were crowded from the curriculum. The readers used between 1775 and 1825 devoted 22% of their space to religion and 28% to morals; between 1825 and 1875, these numbers were reduced disproportionately to 7.5% to religion and 23% to morals; and between 1875 and 1915, only 1.5% of their space was given to religion and 7% to morals.

However, *less religious teaching did not necessarily reflect a decrease in the religious mission of the common school.* The sense of an increasing civic threat caused the nation's attachments to *harden* around its Protestant moral and civic heritage. Glenn argues that decreased religious instruction reflected a reasoned strategy to broaden Protestant influence. During the latter half of the 19th century, religion was "increasingly removed . . . largely as an attempt to enroll and thus to assimilate the children of Catholic immigrants, *the mission of the school itself became more rather than less truly 'religious'*" (1988, p. 178, emphasis on the original).

This insight deflects the assumption that religion declined due to its ir-relevance to the public mission of education. To the contrary, the spread of "American" moral and civic values *was* a religious mission. Religious teaching appears to have declined as a "best choice" that enabled the nation's Protestant civic vision to gain state power while also acknowledging growing concerns regarding state impositions upon conscience.

The 19th century's civic education ended quite differently than it had begun. The curriculum spoke less of religion, yet the Christian context assured parents that the material aligned with their religious beliefs, which the public accepted as the foundations for political and social endeavors. Elson finds that

> by the last three decades of the century ambivalence toward religious free-dom is gone, and the United States is proudly described as Christian, but [quoting from an 1892 geography book]: "There is no established religion in the United States. Every man may worship God according to the dictates of his own conscience. But Christianity is the basis of the government and institutions, and public opinion is enlisted in its favor." (1964, p. 58)

By the end of the 19th century, school texts had followed the common school's predictable path of secularization, but they held strongly to broad conceptions of religious truth. Elson writes, "As systematized theology, religion almost disappears from the later books, but it always maintains a prominent place with regard to man's moral behavior. It has become a religion of ethics rather than one of theology" (1964, p. 43).

Thus, the decline of religious instruction did not necessarily reduce religious concerns regarding common schooling. However, it would become apparent in the 20th century that religious missions rely upon overt teaching and grounding to support their goals. Those who hoped to spread their faith through a diluted message may have found they won a "Pyrrhic victory."

Reflections on the Success of the 19th-Century Common School

Summary

The American public chose the common school model of education for a plurality of reasons within a particular historical and social context. The model began with a robust view of the individual and good citizenship and relied upon linking with religious conceptions of truth, but due to growing ideological diversity, it was forced to draw more shallowly from these religious foundations. The preceding chapter has documented:

- Sectarian religious schools had been working to meet the growing concerns related to educational quality and availability so that "locally controlled, voluntary elementary schooling was a common feature of life in most American communities by 1830" (Kaestle, 1983, p. 62). However, public leaders proposed that common schools could more decisively address the public's educational concerns.
- Although the public could have invested in a plural public education system, the common school more forcefully aligned public power *against* what was perceived to be an un-American philosophic foundation.
- Although common schools proved to alienate many because of what they taught or failed to teach, they were believed to promote the foundations of public morality and unity by exposing children of all faiths to American ideals in a context that was both inoffensive and meaningful.
- Early common schools were not secular. The common school's religious affirmations aligned with the beliefs and values of most Protestants and thus showed a measure of success in linking the motivating force of their religious views with American moral and civic ideals.
- Many education leaders claimed that common school would accommodate concerns of conscience in spite of the fact that it did not accommodate beliefs that differed drastically or beliefs that their holders refused to separate from the school day.
- Although it provided a shallower religious education, the common school won over many of its early Protestant opponents, in part, because it complemented their evangelical concern to spread aspects of America's godly understanding and concerns to the unenlightened.

Ultimately, the national majority chose the common school model to support the civic uncertainties of the day because it was believed to be effective toward the moral formation, national unification, and conscientious accommodation of a diverse population. However, though its goals were lofty, the model provided mixed success as it dramatically alienated some groups and lost moral and intellectual force among its supporters by undermining the philosophic foundations that had given rise to the American vision. Additionally, hindsight provides evidence that Catholics and others were more capable than presumed of assimilating American ideals apart from common school attendance.

Though the experience and bias of the day seemed to provide substantial reason both to favor the teaching of Protestant moral and civic ideals and also to question the ability of Roman Catholics to instill the moral and democratic attachments valued for American citizenship, the effect of the common school was to alienate those it most desired to reach. Using the pressure of an education tax, it required that parents and children consider the ideals of the state to override many of their concerns of faith. Though the precise influence of 19th-century common schools cannot be known, it may likely be that common schools did more "preaching to the choir" than they did "winning of the lost."

The 1800s were transitional years for American education. The century began with public and private schools that were taught from fully integrated religious perspectives. By the end of the century, the key religious concepts that undergirded the "American way of life" were transposed into a "civil religion"—or religion of the state. Though many faith tenets were rejected as divisive, those that remained not only made common schools acceptable to most families, but also anchored the moral and civic concerns of the public in the deeper beliefs of most Protestant citizens.

The public was stepping deeply into the parental role of raising children toward a moral and ideological maturity defined by the needs of American society. Was the common school model, torn between concern for religious conscience and the needs of moral and civic propagation, a sufficient ideological platform for this task once conceived to be deeply religious? Although the unitary model chosen was created to link public power with a Protestant-leaning ideological view, this public power was limited by an evolving concern for religious conscience. To what degree could non-Protestant religious foundations provide "soil" for the growth of American ideals? Would a *continued* distancing of American ideals from religious contexts weaken/undermine the mission of public education? As public education secularized, would new educational methods or curricula be found to enable public schools to successfully meet the public's educational concerns? Or might public education merely become so inclusively shallow as to fail to inspire the meaningful learning and buy-in thought necessary for the success of the American experiment?

Legitimacy and Effectiveness

That some disapproved of the common school does not negate the public concerns that drove it. Liberty required broad individual freedoms, and "liberty for all" required a citizenry with the character and commitment to support the rule of democratic law in a peaceful manner. Thus, public concerns toward American moral and civic education were well founded. Also, since the civic concerns of the state relied upon shaping the moral and ideological convictions of children, the public rightly sought an education model that could not only teach those of various religious views, but also teach them in settings that positively engaged their religious views. However, though the public may have been right on these two concerns, the common model of education may not have been their best choice. Their efforts to achieve the public's concerns were losing traction under a school model increasingly distanced from the moral and philosophical grounds of student convictions.

Thus, this chapter ends having demonstrated the conflict central to the history, development, and philosophy of common education. The conviction that shared religious beliefs could adequately support the public's moral and civic education interests was unraveling. Common schooling forced a choice between a depth of ideological motivation and a breadth of inclusiveness. Proponents hoped that the common school would influence citizens to accept "American" moral and civic ideals as true and to incorporate them into their life-guiding systems of belief, but growing ideological diversity increasingly forced common school discussion from this field of deep philosophical grounding and advocacy.

Into Modernity

By the end of the 19th century, a new philosophic ground became available for the exploration and utilization of public researchers and educators. While social and technological change stretched the national fabric, and traditional religion became increasingly unsatisfactory as a common ground for public truth, public educators would have to make a choice between three options. They could continue to ground public education in the increasingly shallow philosophic soil of nonsectarian religion, they could find an acceptable nonreligious source of truth, or adopt a public education model that circumvented the quagmire created by common education. Whereas the first was rejected because it was becoming increasingly difficult to teach morality without stepping on religious particularities, and the third option remained off the table due to the continuing uncertainties elicited by widespread immigration, the second choice remained a possibility. The scientific methodology posed a solution that promised to be both effective and nonoffensive to people of all faiths.

Academic reflection on the educational implications of scientific and positivistic models of truth began in the last decades of the 19th century. The application of this reflection would strongly influence the nature of public education throughout the 20th century and into the 21st. Whereas early Protestant schools had sought to deal with the depravity of human nature within traditional religious paradigms, the "scientific" philosophy of modern schools would be less skeptical of student nature; that which previous generations had accepted as fallen, modern generations would view as needful only of the shaping forces of reason and experience.

However, though the academic community widely accepted this new view, much of the population continued to hold to religious perspectives. For the purposes of this study, I will view the academic shift away from religiously based civic development as a variable in the public experiment regarding civic propagation. Would this alternate view of human nature respond to the new pedagogy of scientific public education? Could traditional religion be successfully replaced as a ground for the public's education efforts to nurture morality, civic character, and the public values of citizens?

Public education in the 20th century would face the need to accommodate a less assured ground of truth as it attempted to propagate the civic values of modernity under the common school model of education. Thus, the trajectory of the following chapter is to discover how the issues of modernity affected not only the common school model but also the success of some of the key educational theories of the 20th century.

3

Religion Within Modernity's Public Schools

By the end of the 19th century and under the influences of modernity, religiously "common" schools were becoming simply public schools within which traditional religion was conceived by reformers to play little (if any) necessary role. Whereas the previous chapter confronted the "common religion ideal" of public education, this and the next chapter will confront two variations of the secular education ideal. Here, I will show that modernity's conception of "secular" education largely overlooked the religious nature of its project; religion continued to play a vital role in public education, both through features that remained and features that became absent. Though the schools of the 20th century were much more secular than those of the preceding century, the distancing of public schools from the ideological cores of attending families seems to have weakened rather than strengthened many of the public's educational efforts.

Some educators blamed conflicts over religious truth as the cause of school secularization (Giordano, 2003, p. 114). Though both a reason-

Education Reform, pages 53–76
Copyright © 2013 by Information Age Publishing
All rights of reproduction in any form reserved.

able and a popular idea, this explanation is incomplete and provides limited insight into the thinking of families and education reformers of the day. At the heart of the school secularization movement was a triad of influences that worked together to bring about secularization but not necessarily to strengthen the public's educational efforts as intended. These three influences were

- A nontraditional (secular) philosophy of knowledge, learning, and human nature.
- A predominant religious perspective that approved a limited place for "secular scientific inquiry" and the schools it spawned so that they retained religious meaning.
- A legal collision between traditional religion and the rights of conscience caused by the common education paradigm.

Public schools retained the mission of cultivating a robust vision of the strong American citizen—a life-shaping endeavor shaped by Protestant beliefs. However, 20th-century educators would experiment to nurture this citizen in public schools that were meaningful, motivational, and supportive of the public's educational goals, yet not overtly religious.

Though educational secularization represented many philosophical, organizational, and curricular changes, most religious Americans continued to accept the strengths and weaknesses of the common education model that allied state power with "common" conceptions of civic and moral education. Dissent also continued from outsider communities, with Catholic, Lutheran, and Seventh Day Adventist churches operating the greatest numbers of private schools.

Whereas 19th-century common school advocates linked a nonsectarian Protestant worldview with American values, public education reformers of the 20th century looked for other philosophic sources to support their civic curricula. Whereas early common school advocates removed controversial religious material from public schools for pragmatic reasons, by the early 20th century, the academy, with its naturalistic and scientific orientation, secularized schools for ideological, not just pragmatic, reasons. Rather than looking to religious beliefs, scholars proposed moral and civic ideals (with accompanying methodologies for their inculcation) that they described as common, scientific, progressive, and finally, noncomprehensive.

Though the Protestant majority in America held on to the common education school model with its predisposition for secularization, traditionalists in the Netherlands criticize the model. Abraham Kuyper, Prime Minister of the Netherlands from 1901 to 1905, was instrumental in the successful national struggle against common education that lasted from 1869 to 1920. The struggle reflected a rejection of common education and the Enlightenment premise that society should share a common civic identity. It recognized that education rested upon different sets of foundational assumptions and that common education was civically divisive. Kuyper's successful leadership aided in the establishment of a public education system that reflected diverse religious schools funded with public money. Whereas in America, the civic identity was linked to Protestantism, in the Netherlands, neither Catholicism nor Protestantism was dominant. Thus, Glenn attributes the success of this educational path to the equally matched interests of Protestant and Catholic communities that each deemed education inseparable from their faiths (1988, pp. 244–249).

Public Truth Shifts From Revelation to Acceptable Scientific Inquiry

How a religious people came to accept secular education is a fascinating study in itself, but the significance of the subject warrants at least a brief discussion here. The incremental shift away from traditional religious views of truth grew out of an increased confidence in the role of enlightened reason toward the pursuit of truth. Truth was not found merely from the study of Scriptural revelation, but it could be discovered and even expanded through methodological research. From its founding in 1746, Princeton was an early entry and dispersal point for Enlightenment thought. As science found explanations for much of what had hitherto been attributed to God, enlightened thought spread throughout the nation in higher education. In scholarly circles, God increasingly became a secondary rather than a primary cause, and the natural world became separated from the supernatural.

As the academy's source of truth, Enlightenment science validated and preferred experience to revelation. Agreement arose that "empirical truths were more reliable than those that transcended physical reality" (Turner, 1985, p. 134), and academics attempted to separate religious belief from scientific study. Even if God remained present and active in one's private life, in the world of the natural sciences, "He pulled a quick about face. There an abstract Supreme Being made the universe, laid down its rules, and sustained it, but in effect stepped back and let the mechanism run with little if any direct intervention" (1985, p. 38). Later, doubt was cast upon religious belief itself as Darwin provided a nontheistic explanation for the origin of life. From the late 19th century, positivism challenged Christian thought.

Stemming from the ideas of Auguste Comte (1798–1857), the founder of the field of sociology, positivism need not consult religious beliefs.

> In Comte's construction of history, humans were rising from a religious state in which questions were decided by authority, through a metaphysical state in which philosophy ruled, to a positive state in which empirical investigation would be accepted as the only reliable road to truth. (Marsden, 1994, p. 130)

Positivism "devalued theology and metaphysics and regarded the findings of empirical science as the only knowledge worth having" (McClellan, 1992, p. 69).

Noah Porte modified Comte's ideas to assert that an absolute must exist for us to know anything. He argued that God must exist for all else to exist, and from this starting point, the scientific method could be used in what he called Christian positivism. Though accommodating religious belief in the academy, Porte's accommodations of faith failed to gain traction as the shaping force of academic pursuits. Comte's confidence in reasoned inquiry alone would reign with little challenge for the better part of a century (Marsden, 1994).

With positivistic assumptions and a new faith in the scientific methodology, higher education's historic linkage with church bodies was philosophically undermined—*both from within and without*—leading to a predictable shift of control. Religiously affiliated colleges not only secularized philosophically, but many changed their names and became public institutions in the states in which they resided. As the physical sciences presupposed natural explanations for physical realities, the social sciences presupposed natural explanations for human beliefs and actions. The successes of these scientific presumptions and methodologies elevated their credibility and emboldened their pursuits. Soon, according to Turner, "evolutionary explanations of the origin of belief in God, carrying the imprimatur of social science...acquired far more plausibility than ever before" (1985, p. 174), and some left their faiths. But many more integrated the new way of thinking into their faiths. Marsden notes,

> Across the nation at the turn of the century, one could find academic leaders, both conservatives and progressives, who would not have been ashamed to view themselves as missionaries for the higher culture based on science and the unifying ethical ideals of Jesus. (1994, p. 256)

With these shifting patterns of faith, the public place of religion was shrinking, and this left a broader place for "unbiased" scientific thought. Enlightened thought that had once vindicated God's existence was now used to refute it, and religion, though still a foundation for "private" life, seemed to be less relevant to public endeavors.

Religious historian George Marsden (1990) reflects that the relative lack of resistance to the secularization of higher education implied a wide agreement that education *should be* secular. It follows that since institutions of higher education trained the nation's leaders and defined that which was viewed as authoritative, the beliefs of modernity's scholarly community regarding the role of religion had broader influence than is measured by adherent numbers alone. The relatively few scholars multiplied their influence as they trained the teachers, administrators, textbook authors, and public policy experts of society.

Not only did scholars question the place of religious views in scholarship, but they questioned the need for religion as a shaper of morality. The earlier writings of Scottish philosophers Francis Hutcheson and Thomas Reid contradicted the need for traditional beliefs. Reid had argued that the moral sense was just an innate, independent, and perceptive power of the mind. This philosophy, when complemented by 20th-century positivism, supported the move away from religiously based moral instruction in the schools. In the academy, enlightenment faith, evolutionary philosophy, and the progressive discoveries of the physical sciences encouraged the belief that even moral and social knowledge advanced with study; the certainty of one generation would be modified in the next to provide a higher degree of moral truth (Turner, 1985). Two effects of this presumption were to place an undue confidence in new social theories and to lose confidence in traditional views. Brought into the realm of the natural, morality became accessible to modern social scientists, and public schools drew from their research to formulate new foundations and methodologies in support of the public's educational mission.

This would enable John Dewey and other modern progressive philosophers to present civic concerns without any appeal to traditional faith. Concerns regarding citizenship and public education would find this "naturalized" or secularized moral theory as the least controversial and perhaps the most dependable support of the public interest toward the moral and civic development of its citizenry.

In summary, by the end of the 19th century, enlightened religion was rapidly losing its role as the common and secure source of public truth. The evolutionary theory had provided validation for nontheistic beliefs, German higher criticism had opened the Bible to reinterpretation, questions of theodicy (brought to the fore by the evolutionary paradigm in which progress came at the expense of the weak) had cast doubt upon God's goodness, and immigration and revival had diversified traditional beliefs. Though relatively few disavowed faith entirely, agnosticism was becoming an American phenomenon (Turner, 1985), and the reliability of nonsectarian religion as a source of public unity, moral knowledge, and civic commitment became increasingly controversial. While earlier generations had looked to the Christian faith as a key educational resource, modern public schools relied heavily on positivistic sociology for its moral and civic education programs.

The reduction of public education's reliance upon religion faced relatively little resistance from the general Protestant populace, at least not enough to motivate families to pay to attend private schools. In 1900, only about 8% of American school-age children attended private schools, and only 27% of these were non-Catholic (Carper & Hunt, 2007). Though Catholic schools steadily grew in number through the modern period to a peak in 1965, the Protestant trend was not toward an exodus from the public schools. Lutherans had the largest number of non-Catholic schools, but rather than expanding to reflect opposition to secularism, between 1900 and 1936, about 1,000 Lutheran schools closed out of a total of 2,500. An additional 300 closed by 1954 (Curran, 1954). The changing numbers of other religious schools does not reflect a strong opposition to increasing secularization either. However, this general lack of resistance need not be considered to reflect religious apathy; rather, when one views this acceptance in context with the philosophic dynamics mentioned above, it seems to reflect the compatibility of secular curricula with many religious beliefs.

Though the academic philosophy of modernity did not accept religion as a source of truth, most religious Americans failed to understand or foresee the broad implications of the new philosophy. Rather, they accepted science-based research not just as compatible with but even as an extension of their faith. Thus, in spite of fewer acknowledgements of valued religious beliefs, as long as public schools seemed to reflect a Christian ethos, most Protestants accepted scientifically based education. In the words of historian Robert Lynn, there was a sincere belief in "the inherent and inevitable harmony of public education and the Protestant cause" (1964, p. 121). Accordingly, most religious Americans supported both the common school and more secularized public schools, and 20th-century civic education was shaped by scientific presumptions in a manner similar to the way in which 19th-century civic education was shaped by religious presumptions.

However, though most of the religious public accepted secular curricula, this acceptance did not imply that religious people would give scientific methods and conclusions greater—or even equal—authority than religious conclusions. Nor did this religious acceptance speak to the formative power of secular curricula. Unless curricular claims were meaningfully integrated into the faith of the believer, they seemed to be held at a relatively larger distance from the individual students life-shaping "religious" beliefs. The following sections will show that secular educational methodologies led to a weakening of programs intended to nurture the human qualities of American citizenship. In addition, as secularization distanced curricula from the religious beliefs of attending families, opportunities for conflict increased and served to alienate or divide sectors of the population counter to the unifying vision of common education.

Religion: Less Overt, But Still Active

Though it is clear that public education secularized through modernity under the general approval of a religious population, religion was *not* disappearing from or becoming irrelevant to the public education project. Rather, it *continued* to play important roles in the increasingly secularized settings of 20th-century public schools, some of which countered the public's educational efforts. In these schools, "scientific" curricula relied upon student reason and exposure without overt religious guidance or appeal. Though educators increasingly avoided traditional religion as a source of truth and value, public educational interests remained strongly indebted to religious views for its *acceptance, empowerment,* and meaningful *conceptualization.* The *acceptance* of public education's moral, civic, and even academic curricula required the acceptance of attending families who often framed their judgments around religious views. When curricular material aligned with family beliefs, it was supported, but when it contradicted home beliefs, the curricula was opposed and even served as a possible source of public disunity. Evidence for this will include an analysis of the religious acceptance of the reasoning and scientific methodology underlying many secular curricula, descriptions of some of the religious contentions surrounding certain moral/civic/academic curricula, and a review of religious claims that led to the rejection or reshaping of unacceptable curricula.

Likewise, the public's educational interests remained indebted to religious views for the *empowerment* of moral, civic, and academic curricula. The relative success of education efforts (measured broadly) was associated, in part, with the degree to which public schools positively engaged the religious views of students and their families. Curricula were empowered and re-enforced when they actively drew upon the important religious concepts of believing families, whereas curricula were less likely to become a life-shaping force when they conflicted with or neglected to connect with the religious beliefs of students. Thus, I will show that the 20th century's education theories increasingly neglected to actively engage the religious views of citizens with a predicted decline in effectiveness. Evidence for this claim will include the results of academic studies that failed to find support for the effectiveness of public moral and civic curricula, implications drawn from the decisions of both educational leaders and the public that evidence dissatisfaction with secularized programs, and public responses to these curricula that served to counter civic goals.

Finally, the public's educational interests remained indebted to religion as education leaders drew from their functionally religious views (or secular worldviews) to *conceptualize* meaningful curricula and teaching methodologies. Here, my concern will not be to merely show that many educational programs that pass as common or secular reflect a religious perspective, but to show that good education engages the presuppositions, the internal logic, and the prioritization of value that every meaningful education program reflects. In other words, since even most "secular" programs have some manner of functionally religious roots, they are best taught in settings in which these roots can be revealed, discussed, and even advocated. I will look to the writings of John Dewey, Mortimer Adler, and Bernard Iddings Bell to illuminate this claim.

Modern Public Education Accepted and Empowered by Religious Views

Though earlier I noted that religion actively plays distinct roles in both the *acceptance* and the *empowerment* of modernity's public education efforts, the two roles frequently become evident in situations of conflict. This should not come as a surprise, because our religious beliefs, as the ideological and motivational frameworks for our lives, not only legitimate truth claims and move us to action, but are controversial to nonbelievers! Thus, rather than addressing these roles in separate sections, I will illuminate these two roles of religion in public education in a series of historic conflicts and follow them with a brief analysis.

Conflicts Regarding the Acknowledgment of God

Conflicts regarding prayer and Bible reading were the first broad religion and education conflicts addressed at the legal level during the modern period. In 1900, only Massachusetts had a law mandating prayer and Bible reading in its public schools. By 1930, eleven states had joined Massachusetts to require prayer and Bible reading, while Wisconsin plus five other states had banned these exercises as divisive (Handy, 1991, p. 160).

Though one may view these laws regarding the place of a few moments of prayer and Bible reading as simply the presence or absence of religious rituals, their significance for many Protestant believers seems to have been much greater. Whereas the Protestant public had generally not viewed curricular secularization as anti-God, the removal of *all* faith practices seemed to not only reflect an aggression against their faith but to undermine the trustworthiness of public schools. A simple prayer and a moment of Bible reading seemed minimally sufficient to make the increasingly secular curriculum acceptable, and a school day that began by acknowledging God and his revealed truth was presumed to imply an awareness of his presence and truth throughout the day. The public response to later Supreme Court rulings that prohibited these "rituals" (to be addressed below) provides evidence for the high degree of value many Protestants placed not only in prayer and Bible reading but in an education day that seemed to draw from and acknowledge their faith.

Conflicts Regarding the Nature and Origin of Life

The teaching of evolution was a second issue of truth that caused conflict with sectors of the Christian public, and during the modern period, politician and orator William Jennings Bryan was at its center. He debated the right of public schools to teach the scientific theories that many Americans opposed for religious, moral, and civic reasons. Before the West Virginia legislature, he argued, "Teachers in public schools must teach what the taxpayers desire taught. The hand that writes the paycheck rules the schools" (as cited in Larson, 2006, p. 44). In particular, his concerns extended to legislation that would restrain the exposure of children to evolutionary teaching. The legislatures of six southern states considered measures against teaching evolution in 1923, and Bryan was involved in most of their discussions. In Tennessee, the Butler Act (1925) was enacted to prohibit the teaching of evolution in public schools. It stated,

> It shall be unlawful for any teacher in any of the Universities, Normals and all other public schools of the State which are supported in whole or in part by the public school funds of the State, to teach any theory that denies the story of the Divine Creation of man as taught in the Bible, and to teach instead that man has descended from a lower order of animals.

Opponents challenged the act in court. The Scopes Trial (1925) highlighted a distinct curricular threat—academic content antagonistic to theological beliefs. The trial reviewed the case of John Thomas Scopes regarding a violation of the Butler Act, and it won the attention of the nation by pitting the claims of naturalistic science against widely held religious conceptions of truth or, in Scopes' words, "against bigotry and prejudice" (n.d.). In many venues, this philosophic battle was popularly portrayed as one of tradition and ignorance against science and progress. The condescending attitude of much of the population reflected the scientific confidence of the period, even as it obscured the trial's deeper questions associated with the mission of public education regarding the nature of humanity, truth, and worldviews.

The regional popularity of anti-evolution legislation following the trial stood not only upon beliefs regarding the origin of life but upon the public value and effects of those conceptions. Bryan, who famously prosecuted the case, held a stance against evolution's religiously offensive naturalistic presuppositions and their "dangerous" civic implications. In a 1905 speech, he said,

> I object to the Darwinian theory because I fear we shall lose the consciousness of God's presence in our daily life, if we must accept the theory that through all the ages no spiritual force has touched the life of man and shaped the destiny of nations.... But there is another objection. The Darwinian theory represents man as reaching his present perfection by the operation of the law of hate—the merciless law by which the strong crowd out and kill off the weak. (Cited in Cornelius, 1996, p. 42)

Additionally, Bryan blamed evolutionary philosophy for the World War and argued for society's need for transcendent grounds. He said,

> Nietzsche carried Darwinism to its logical conclusion and denied the existence of God, denounced Christianity as the doctrine of the degenerate, and democracy as the refuge of the weakling; he overthrew all standards of morality and eulogized war as necessary to man's development. (as cited in Larson, 2006, p. 40)

Bryan saw that to commit public education to naturalistic presuppositions could undermine not only religious beliefs but also the education of children and the integrity of the nation.

The Scopes trial served to ignite philosophic fears that had been smoldering across the nation, fears that held both individual and public relevance. According to Larson, "Concern about the social and religious implications of Darwinism had been a secondary issue within the church for two generations. . . . It took Bryan to transform them into a major political issue" (2006, p. 46). He rejected evolution as a theory being posited as true upon a public that generally held other transcendent conceptions, but also, and perhaps more important to his public stance, he rejected evolution under the conviction that the public implications of Darwinism undermined the moral and even political fabric of society.

Following the Scopes Trial, public education reinforced its alignment with prevalent religious conceptions of truth as bills forbidding the teaching of evolution passed in 37 states. These new laws were so successful that for nearly 30 years, biology textbooks made almost no mention of the theory (Arons, 1983, p. 18). But not all states banned the teaching of evolution, and, for example, during the 1920s, a California textbook selection committee opposed the trend and required that evolution be *included* in all of its biology textbooks. In spite of the frequent opposition of parents, the theory of evolution renewed its place in the curriculum over time with a powerful force coming from the Cold War fear of Soviet technological superiority. This round of attempts to support a particular biblical view of human origins came to a legal close in 1968 when the Supreme Court struck down all such public school laws as violations of the First Amendment's establishment clause through the case of *Epperson v. Arkansas* (1968).

Other Conflicts Surrounding Offensive Curricula

Sociologist William Martin (1996) documents some of the other political revolts erupting around the "neutral" but progressive dealings of state governments regarding their moral and civic education curricula. Conflicts arose regarding sex education, textbook selection, and moral instruction. Attempts by state governments to avoid some conflict-laden topics also stirred controversy as citizens, whose views of truth and morality held that good education required the advocacy of particular values, called for particular moral instruction. Reflecting the difficulties created by the common school setting, many religious parents believed that sex education curricula without a "specific doctrine" taught an atheistic or relativistic view of morality.

Textbooks exposed children to multiple cultures, beliefs, and meanings that many parents opposed or felt were inappropriate for the age level of their children, while other parents advocated for the exposure of children to the "real world." Avoiding issues of conflict and finding positions of compromise reflected the alternative responses possible within the common education model. However, since conflicts were generally rooted in strongly held beliefs, solutions that circumvented or compromised these beliefs found resolution at the expense of a separation from the motivations associated with those deep beliefs. For example, to avoid school prayer eliminated conflicts over the nature of the prayer, but it also served to alienate motivations associated with acknowledging God's concern for the school day. These solutions served to satisfy only those willing to reduce the overt role of their beliefs in the school day; they distanced religious parents who held that their religious beliefs and traditions should pervade their child's education.

Analysis

Thus, religious views regarding prayer and Bible reading, human origins, sex education, textbook selection, and other ideological education issues served to energize broad sectors of the U.S. population to accept or oppose public schools that had not or did not support their views on these practices. Religion acted as an ideological filter for school *acceptance*. Though some parents willingly set aside some of their beliefs and values for the sake of those of other faiths, it is clear that for many, agreeable religious values and practices also served to *empower* the public's education efforts.

Acknowledging God not only called upon His potential help in the classroom, but it also provided an authoritative foundation of moral and ideological expectations among the broad community of believers. Holding to God as creator empowered moral and civic instruction regarding the rights and value of others far beyond the ideological potential an evolutionary framework offered. Similarly, when traditional religious foundations were exchanged for secularized foundations for sex education and other curricula, education programs lost the support of ideological foundations that had successfully shaped generations of children for society. And these foundations were not necessarily rejected for their lack of success but because traditional religion did not fit within the common education paradigm.

Lastly, religious beliefs empowered public school curricula by providing or deepening a sense of community between the public school and like-minded attending families. Many contemporary studies affirm the importance parental support has in a child's educational attainment. Though no studies were conducted at the time to attempt to discern the influence that school acceptability had upon student outcomes, it can logically be assumed that parents were less likely to support the school's education program from home when it opposed the deep religious beliefs of home.

Still, some readers may be quick to look at these conflicts as evidence to reinforce the idea that religion is a problem to be overcome, not an asset to be utilized. However, this response misses the mark. The protection of conscientious beliefs was a foundation of our sociopolitical heritage; public officials should not directly or indirectly act to undermine the beliefs of individuals. Most people adhere to a functional religion that frames their perceptions, judgments, and values, and we cannot escape the reality that religious ideas will conflict with one another. Our social goal should be to draw out the strengths of our religious views while trying to minimize their public conflicts. The common education paradigm of public education has not done either well; it caused conflicts while distancing the religious beliefs of families from their support of public education goals.

Secular Character Education

The roles of religion in public education became apparent not only when ideological conflicts brought them to the fore, but also when modern efforts attempted to avoid using traditional religious methodologies. Whereas 19th-century Americans generally believed religious convictions were to drive the moral and character education of children, by 1910, civic pressures extensively forced public education away from its reliance upon these convictions as the framework for its moral and civic curricula. Whereas early common schools taught Biblical moral precepts, modern public schools taught ideals that required less theological sanction. Old textbooks contained "explicitly religious passages," and new textbooks often secularized moral lessons and rarely asserted the importance of religion (Giordano, 2003, p. 117). The efforts of the 20th century provide experimental data that we can use to evaluate not only the relative success of their efforts but the religious nature of moral and character development.

"Character education" was the first attempt at a replacement program for moral religious instruction. Character educators, recognizing the growing conceptual diversity of the population and common education's growing need for secular curriculum materials, relied less upon traditional moral constraints. Rather, they taught civic values as true and right without an appeal to higher ideologies. Schools published behavioral codes and developed strategies to teach them in the classroom, including the use of the formative influences of duty and a desire for approval. Group activities that utilized the pressure of peer influence became the means of imparting the codes. Free of the appeal to controversial tenets of faith, moral codes listed virtues and defined behavioral expectations. "The aim was to use the codes as a way of suffusing every facet of school life with moral education" (McClellan, 1992, p. 58). Character education would predominate in the classroom until the mid-1920s, at which time, its competitor, found among progressive educators, would propose an entirely new base for moral education.

A Weakened Effort

Character education programs from the 1890s to the mid-1940s attempted to advocate virtues similar to those of past generations, but their more secularized presentations hampered the linking of faith motivations with civic concerns. The secular civic strategy required greater extracurricular involvement, thus parents and civic groups formed home and after-school clubs with moral codes of behavior (often with religious grounds) such as the Boy Scouts, the Campfire Girls, and 4-H.

Cause-effect relationships are difficult to discern (or prove) in the realm of human moral behavior, but the populations of the day called for better character education curricula that were, in part, a response to a perceived moral decline under secularized curricula. The neglect of poor and immigrant communities, the immorality of the "Roaring Twenties," the illegal activities associated with Prohibition, and the questionable nature of labor movements motivated social leaders to call for stronger moral guidance than the secularized schools seemed able to provide. However, the effectiveness of these programs in relation to the religiously based moral education curricula of earlier generation is difficult to discern. Most education leaders disbanded their reliance on character education curricula by the mid-1940s (Howard, Berkowitz, & Schaeffer, 2004), disbandment that was motivated, in part, by studies by Hugh Hartshorne and Mark A. May, which found the prevalent character education curricula to have little positive effect.

Character education curricula of the period compounded the weaknesses found in earlier secularized moral education curricula. Opponents sometimes criticized character codes for reflecting the values of a class or culture without respect for the differences found in society. With a focus on conformity, they also failed to build a character favorable to a growing concern for autonomy. "By combining moral prescriptions with a heavy-handed patriotism, reformers cast their lots with those who sought to deal with diversity by creating rigorous assimilationist schooling" (McClellan, 1992, p. 60).

Though it was to reappear at the end of the 20th century, ungrounded character education enjoyed a short tenure in many schools of modernity.

Its moral and civic education replacement would move further from engaging the aid of deeply held religious beliefs. Progressive scholars believed religion and tradition hampered social development by yoking children with outdated ideas and scientifically indefensible moral restraints. Progressives believed a more secure source of social progress would be found by attempting to nurture rational, intelligent individuals who were guided by a process of scientific inquiry and decision making (Turner, 1985).

Religion as the Source of Meaningful Conceptualization

Character education declined in the face of its competitor from the progressive education camp throughout the 1930s. Progressive moral education gained the support of "liberal Protestant clergy, intellectual leaders, professional elites, and educators associated with major universities and large urban and suburban school systems" (McClellan, 1992, p. 61). Some believe the tide turned away from the advocacy of virtues as the previously mentioned studies of Hartshorne and May, published between 1928 and 1930, cast doubt on the effectiveness of character education. Though the authors only meant to provide critical proposals to modify character education curricula, progressives used the studies to argue for its replacement.

Progressives Refute Religiously Based Moral and Civic Education

Academic reformers embodied the beliefs of the modern university. Since many scholars consider progressive education leader John Dewey to be America's most influential philosopher, his civic ideas are a key source for the ideas related to the progressive education movement and its interactions with the religious beliefs of students.

Dewey believed that by following a methodology adopted from science, children would learn to effectively define social problems and implement solutions. He did not believe in the overt teaching of moral and civic values, but that children would glean them from his methodology, which included group discussion and reflection upon experiences. He believed that encouraging children to analyze and solve moral and social problems apart from religious or cultural traditions would advance civic progress. But this concern to free children from tradition did not imply that education should not intentionally form a child's character; he believed that public education should work to see the child's potential formed around social concerns rather than just individualistic concerns.

Dewey believed that a good education should enable children to flourish in their unique abilities rather than attempt to fit them into the molds of others. Thus, in his words, he supported child-centered strategies, envisioned to "permit the intrinsic wonder and value which attach to all the realities which lie behind the school curriculum to come home to the child, and to take him up and carry him on in their own onward sweep" (as cited in Westbrook, 1991, p. 169). As an early ideological liberal, Dewey opposed moral absolutism, but this did not imply the lack of moral education concern. "Rejecting the notion that the school should teach specific moral precepts or encourage particular traits, progressive educators hoped to cultivate in students both a quality of open-mindedness and a general ability to make moral judgments" (McClellan, 1992, p. 63).

Progressives advocated a dynamic ethical process in which individuals judged and decided upon relative values in accord with the situations in which they arose. The 1932 Character Education Committee report of the National Education Association's Department of Superintendence articulated the essence of this new, scientifically based values education curriculum. The report stated, "Relativity must replace absolutism in the realm of morals as well as in the spheres of physics and biology.... No such system is permanent... it will have to change and grow in response to experience" (National Education Association, 1952, p. 11). This idea of relativity was to serve as a presupposition of the moral and civic curricula of progressive public education, and it further distanced civic curricula from their 19th-century connection with traditional religious roots that affirmed invariable moral values.

Dewey proposed a moral framework for education that avoided the "pitfalls of a transcendent and potentially authoritarian conception of 'making the best of oneself' which stood apart from the particular powers and particular desires of particular individuals" (as cited in Westbrook, 1991, p. 165). He and other progressive educators called for a redesign of public civic education from the ground up. They questioned whether "indoctrination" into traditional values prepared children for citizenship in the new and diverse social settings of the modern world. They believed that moral character should grow apart from theology or other traditional conceptions of truth; education should be practical and experiential. They conceived human motivations to be intrinsically good and rational rather than willful, thus moral education required not the formation of moral habits and the teaching of transcendent truths, but it required the formation of a socially oriented, self-realized character equipped with the scientific skills of social problem solving.

Struggle Between Naturalism and Traditional Faith

Though much of Dewey's educational theory continued to influence succeeding generations, much of "progressive thought" would be short-lived. The social and economic pressures of the 1930s accelerated the collapse of the excessively broad faith that modern society placed in science as a ground for all truth and the hope for society's salvation. Science had been unable to predict, avoid, or solve the problems that the depression brought upon the nation, and many even questioned the tenets of the democratic system. Into this concern, Mortimer Adler argued that for science to help society, *science had to operate within a context of metaphysical truth* (Marsden, 1994, p. 378). In other words, the scientific method operated within religious contexts; it could not access truth apart from some "faith" presuppositions. Monsignor Fulton Sheen, Robert Hutchins, and others supported Adler's views, but many progressives (as noted above) continued to affirm that traditional religion was an authoritarian danger to democracy.

In 1944, John Dewey and Sidney Hook held a conference in New York to counter the perceived threat of those advocating traditional moral formation. The conference's name, "The Authoritarian Attempt to Capture Education," reflected the ideological perspective of Dewey and Hook. Whereas some academics now claimed that transcendent truths were necessary foundations for democracy, Dewey and others claimed that the authoritarianism they linked with religion undermined the freedom and tolerance that undergirded democracy. George Marsden describes the fear of this latter group: "Authoritarianism, especially religious authoritarianism, was not only a superstitious denial of free inquiry but ultimately incompatible with true tolerance. If the religious authoritarians gained control, the United States would be well on its way to its own brand of totalitarianism" (1994, p. 384).

This academic debate was relevant to public primary and secondary education, because it sought to define the degree to which truth, still relied upon for social cohesion, was accessible through scientific methodology. Religious truth was controversial, and scientific reasoning seemed to be a more acceptable replacement. If this were so, then the state could advocate scientific curricula without fear that they represented a secular form of religious establishment. However, Adler's claim that science operated within a framework of metaphysical truth placed scientific conclusions in the religious realm of belief.

Whereas progressives had sought to free education from the authoritarian assertions of religion, Adler's reasoning led to the conclusion that *naturalistic science could also be a source of authoritarian education.* If metaphysical presumptions provided the base for scientific inquiry, then public educators would be obliged to evaluate which aspects of "scientific" curricula they could teach as true. Thus, Dewey's attempts to leave the arena of religious views betrayed his own worldview that many would find controversial. He rejected a traditional view of human nature and proposed the public advocacy of his belief regarding ultimate values and human motivations. He believed that through exposure and discussion, children would learn to value the political community above all things and that serving the community was equivalent to the greatest commandments of other ethical systems. In Dewey's words, an

> interest in the community welfare ... in perceiving whatever makes for social order and progress, and for carrying these principles into execution—is the ultimate ethical habit to which all the special school habits must be related if they are to be animated by the breath of moral life. (1903, p. 15)

This view of an ultimate good betrayed what postmodern analysis would view as evidence of the comprehensive beliefs often attached to the proposals of academicians claiming to represent a scientifically neutral perspective.

Analysis of Progressive Moral and Civic Approaches

Though popular and influential, progressive ideas were not universally accepted. Dewey theorized that tradition and religion hindered the progress of moral development. He said, "The moral has been conceived in too goody-goody a way. Ultimate moral motives and forces are nothing more or less than social intelligence—the power of observing and comprehending social situations" (1909, p. 43). He lauded the potential of human reason, but he sought to destroy standing social foundations before he had a proven replacement. He neglected to value religion as a source of historically tested, motivating, and accumulated social understanding.

However, in discounting religion and tradition, Dewey failed to adequately evaluate the place that reason and experience held in each. Bernard Iddings Bell, a social analyst who witnessed Dewey's scientific philosophy of life, which became prevalent in the culture by the 1950s, offered this critique:

> We separate ourselves ... from the past. We neglect the store of humane wisdom painfully acquired down the millennia by experimenting man. We are conceitedly, absurdly, of the opinion that almost everything worth man's knowing about himself and his society has been discovered only recently. (1952, p. 128)

Public common schools were unable to provide children with the moral and civic education that transcended the physical, and thus they provided an education that was "nontheistic and merely patriotic Secularism" (Bell, 1952, p. 67). Bell (1952) wrote against the lowest-common-denominator values of the postwar period in *Crowd Culture*. Here he criticized both American religion and public education as having aided in the formation of a dangerously immature and childish citizenry that overvalued possessions, found personal identity in wealth, made comfort a priority, valued conformity over integrity, found the highest satisfaction in physical sensation, and was superficial in its depth of understanding. In his book, Bell argued (much as I do) for the public funding of separate schools of comprehensive orientations so that deep reflective contexts could support moral and civic nurture. Perhaps if Dewey had given greater credit to the rationality and experiential learning of religious people, he may have discerned that religions and traditions could be repositories of social wisdom that held value to contemporary problem solving.

Instead, progressive educators liberated students from tradition and supplied a socially oriented morality to replace religiously oriented ones. Opponents criticized them for devaluing much human and cultural authority and for leaving students vulnerable to the popular wisdom of their peers and the popular culture. Presupposing that human nature was rational rather than willful, innately good rather than needful of regeneration, merely in need of information and experience rather than heart transformation, progressives focused on reasoning toward a social good and failed to adequately address the relationship between the moral values of the individual and the social good.

Progressives brought needed focus to the child, but they advanced a disputed and comprehensive conception of human nature and public value through the public schools. Though they claimed a neutral scientific base for their theories, they advanced curricula that were often controversial and of less than scientifically reliable civic effect. In reality, *Dewey and those of like mind formulated educational methods and goals from their own religious views.* They failed to see that naturalistic scientific philosophy actually represented a comprehensive metaphysical claim that was unproven by the scientific reason they relied upon for authority. It would require later, "postmodern," generations to recognize the faith and the fallacies that underlay many of the "universal scientific truths" promoted during modernity.

Though progressive leaders were frequently blind to their own religious presuppositions, their efforts serve here to demonstrate one of the important roles of religion in public education. Without the coherent rationales and values found in progressive views of human nature, life meaning, the social good, moral and rational integrity, and of course, a vision of human progress, they would not have been able to conceptualize their educational vision in such a compelling manner. Though I oppose much of Dewey's philosophic project, from the first time I read his work, I recognized him to be not merely an "academic," but an evangelist of his deeply held beliefs. He was impassioned to see society made whole by his vision of people and of the good society. Regardless of his success, other scholars confronted Dewey's ideological conceptions and commitments, and the confrontation helped to illuminate the religious foundations of the public educational project. Though ongoing generations have continued their attempts to separate public education from religious foundations, their attempts have been at the expense of intrinsic curricular meaning.

Shortcomings of Secularized Textbooks

Not only did modern schools avoid drawing from traditional religion as a human and an educational resource, but they also tended to exclude factual teaching about the role of religion in American history. Students were free to ask questions about the role of faith in history, but for them to ask questions that led to meaningful discussion would first require that they had a preexisting knowledge base. It would also require that teachers had sufficient training in these areas to give meaningful answers. However, both conditions were doubtful under a common education paradigm further shaped by a philosophic bias that viewed traditional religion as irrelevant or harmful to the public's education goals.

In the midst of the secularization process, many education scholars and textbook publishers shunned religion or avoided entering into religious controversies by avoiding its mention. By the 1930s, civics textbooks rarely mentioned religion for reasons such as the fear of offense and even secular bias. For example, one civics book made a single reference to religion as an opportunity or a "way of life" out of 495 pages of text. It followed this reference with ideologically based critique that too many religious differences existed (Giordano, 2003, p. 120).

This avoidance of religion and religious ideas undermined the deep analysis that is often grounded in religious views. A brief study of how textbooks dealt with nationalism (at a time when civic efforts to build allegiance to the nation stirred controversy) illuminates this concern. Conservatives criticized textbooks written under the shadows of the World Wars for failing to support adequately national causes and patriotism. Concurrently, liberals criticized texts for excessively glorifying nationalism. In either case, there is little evidence that these discussions of patriotism and national support were more than confident assertions. In other words, ungrounded civic perspectives were open to shallow attack and unduly presented students with few reasons to undergird their civic convictions. For example, one conservative New York bill stated,

> No textbook shall be used in the [public] schools . . . which . . . ignores, omits, discounts or in any manner belittles, ridicules, falsifies, distorts, questions, doubts, or denies the deeds and accomplishments of the noted American patriots, or questions the worthiness of their motives, or casts aspersions on their lives. (New York Bill on History Textbooks, 1923, p. 349)

These criteria aimed to support a nationalist agenda, but they broadly eliminated texts that may have deepened civic discussion with meaningful (and needed) critique. And this secular perspective was not unique: B. L. Pierce's broad study of textbooks published in 1934 concluded that textbooks were "shot through and through with national spirit [and that] . . . glory of service to one's country is emphasized, and American customs, institutions, and ideals are treated as sacrosanct" (1934, p. 119).

Liberal criticisms of textbook nationalism were equally shallow. For example, following the First World War, E.W. Nolen, a critic of textbook nationalism stated, "If the children of all countries could be real and close and friendly to one another, there could never be another war" (1942, p. 348). Other examples could be cited, but their relevance to my argument is that, within a secular context, discussions of weighty matters (such as nationalism) tend to either neglect concerns that oppose the current political vision (and lean toward nationalism), or they deal with weighty issues without delving into the deeper metaphysical beliefs that underlie the values associated with the issues. As evidenced by Catholic discussions on "just war theory," without the resources of deeper beliefs and values, secular education settings served to limit discussions of patriotic concerns to shallow debates over issues of propriety and neglected to inspire deep reflective discussions of benefit to the public.

In contrast, to those who succumbed to the popular trends of modernity, a few textbook publishers worked with the reality of religious differences and either modified their texts or wrote new ones for particular religious audiences. One such 1945 social studies textbook for Catholic parochial schools was written with the goal of providing a civic education "guided and strengthened by clear Catholic convictions" (as cited in Giordano, 2003, p. 121). Though some may have seen efforts such as these as counter to the public good, it serves as a model to demonstrate that religious ideologies can be used to "guide and strengthen" civic education curricula.

Summary

The modern period was a time of concentrated cultural and educational change. As demographics shifted, science exploded, religion was reconsidered, public philosophy was remodeled, and personal and societal foundations were shaken; parents and society entrusted public education to keep pace and prepare children for the future. Though religious views and the public place of traditional religion shifted, personal faith continued to play at least three important roles in the public education project. Religious beliefs judged the *acceptability* of public school curricula, *empowered* public school efforts, and served as a source of educational *conceptualization*.

This chapter's brief survey has shown that modernity's educational efforts were both strengthened and weakened by the ways they dealt with religion. As the common school paradigm forced the removal of traditional faith-based philosophy and practices, believers were less attached to their local school programs. Public schools often became places of societal conflict rather than of unity. However, in spite of punctuated times and places of conflict, public schools continued to be favored and accepted by most of the population, who felt a large degree of local control over their children's schools. However, even in schools that remained "inoffensive," curricular teachings and philosophy were subtly disengaged from the meaningful and life-shaping beliefs of not only families but also education professionals. Religious beliefs that had informed and empowered moral standards, character development, public commitments, academic knowledge, philosophic understanding, and professional educational insight were replaced with "research based" secular alternatives that for all their academic promise, rarely seemed to captivate the hearts and minds of students or the favor of the education community for extended periods of time.

Dewey spoke to public education near the junction of nonsectarian religious public education and the more fully secularized education to come. Much of his educational vision impassioned the nation because the most obvious of his ideas found a coherent place in the religious convictions of the general population. His proposals skirted traditional religious practices without overtly seeming to oppose them. Though he did not speak in traditional religious terms, his concerns for the individuality and flourishing of children and the moral health of society resonated with the Christian ethos of the public; one might even argue that his outlook and values were indebted to a Christian upbringing that he believed would be a hindrance to future generations. However, religious *acceptability* does not necessarily lead to religious *empowerment*. The lack of direct grounding in the religious beliefs of students and families seemed to weaken their effects.

Dewey's religious framework of beliefs gave rise to his educational ideology and predictably became a subject of controversy, *but his beliefs had given vitality, coherence, and meaning to his own efforts.* Later generations of public education leaders, with both a greater awareness of what passed as religion and a more strict "separation of church and state," would conceptualize and implement education programs with fewer religious resources from which to draw. Under the common model of public education, conflicts over the nature of a good education would expectedly continue to mar public education's mission as an instrument of public unity, but this would not reflect public education's greatest inadequacy.

Through the 20th century, both conscientious and pragmatic followings of the common education model forced an increasing detachment of civic curricula from the worldviews of students. Moral and ideological formation more extensively relied on ungrounded moral assertions or alternative secular curricula. Most early modern citizens accepted this philosophical thinning under the presumption that scientific substitutes were compatible with their faiths. In many states, they were further reassured of the philosophic acceptability of public education because of laws that insured a place for prayer and Bible reading. These activities provided a means by which public education kept the trust of the predominantly Protestant population for purposes of unity, but the civic curriculum made little attempt to connect deeply with or draw upon the worldviews of the children and families they represented.

While I argue that the religious beliefs of students provide a framework for reason, motivation, and value regarding the moral and civic goals of education, Dewey, and other progressive educators disparaged traditional religion as nonrational, authoritarian, and regressive. This philosophic shift from a religious to a secular moral and civic curriculum represented a distrust of traditions, an optimistic view of the "human will," and an expansion of the role of reason regarding conceptions of human moral and civic behavior.

Before this shift, traditions had been valued as sources of accumulated wisdom, and many considered self-centered antisocial behavior to be most successfully turned toward a concern for others through religious beliefs and commitments. Additionally, to be of the greatest public value, reason had to be matured through in-depth knowledge and reflection upon transcendent truths and the wisdom of the past. Civic education relied upon the submission of the individual will to the goodwill of God and the individual acceptance of a new paradigm for rational thought and moral behavior contained within religious traditions.

Modern public education leaders embraced a distrust of traditional ideology as rigid, supernatural, and presumptive; progressives believed that rational processes could be trusted to overcome issues of the will. They viewed human behavior to be naturally and positively governed through a rational engagement with experience; thus, the informed rational citizen would advance the good of society more than would the informed, rational, and religiously faithful citizen. These presumptions not only optimistically revised the assessment of humanity's rational nature in accord with nontraditional views and disconnected citizens from the experiential wisdom of the past, but they diverted concern from the role of deep belief in education. This diversion not only neglected discussions of traditional belief, but it obscured the philosophic nature of progressive morality and the modern scientific method.

Looking Forward

Public education in the postmodern period, more philosophically and legally dissociated from religious foundations, would suffer most; not from a lack of personal effort, professional expertise, public resources, or educational research, but from a lack of meaning. High familial, educational, social, and national ideals, once defined in meaningful terms of truth and value and closely tied to the public education vision, would be replaced by increasingly shallow common values. Removed from coherent views of human flourishing, which provided a ground for subject-area significance and holistically nurtured the child, public educators would have few philosophic resources with which to evaluate curricular value, and students would have decreased motivation to learn. Liberal tolerance, material prosperity, and environmental preservation would function as school ideals, but would prove to anemically inspire human growth, social compassion, or educational excellence. Without the intrinsic meaning associated with religious beliefs, the public's educational goals would become increasingly illusive.

4

Postmodern Public Education

Redefining American Identity

Both America and its public education system were founded upon a belief in particular American ideals and a concern for the protection of individual religious conscience. While the former served to define the national identity, the latter insured the continuance of personal liberty. Both coherently flowed from America's founding principles. However, as noted previously, the two concerns would conflict if not managed properly. Either the state, while attempting to assure the propagation of its undergirding ideals, could use its corporate power to trample on the rights of conscience of individuals deemed in need of "American" moral and civic nurture, or the state could so focus on the conscience-based liberty of its citizens that it fails to support the moral and ideological foundations that make liberty possible! In the end, both routes lead to the demise of American liberty—one route sanctioned by a distrustful state, the other sanctioned by a state that has abdicated a vital core of its public responsibility.

Though history clearly records that educational state power was used in a distrustful manner toward Catholics of the 19th century, the same ideological vision to define and nurture strong American citizens continued

Education Reform, pages 77–94
Copyright © 2013 by Information Age Publishing
All rights of reproduction in any form reserved.

through the first half of the 20th century. The descriptive terminology of modernity used less religious language, but "good Americans" were still thought of as reflecting the moral and civic commitments of their Protestant predecessors of the 19th century. Then, the cultural and philosophical revolts of the 1960s, built upon growing discontent with the perceived self-interest and superficiality of the American status quo, spurred the reshaping of public education along postmodern, pluralistic lines.

American identity would no longer be narrowly conceived of by a state that presupposed a Protestant—or even a Christian—heritage, but the identity would be conceived of so broadly as to be nonoffensive to an ever-increasing number of life visions. Separated from alignment with any religious perspective or methods, yet still responsible to nurture strong citizens, public schools would now nurture children toward a merely shallowly defined "moral and civic ideal" utilizing unproven secular resources. Following the recent course of educational history, this chapter will not only continue to illuminate the religious nature of public education, but it will reveal how the late 20th-century state, by following the common education model's secularizing trajectory, has abdicated many of its educational responsibilities toward the nurture of children and future citizens.

Precursors to the Fall of Robust Conceptions of Civic Identity

At the end of World War II, education leaders still addressed diversity under the melting-pot conception of civic formation in which un-American dross would separate from new citizens as they were purified and blended into the molten being of the nation. "Non-American" particularities were expected to diminish over time as new citizens took on the civic values, beliefs, habits, and commitments of the nation. Acceptable diversity supplemented the American civic identity without playing a deep role in defining it. Catholics and other minorities may have had the legal right to vote, but they would not have been displayed as "model" citizens. Originally viewed as a religious endeavor, the nurture of an American civic identity was increasingly reliant upon reasoned exposure to American claims and the shared celebration of public traditions. Within the public school, secular civic identity formation was built upon the presumptions that

- American morality and civic identity were indebted to and reliant upon a "common American" view of the world,
- this view of the world was accessible to all rational citizens,
- this view was nonsectarian,

- this view reflected sufficient meaning and value to motivate individual moral and civic behavior, and
- common civic education was superior to religious schooling toward the nurture of moral and civic health.

However, not all agreed with these tenets or agreed that secular education was sufficient to nurture good citizens. In 1958, Will Herberg, the respected analyst of America's three-faith pluralism, argued that Americans did not seem to have chosen secular education as an ideal, but that their overreaction to perceived threats had pushed them into favoring secular education. He observed, "Virtually all Americans who have given any thought to the matter are thoroughly dissatisfied with the present state of the relations between religion and education, particularly public education" (as cited in Marsden, 1994, p. 412). Catholics repeatedly tried to get public funding for parochial schools, but according to Herberg, "a powerful coalition of Protestants, Jews, and liberal secularists effectively blocked every significant Catholic effort to obtain federal support" (Marsden, 1992, p. 43).

Herberg insightfully reflected that the Protestant majority reacted to what they considered to be Catholic encroachment as if they (rather than Catholics) were in the minority—as if their way of life was endangered. Protestants acted defensively with a characteristic overresponse. He argued,

> This minority-group defensiveness has contributed greatly toward turning an important segment of American Protestantism into a vehement champion of an extreme doctrine of the separation of church and state, of religion and education, despite a disturbed awareness of the growing "religious illiteracy" of the American people. (1960, p. 235)

Perhaps blinded by a progressive bias, an influential segment of the population failed to see the debt it owed to religious faith.

Thus, Catholics desired to build their personal and civic identities upon a deeper religious foundation, but the public would not support their schools, which it still viewed a source of civic authoritarianism and division (Marsden, 1994). Harvard's president James Bryant Conant reflected the thoughts of many when he deflected those who criticized secular public schools as being too ideologically shallow in saying "our tax-supported schools have had as a great and continuing purpose the development of moral and spiritual values" (as cited in Marsden, 1994, p. 403). He was right in referencing a key historic purpose of education, but he failed to address how one might promote spiritual values within an increasingly diverse population through an increasingly secular common school.

The implications of secular civic identity formation were soon to be further tested. The courts would soon place the "wall of separation" asserted to exist between the state and Catholic schools within public schools. Here, it would separate even favored Protestant religious support from state endeavors to nurture the moral and civic values of its citizens.

Ideological Struggles Regarding Civic Identity and Conceptions of Truth

By the end of the first quarter of the 20th century, by some measures, it seemed that the scientific rationalism of Sigmund Freud, John Dewey, and others of the philosophical elite would displace the conceived irrationality of religious belief in America. But by the mid-1950s, traditional American religion was thriving, and the broad claims of scientific rationalism (especially in the social realm) were beginning to show their limits regarding the neutrality of their presuppositions. Within a decade, religion would diversify with alternative philosophical movements in the "spiritual awakening" described by historian Robert Elwood (1994, 1997).

In the social reanalysis of the awakening, not only would the morality and civic commitments of the nation be challenged, but they would be overturned. Earlier robust conceptions of American identity held that a *single* intellectual framework could support a deeply meaningful and widely agreeable conception of public truth, and this truth was to be the support for the moral and civic education curricula of the public schools. Breaking with past civic expectations, the awakening marked the "reconception" of national philosophy to acknowledge and legitimate the deep philosophic diversity of America's citizens. The civic identity once broadly defined in enlightened Protestant terms and later blended with a general confidence in scientific rationalism, would hence attempt to remain aloof from the advocacy of all comprehensive conceptions of truth for the sake of individual conscience. Without delving deeply into church-state philosophy, I will argue that this conscientious concession further hindered the civic mission demanded of public education by increasing the distance between civic curricula and frameworks of religious belief, value, and understanding.

Public education secularized; however, it was the choice of a common model of education to serve the needs of a diverse, liberal, and democratic society that compelled the separation of faith from education—*not popular will or a proven superiority of secular education.* Catholic scholars such as Francis Curran and Neil McCluskey argued for the opportunity to engage a plurality of comprehensive perspectives in support of moral and civic nurture by the adoption of a plural model of public education. But the idea failed to gain broad support outside of Catholic and other religious communities long in opposition to common education. Most education scholars, public educators, and the public supported the common school system in spite of its weaknesses. Not only did they consider entrusting the public's educational concerns to a plurality of sectarian schools to be divisive, but the liberal viewpoint of the progressives continued to present religious schools as authoritarian and incompatible with their liberal views.

The Common Education Model Under a Pluralized American Identity

Public Schools "Neutralized" by the Court to Conform With Pluralism

Public education leaders of the 18th century, with less federal and state legal definition regarding religion in the public schools, often violated the conscientious liberties of religious minorities. But after a decade of national self-reflection and action regarding America's poor record associated with racial civil rights, the courts of the second half of the 20th century were willing and prepared to stand in defense of the religious rights of minorities in the common public schools. Awareness and tensions had been building throughout the century as Protestant majorities conscientiously fought to preserve some degree of spiritual meaning associated with the school day, while those with differing spiritual and social understandings conscientiously opposed them. Though Midwestern state courts upheld bans on public school Bible reading, it was required in the public schools of 12 states as late as 1949, and Bible reading was state sponsored in 21 other states until much later. As Catholics worked to make public funds available to religious schools, the Supreme Court adjudicated Establishment Clause rulings that affected the religious practices remaining in some public schools. The Supreme Court declared state-sponsored school prayer unconstitutional in *Vitale* (1962) and state sponsored Bible reading unconstitutional in *Abington v. Schempp* (1963). Prohibitions regarding postings of the Ten Commandments and the teaching of "Creationism" followed.

These rulings served to reduce traditional religious activities in many public school classrooms, but they alienated Protestants who held that their religious beliefs played a vital role in their children's education. Public officials responded to the removal of even relatively benign and nondenominational official school prayer with strong negative reactions. President

Eisenhower denounced it, it found no vocal support in Congress, former president Hoover described it as representing the "disintegration of a sacred American heritage" (as cited in Jeynes & Robinson, 2012, p. 26), and Congress responded to it with an unsuccessful attempt to impeach Supreme Court Chief Justice Earl Warren.

Individuals were equally condemning. A 1963 Gallup Poll survey found that Americans disapproved of these court decisions by a margin of three to one (Jeynes, 2007b, p. 338). One of the outgrowths of this disapproval was to be the Protestant day-school movement, which currently represents about half of those attending religious schools. Others responded to the removal of school prayer with a type of civil disobedience in which many homogenous communities of the South continued to make room for public school prayer with the support of local public opinion and the absence of legal challenges. Both of these actions represent not only a diminished trust of the public education system but the partial civic alienation of a broad segment of the public that, in part, felt the nation had rejected its transcendent roots.

As an aside, it is important to distinguish between the growth of religious schools following the desegregation of public education and the Christian Day School movement of the next decade. Both reflected a move from public to private schools but for vastly different reasons. Whereas the former was based on racial prejudice, the latter was clearly based on religious concern. Following the *Brown v. Board of Education* (1954) decision that mandated the desegregation of all state public school systems, a massive resistance movement coalesced under the leadership of Senator Harry F. Byrd (D-Va.). Some 101 out of 128 southern congressmen signed what became known as the "Southern Manifesto," which claimed that federal powers were overstepping their Constitutional boundaries (see Salisbury & Lartigue, 2004). Under the banner of "freedom of choice" in education, six states (Virginia, Louisiana, Arkansas, Alabama, South Carolina, and Mississippi) established variations of tuition reimbursement or voucher programs that opened the doors for Whites to freely leave the mandate of *Brown* by attending segregated private schools at state expense. Program proponents accomplished their goals, which even led to the closing of several public school systems in Virginia.

Over a decade was required for the U.S. Supreme Court to close these voucher systems. In the Virginia case of *Griffin v. County School Board* (1964), the Supreme Court ruled that the closing of public schools linked with the state funding of racially segregated private schools violated the equal protection clause. The ruling required that public schools be reopened. Five years later, with 10 million dollars of state money still going to support private segregated schools, the federal district court, in *Griffin v. State Board of Education* (1969), ruled that Virginia's entire tuition grant system violated the equal protection clause. The avoidance of "freedom of choice" educational systems of other states in *Brown* fared similarly in their own state courts. When segregated private schools lost their access to public funding, those who simply sought to escape desegregation generally returned to the public schools.

Returning to religious concerns within the public schools of the 1960s, the Supreme Court's interpretation of the First Amendment forced public schools toward a position of attempted neutrality regarding comprehensive views. This philosophical shift was due to the nature of public schools as government organizations, not necessarily due to the value of neutrality as an effective tool for moral and civic education. Some may rightly say that efforts toward religious neutrality made public schools more acceptable to outsider groups, which was one of the goals of common education, but it opposed the second goal of common education: the building of religiously meaningful democratic civic identities.

In a chapter entitled "Culture War," William Martin (1996) documents the depth of conflicts surrounding textbook values and perspectives during the last quarter of the 20th century, but he does not address the source of these problems. In describing conflicts involving deeply held "religious right" concerns, he leaves his readers with little hope for the reduction of ideological conflicts of this nature. But his conclusion accepts common education as the only form of public education. However, the genius of liberal democratic government was to withdraw government power from the support of particular worldviews. The "wars" directly associated with common education that Martin has documented may not have occurred had public education reflected a diversity of religious perspectives rather than merely "secular" perspectives. Other Western nations have supported religious schools of differing faiths with little public conflict (see Chapter 5, this volume).

Since the 1960s, the fastest growing group of public school dissenters has come from conservative Protestant denominations. The federal removal of prayer and Bible reading were key contributions to the sudden growth of the Christian day-school movement (Carper & Hunt, 2007), but philosophic conflict regarding the philosophy of the moral education curriculum was also a strong factor. In short, Protestants have left the public schools due to concerns regarding secularization and its growing hostility to their beliefs (McClellan, 1992, p. 44). Public education, which is indebted to religion for its acceptability, motivation, and conceptualization, was further undermined. Though the removal of Protestant and other religious particularities from public common schools was necessary to accommodate the religious rights of others, it not only made the public's education system unacceptable to many, but it concurrently weakened public education's capacity to support the moral and civic foundations of America. The following sections describe how the improper management of the public's educational responsibilities, caused by the common school model, has undermined the nurture of healthy moral and civic identities.

Secular Civic Education Curricula of Early Postmodernity

After the 1960s, psychology, with a concern toward the self-actualizing individual, drove the moral and civic education curricula of public education (Arthur, 2003). In spite of growing concerns regarding the objective neutrality of scientific methodology, the academic world still did not consider traditional religious perspectives to be respectable. Marsden writes, "Old secular liberals and postmoderns, despite their differences, typically agreed that acceptable theories about humans or reality must begin with the premise that the universe is a self-contained entity" (1997, p. 18). In other words, they agreed that the integration of traditional religion was either false or irrelevant. Though the social sciences had been at the center of public educational curricula since the turn of the 20th century, the legal and philosophical climate of modernity further distanced religious conceptions from the curricular philosophy and methodology of public education.

Values Clarification and Moral Reasoning

Following the attempted separation of public education from all comprehensive views in the 1960s, educators disputed which values should direct the moral and civic education curricula of the public schools. With growing diversity, sectors of the population attacked attempts to establish a moral consensus "as narrow, sectarian and not inclusive" (Hunter, 2000, p. 77). The fear of advocating controversial views reduced the amount that many teachers addressed moral issues (Jeynes, 2007b, p. 340). Values-clarification curricula stepped into this place of neglect as an opportunity to advance the public interest in moral development without the advocacy of controversial moral values. Introduced in a 1972 book by Sidney Simon, Leland Howe, and Howard Kirshenbaum, education scholars Thomas Hunt and Monalisa Mullins describe values clarification as a "pedagogical method that would purportedly clarify ethical behavior for students." Central to both the philosophy and the methodology of values clarification curricula was the authors' suggestion that "teachers should encourage students to make fully autonomous ethical decisions based on personal choice and analysis of particular situations that presented themselves as moral dilemmas" (2005, p. 181).

Values clarification was strongly supported by the liberal educational ideals of John Dewey. It also accommodated the conscientious concerns of the Supreme Court regarding public education because it was purported to be unaligned with any worldview and to advance the public's concerns regarding the moral development of children. However, as parents and public leaders became aware of the program and its effects, values clarification was criticized as failing on both accounts, because it promoted a relativistic moral framework that actually seemed to support some behaviors such as drug use and adolescent sexual activity deemed to be counter the public interest (Kilpatrick, 1992). With the deep controversies that values clarification curricula elicited, it largely fell from public use by the 1990s (Hunt & Mullins, 2005).

Attempting to provide a new program, Lawrence Kohlberg proposed a philosophy of moral education that he distanced from both the framework of relative values attributed to values clarification and the authoritarian teaching of character ideals that he pejoratively referred to as "a bag of virtues" (1981, pp. 2–3). Supportive of both a liberal view of personal autonomy and a vague sense of public good, he argued that the democratic end of education is the "development of free and powerful character" (p. 94).

From his primary works, Kohlberg (1981, 1984) proposed a public moral education curriculum based upon the belief that moral development was primarily a cognitive process. Kohlberg asserted that the rational moral faculties of individuals developed sequentially in a manner similar to Piaget's stages of cognitive development and could recognize universal moral values even if individuals applied them differently. The focus of Kohlberg's moral education curricula was to advance the child through the stages of moral development toward the universal claims of justice.

Though his program avoided drawing from traditional religion, its results were found to be lacking. Even with Kohlberg's (1981) philosophic assertions as to the differences between values clarification and his proposals, the study and experience of many found the curricula to promote a similar sense of relativism. Without the authoritative advocacy of higher moral behaviors, students tended to follow their own desires (Kilpatrick, 1992). Character education scholar James Leming gives us an understanding why

although the two approaches were different in many ways, they both emphasized that teachers were not to moralize. In Kohlberg's moral dilemma discussion approach, the teacher facilitated student reasoning, assisted students in resolving moral conflicts, and ensured that the discussion took place in an environment that contained the conditions essential for stage growth in moral reasoning. Values clarification sought to have each student clarify his or her values by following the prescribed seven-step valuing process. The teacher only facilitated the valuing process and, for fear of influencing students, withheld personal opinions. The teacher was to respect whatever values the students arrived at. (1993, p. 64)

These specific experiments with moral self-direction were short-lived and served to support the public value of actively promoting certain moral goods. Nevertheless, concepts of moral self-direction still influence some scholars and some educational approaches under the rubric of student autonomy.

Following a controversial view of human nature, many educational scholars from Dewey to Kohlberg philosophically equated cognitive development with moral development (Hunter, 2000, p. 84). They assumed that the key to socially valuable behavior was adequate intellectual development and knowledge. Though this presumption supports curricula requiring minimal moral authority, it neglects a vast amount of religious and traditional experience that supports the obligation of mature adults to help children to not only understand what behaviors are most valuable but to strengthen their wills to act in accordance with concerns of the highest value.

In acknowledging individual autonomy, Kohlberg dismissed concern for all the virtues except justice; and to understand justice, one needed to develop one's intellect. However, one's conceptions of other virtues support one's conception of justice. Kohlberg's attempt to provide for autonomy relied upon an unproven and controversial view of human nature that assumed that knowledge of the good would lead to doing the good. Further, his concerns regarding autonomy led him to fail to provide the moral scaffolding that traditional religious views have long held were necessary for the moral development of children and the social health of a just society.

The Return of Character Education

The past two decades have seen a return to a form of character education reminiscent of the early modern period. It promotes widely held public values apart from any deep moral frameworks. Though not a proponent of character education, Robert Nash rightly identifies this requirement: "I believe, that if the virtues of humility, faith, self-denial, and charity are to have any functional utility in secular educational institutions, and in a democratic society, then they have to be 'decoupled' from their religious roots and secularized" (1997, p. 166). Kevin Ryan and Karen Bohlin argue, "We are born both self-centered and ignorant, with our primitive impulses reigning over reason. The point of a nurturing upbringing and education is to bring our inclinations, feelings, and passions into harmony with reason" (1999, p. 5).

Much of the character education movement is premised upon the belief that the moral education of the 1970s and 1980s proved to be insufficient. James Leming argues that moral education based upon reason alone fails to align with our understanding of child development. He writes,

> As the British philosopher R. S. Peters has succinctly stated: "The place of reason must be entered through the courtyard of habit." I conclude, therefore, that there is no alternative to the use of non-rational methods to internalize in children a commitment to certain cultural traditions. (Leming, 1997)

Character educators build upon virtue education with an added focus on behavioral formation (Arthur, 2003). Character reflects upon what people do in secret and under pressure; it is the sum of moral and intellectual habits (Ryan & Bohlin, 1999). The goal of educating for character "appears to be to instill certain virtues so that they become internal principles guiding both the pupil's behavior and decision-making for operation within a democracy. Its focus is upon the formation of the individual, and it is intimately connected with citizenship" (Arthur, 2003, p. 2). Though advocates of liberal autonomy consider character education autocratic and indoctrinating, its proponents refute this criticism and conclude that children require some authoritative moral instruction. "Children especially need to understand and acquire the strong moral habits that contribute to good character" (Ryan & Bohlin, 1999).

Character education uses the teacher as a role model, calls for parental support and involvement, and relies upon the community effect of school climate. Edward DeRoche and Mary Williams find that there are few studies supporting the effectiveness of secular character education programs that merely utilized didactic teaching methods or that focus upon the development of moral reasoning. Thus, they advocate community-based character education programs in which the school community seeks to address moral concerns that lead to a good and worthwhile life (DeRoche & Williams, 2001). James Arthur argues that character education is "ultimately experienced in action.... But it is particularly transmitted through the witness and example of parents and teachers, especially through their storytelling or narratives" (2003, p. 5).

─────

Critiques of Character Education

Nash opposes character education, in part, because he believes the diversity of our ideological perspectives will lead to social conflict regarding what is right and what should be taught. Instead, Nash argues that children need to be taught to be sensitive to the differences found in pluralism's anti-foundationalism; schools need to nurture a capacity for dialectic conversation, and hermeneutical sensitivity (Nash, 1997). While Nash opposes character education as too substantive, Alasdair MacIntyre argues that it is substantively deficient. He writes, "Education that purports to teach a morality neutral between rival controversial standpoints concerning the virtues will end up in teaching a largely indeterminate morality" (1999, p. 127).

The wide and relatively nonconflictive implementation of character education curricula seems to oppose Nash's concern, but MacIntyre's insight calls for deeper moral foundations than common schools can provide. While appropriate for common school curricula, the decoupling of moral education from personal religious beliefs remains a systemic weakness that government schools are constitutionally unable to remedy in a meaningful manner. Although the shallow moral advocacy associated with character education has proven to be of greater public value than that of rational moral training alone, religious schools still provide the potential for more meaningful and successful moral advocacy than secular programs appear capable of. Though those with philosophically liberal perspectives still oppose religious schooling, I will later discuss why these concerns cannot be used to shape America's entire public education endeavor.

Reflections on 20th- and 21st-Century Moral and Civic Education

Since the following is a deeper analysis of not only the religious nature of public education but of the relative success of the common or secular paradigm, I will present an evaluative framework for public education. I will define successful moral and civic education as education that is

- effective at nurturing a concern for the good of others,
- effective at building a character governed by moral principles,
- capable of linking democratic tenets and virtues with the convictions of students,
- effective at promoting social cohesion within our nation's ideologically plural context,
- concerned with the development of each child's individuality and the maturation of his or her decision-making abilities, and

▪ successful at promoting civic and social involvement.

An effective moral and civic education program should complement the ideals of exemplary parents and provide meaningful guidance for students with deficient home nurture. Since morality undergirds and provides integrity for many of our social and political institutions, successful programs should evidence increasing social stability, economic welfare, public safety, and personal liberty.

Though a generally "common" understanding of the "good of others," "good character," and so on can be accommodated by secular schools, the *ideal forms* of the concepts can be promoted (without conflict and infringement on the rights of conscience) only in a freely chosen religious context within a plural public education context. Although the *acceptability* of secular schools has continued to fall under the scrutiny of the religious beliefs of families, the secular school day has few ways it can overtly draw from religion for its *empowerment* or *conceptualization*. Surely, many teachers, principals, students, and educational researchers draw from their faith throughout the day, but the secular education paradigm forces them to "screen" their outward expressions of faith. School personnel can pray secretly, but not in a way that influences students. Students have wide religious liberties, but these are constrained by peer pressure in an environment that seems to consider religious expression irrelevant, inappropriate, or inconsiderate. Researchers, too, are free to draw from their faith, but they are trained to avoid or discard pedagogical proposals that overtly draw from or promote religious sources. Again, while the secular filter may be appropriate in the church-state context of the common school, evidence seems to indicate that it opposes the public's educational goals.

The secularization of modern and postmodern moral and civic education had several sources. Some educators pragmatically secularized curricula to accommodate growing social diversity. Some educators held views of human flourishing and human nature that conflicted with predominant religious views, and they secularized curricula to accommodate their own views. Others secularized curricula simply to accommodate court orders. The decisive influence that appeared to validate each of these motives in an attempt to meet the moral and civic needs of an increasingly diverse society was the established and constraining system of common public education. Within common schools, pragmatic concerns regarding unity seemed to necessitate the removal of many traditional religious meanings and methods from moral and civic curricula. Philosophic views deemed to be common and "nonreligious" were needed to fill the vacuum created by the departure of religious meaning, as First Amendment concerns regarding conscience rightly required that public common education not advocate a particular comprehensive view. In the end, curricula tended to avoid traditional religion and to rely upon secular conceptions of human nature, personal autonomy, and value.

Though a minority of Christians believe that our current public education system should support America's early Christian convictions, this is not compatible with our American liberties; for the state to favor or to impose any comprehensive view violates the religious liberties of the individual. I support the secularization of *common* public education as being consistent with the "essential rights and liberties" of religion which, as John Witte writes, include "(1) liberty of conscience; (2) free exercise of religion; (3) religious pluralism; (4) religious equality; (5) separation of church and state; and (6) disestablishment of religion" (2000, p. 37). However, I also believe that a public system of plural education in which parents have the freedom to choose to attend public schools that support their religious views is compatible with these religious liberties. Plural public education is not only compatible with religious liberty, it is a greater support of these liberties in that it not only prevents government from *favoring* particular nontraditional religious views, but it prevents government from tacitly *opposing* religious views that play a vital role in the education of American youth.

Following the disestablishment of public education in the 1960s, moral and civic education curricula increasingly reflected values-neutral perspectives that the public did not find to be particularly effective at instilling moral behavior. Though perhaps educators hoped that democratic tenets would take root in the deep convictions of students, authors did not intentionally design their curricula to facilitate this task. While non-Protestant groups often found increasingly secularized public schools less offensive than the more overtly Protestant schools of earlier times, the increased secularization of public education increased Protestant opposition to common schooling.

Secular common public education became an increasing source of controversy for reasons related to religion as well as moral effectiveness. Curricula that developed around modern and postmodern conceptions of human nature, autonomy, and reason were highly controversial and of questionable effectiveness in their advancement of publicly valuable moral and civic goals. Though the moral decline that followed the 1960s cannot be narrowly linked with Supreme Court rulings, the correlation, which will be discussed further, must not be simply disregarded. Many schools did not have prayer and Bible reading before these rulings, and many other schools continued with these practices following the rulings. However, these rulings influentially distanced public moral and civic curricula from the religious beliefs of many people. Two thirds of the population (noted above) disagreed with the rulings, presumably because they believe their religion was relevant to education; and secular moral and civic education programs have failed to stem the moral slide of our nation reflected by family breakdown, public and private debt, crime, and governmental dependence (Jeynes, 2009).

In the absence of religion, secular schools have attempted to motivate, teach, and nurture students toward good American citizenship. On the moral front, they experimented and discarded efforts to promote moral growth through mere intellectual discussion without advocacy. Character education in its varying forms remains the method of choice for many schools, but in reality, secular schools do little to nurture their students toward higher moral development or higher life ideals. If home nurture during "after-school hours" is considered sufficient for the moral and "life" nurture of children, then perhaps our secular education system is appropriate. However, many (most?) parents desire and believe that the school day should complement home nurture and would likely choose to send their children to acceptable religious schools if plural public education made them financially accessible.

Finally, we must not overlook the broad gains of the school choice movement that bolster the concerns of this book in unequal ways. Obviously, public magnet schools and inter/intradistrict choice (the first level of school choice options) do nothing to further the ability of public schools to engage religion in the classroom. Charter schools, though still under a secular mandate, might strengthen moral education concerns because they tend to operate within a paradigm of greater accountability. Not only are these schools held accountable to state education leaders, but they are also held accountable to the interests of families who might move to other schools if they are dissatisfied with the academic and moral influence of the school. Further, the lower levels of bureaucracy and the generally smaller size of charter schools seems to enable them to hold children to higher levels of moral accountability.

A number of respected scholars sympathetic to the idea of religious schooling are putting their efforts behind the promotion of "religious charter schools." These schools are publicly funded and can reflect the perspectives of their religious communities, but as institutions directly funded by the state, they cannot advocate or practice the faith they seem to reflect (Weinberg, 2007). Faced with financial pressures, many religious schools are choosing, for the sake of partial survival, to set aside much of their religious identity for the sake of charter funding, and others groups are taking advantage of the concept to begin new schools that reflect many aspects of their communal identity. I am sympathetic to the plights and motives of groups pressured into the charter movement and those taking advantage of charter opportunities, but I emphatically assert that this brand of "religious school" fails to draw from most of the religious resources that I argue are vital to the public education project. Even if they may pragmatically support religious communities, they cannot advocate or provide the deeper human foundations children require for developing the most healthy identities, perspectives, and civic values.

Lastly, the school choice movement has brought vouchers, credits, and other opportunities to sectors of the nation that help some families make the choice for a religious education. Some may argue (as noted in the Introduction) that the school choice movement makes my argument irrelevant. This would be a gross error. Though vouchers and other plans allow a few children to attend religious schools, as long as the state and education leaders hold that good public education is secular by nature, then the common model will continue to be favored. Thus, vouchers will tend to become available only when the public system of secular schools fails, and education regulation, research, curriculum, and teacher training will continue to be driven by a secular paradigm. Although the school choice movement is challenging the authority of the state regarding the necessity of uniform education and the advisability of state monopolized education, *it is doing little to challenge the philosophic nature of a good public education.* While each ideological community may uniquely define the specifics of a good education, these ideological discussions and expressions will remain marginalized and at immature levels of development as long as secular education remains the paradigm of choice for the advancement of the public's educational interests.

In conclusion, the 1980s may have been the "low watermark" of public education's efforts to nurture the moral and civic identities of children, but high tide is still a long way off. As the moon's gravity pulls the Earth's waters toward itself, so religions draw the emotions, motivations, and understanding of individuals. Whereas secular schools attempt to "move the oceans" by human means, religious schools recognize the natural relationship between the "oceans and the moon" and allow the latter to facilitate their efforts.

Review of History Chapters

The goal of public education from its inception has been to nurture students with the knowledge, skills, morality, and civic identities that they might responsibly live with the liberties of and contribute to the good of our democratic society. To attain these ends, the common school model became legally unassailable to plural public education proponents nationwide. Initially, state-level Blaine Amendments favored common education for exclusive tax support *because* its Protestant ethos seemed to preserve the prevalent American identity. However, after common education was thoroughly entrenched, 20th-century federal law focused on protecting the First Amendment religious liberties of public school students. While the Blaine Amendments initially protected a place for nonsectarian religion in education, federal law rejected the governmental favoring of any faith, which led to the complete secularization of public education.

Though a secularizing trend had long been associated with common education, it was met with resistance by those who valued the place of faith in the school day even as these same people may have understood the conscientious concerns of those of other faiths. Under the common school model, the "nonoffensive" concern of public education is in direct opposition to the concern that education be meaningful in terms of content and motivation. Thus, the secularization of public education led to social conflicts based not just in "religious preference" but also in educational *substance.* With its increasing secularization, public schools had fewer meaningful resources with which to motivate and direct student learning, so in spite of the best attempts of education leaders and researchers, secular public education programs have not proven to sufficiently nurture public morality, civic commitment, or even academic learning. We must ask, did the secularization of public education serve or oppose the public's educational interests toward the nurture of children for democratic citizenship?

Simply, these first four chapters have argued that public education is religious by nature, and because the common education paradigm must increasingly avoid religion with increasing public diversity, our attachment to the model has obstructed the public's educational interests toward the nurture of whole people and strong citizens.

I have attempted to demonstrate how religion is vital education in three ways. First, I noted that religion, defined by its nature, is central to the shaping of an individual's personal and public life through venues of home and school. Second, I demonstrated that the qualities of good American citizenship were originally considered indebted to particular religious beliefs that provided moral and intellectual frameworks and motivations confirmed to be supportive of our social and political order. Third, I demonstrated that secular moral and civic education curricula were generally accepted by the public, not because they were effective, but because they were generally most compatible with the common paradigm of public education. Their unsatisfactory nature has been demonstrated by research or implied by the short life spans of moral education curricular movements and the public conflicts they frequently elicited.

These arguments affirm that the religious beliefs of students and parents may empower even secular moral education curricula when they are brought into engagement with one another. However, they also illuminate the deficits I associate with secular education. The secular setting not only fails to *build* the religious faiths that empower moral convictions, but it also fails to *connect* public moral and civic ideals with the student's primary source of meaning, understanding, motivation, and order. This disconnection weakens the moral and civic goals of public education. Separated from ideological ideals, today's public schools largely attempt to inspire learning through the hope of a diploma and a good job afterwards. However, every subject of a school curriculum *can be* a source of inspiration and meaning when they remain attached to and draw from personal religious beliefs. Meaningful education takes place within ideological communities and are delivered when scholars, curriculum writers, administrators, teachers, and families freely and passionately join in the ideological pursuit of nurturing children toward a reflective view of individual and social good within a context of coherent truth, value, and community.

In summary, as 20th-century public educators came to rely upon ungrounded character education, the curricula of the progressives, and especially the curricula of the early postmodern period, public education's nurture of moral and civic values weakened. Contemporary character education is more successful perhaps because its curricula find strength as they tend to tap into the deeper beliefs and values frequently associated with cultural norms and heroes. However, even with the successes associated with secular character education, the central aims for which public education has been exclusively tax funded have not been decisively met by the *secular* moral and civic curricula of recent or past times.

5

Problems With Religious Schooling

If my previous conclusions regarding the value of religious schooling to the public are accurate, and if there are no overriding obligations or concerns that constrain education leaders, then clearly, the American public should adopt a plural public education system. However, as the continued attachment to common education indicates, many scholars and other education leaders consider that there *are* "overriding obligations and concerns" that oppose the inclusion of religious schools within a plural public education system. Opponents not only argue that *common* education holds critical opportunities for moral and civic development, but they also question the civic value of religious schooling. This chapter and the next will confront their concerns supporting the secular ideal.

Because concerns regarding autonomy lead the opposition to religious schooling, I begin with a brief historical overview of perspectives regarding the nature and role of autonomy within the liberal democratic state. The 19th-century concern that Catholics would educate their children to merely follow the dictates of the Pope was an autonomy concern. Democratic theory has long held that citizens must think for themselves as they

Education Reform, pages 95–119
Copyright © 2013 by Information Age Publishing
All rights of reproduction in any form reserved.

enter the voting booth; other radical variations of autonomy have since come to shape public education. The remainder of the chapter will address the two primary perspectives of those who argue that traditional religious schools do not satisfy public concerns regarding autonomy. I will counter both these arguments to diffuse the concerns they raise in opposition to a broader place in society for religious schooling.

Autonomy and the Public's Educational Interests

Concern for individual liberty, closely linked to conceptions of personal autonomy, has long been a part of discussions regarding American civic education. In his work, *Orators and Philosophers: A History of the Idea of Liberal Education*, Bruce Kimball (1995) writes that there are two very distinct traditions of liberalism expressed in education. One tradition, which dates to Roman times, focuses on the accumulated moral and cultural wisdom and attempted to pass on these ideals to the next generation through instruction. I will refer to this view of autonomy as "democratic autonomy." The other tradition, which he calls the liberal-free ideal, attempted to liberate students from narrow prejudices and to promote open-mindedness by freeing students from tradition and authority. The former view was present during America's founding and first century of public education. It is represented by figures such as Thomas Jefferson and Noah Webster. Though Jefferson feared intellectual coercion, he strongly supported the education of children toward the moral and intellectual commitments of democratic society. He believed that our polity required that schools teach children to think for themselves, but this did not infer that the classroom should be nonauthoritative in areas of fact or morality. Noah Webster, the "father of American education," also supported a view of democratic autonomy. Schools were not to be neutral regarding values and beliefs, but they were to instruct children in proper submission to law and authority, the principles of liberty, moral and social duties, and the principles of virtue.

While the latter view did not pervade education thinking until the modern period, it was encouraged through the writings of Immanuel Kant (1724–1804) and Ralph Waldo Emerson (1803–1882). They were among those to inspired later generations toward a view of liberal autonomy that advocated for a self-chosen view of the good. In his essay, *Education*, Emerson pleaded for a new perspective of autonomy: "Cannot we let people be themselves, and enjoy life in their own way?" (1883, p. 136). Finding broader appeal with increasing pluralism, moral education curricula, such as values clarification, strongly reflected Emerson's view of moral freedom.

Though contemporary approaches to moral and civic education are distinct in many ways from the controversial approaches associated with the values clarification and moral reasoning curricula, they often hold philosophical or structural similarities to them. Some educators continue to reflect the liberal view of autonomy and believe that children are competent or rightfully entitled to determine their own moral and civic identities. They avoid "imposing their morality" on their students, which implies that they do not believe one moral framework is necessarily "better" than another. Others, reflecting a democratic view of autonomy, are less confident of the nature and abilities of children to determine their own moral development and believe that certain moral qualities are good for the child and society. Rather than viewing moral autonomy as a human right, they believe children have a fundamental need for moral instruction and that society is entitled to see that they are taught at least the common moral and civic virtues associated with societal liberty and stability.

Even though some advocates of liberal autonomy support *heavily* regulated vouchers as a means to expand state control over religious schools, they generally oppose the idea of religious education. These opponents of a move to a *lightly* regulated plural public education system tend to believe that religious schools cannot or will not provide the necessary moral and civic support for autonomy that American democracy requires, especially under only light public regulation. I divide these opponents to plural public education into two groups. The first group, reflecting the liberal-free view of autonomy, opposes religious schools because the teaching of any moral perspective as "true" conflicts with their belief in moral autonomy as a human right. The second group argues that the inclusion of religious schools as equal alternatives to secular common schools undermines the development of more traditional democratic autonomy. They believe that by educating from within one religious perspective, children will not develop the understanding or the skills necessary to understand people and perspectives from outside their faith. So, should the concerns of either liberal or democratic autonomy justify the continuance of the common paradigm of public education?

Concerns Regarding the Protection of Liberal Autonomy

Meira Levinson, Rob Reich, Harry Brighouse, and James Dwyer represent the first subdivision of those opposed to the inclusion of traditional religious schools within a system of public education. Though they vary in their particular arguments, they view autonomy not only as a value that contributes to the health of our democratic system, but as a liberal right of every citizen regardless of age. Thus, provision of life options and protection from restrictive moral influences becomes a public duty that places limits upon both the state and parents regarding the manner and degree of their authoritative influence upon the children under their educational care. Since my support of plural public education rests upon the superior ability of religious schools to teach concepts of truth and morality, my proposal clearly conflicts with those who believe no morality should be authoritatively taught.

Liberal Autonomy's Public Value

Reich supports minimalist autonomy as necessary to human flourishing because it is "deeply connected to self-respect, a fundamental or primary good in liberal societies" (2002, p. 120). He further supports autonomy because it "prevents in children the development of servility to the values of their parents or the traditions and norms of the cultural group(s) and state in which they are born" (2002, p. 121). Thus, Reich and other proponents of this view claim that in addition to holding personal value, liberal autonomy holds public value. When integrated within a view of liberal multiculturalism, liberal autonomy is civic, "in the interests of all citizens" (2002, p. 140). It is necessary as a public good because citizens must reflect upon and choose justice and the good apart from the opinions of others (Reich, 2002, p. 124). Reasoning from the writings of Rawls, Levinson also supports liberal autonomy as a central and "substantive *good*... that the state should uphold" (1999, p. 20, emphasis in the original). She claims that autonomy's value to the liberal state derives from its essential roles in legitimating government and in protecting liberal freedoms.

From within her view of liberal autonomy, Levinson argues, "Civic education is a primary aim of American schooling. Its general purpose is relatively uncontroversial: to educate children to participate in a democratic *polis*" (2002, p. 262, emphasis in the original). Further, she argues, "Education lies at the heart of the liberal project" (1999, p. 5), and that liberal concerns for "choice, cultural coherence, and citizenship fit together within an autonomy-driven education" (1999, p. 132). Thus, Levinson argues that the public should support autonomy as a favored and necessary civic ideal and foundation.

Rebuttal: Lack of Evidence Discounts Claim

Throughout its history, public education has positively supported certain moral and civic values. Ryan and Bohlin write, "State codes of education overwhelmingly support actively teaching the core moral values that provide the social glue of civic life" (1999, p. 18). However, supporters of liberal autonomy argue against the authoritative teaching of values in order to provide for an autonomy-driven education (see MacMullen, 2007). I counter this argument by claiming that liberal autonomy lacks sufficient evidence in support of its value to the public to compel the state to support these controversial claims.

Whereas claims regarding the personal benefits associated with liberal autonomy (such as its link with self-respect) are open to individual assessment, its public claims require broader justification. Proponents theorize that autonomy-driven education will advance the public good by providing a more reasoned and unbiased ground for public justice, but they provide no evidence that traditional religious schoolings inhibits the moral formation of students. To the contrary, public morality may be indebted to religious beliefs and communities that serve to preserve and propagate civilizing virtues. Scholar James Leming expresses the concern that "as a society we are currently living on moral savings accumulated over many generations" (1997); the further disconnection of moral and civic nurture from religious traditions may actually undermine the public good rather than advance it.

Scholar Christopher Winch (2002) argues that liberal educational systems are obligated to provide for the needs of traditional, not liberal, autonomy. He reaches this conclusion after distinguishing that liberal autonomy aims to prepare children for *any* reasonable life plan the child may choose, whereas traditional autonomy aims to prepare the child for life plans viewed by parents and educators as worthwhile.

A traditional conception of autonomy still supports the nurture of informed and independent decision makers and is of obvious value to the democratic process. Educators can nurture this conception within the curriculum while also encouraging the authoritative advocacy of common moral and civic ideals. However, when one replaces this advocacy with a liberal conception of autonomous student choice, moral and civic outcomes depend in greater part upon student preference. The broad rejection of values clarification in favor of character education provides evidence (see Hunter, 2000) that without moral guidance, children are less likely to make publicly beneficial choices. The move from a values neutral approach to one of mild, authoritative, moral advocacy indicates the public's support for the latter. A public commitment to *liberal* autonomy would promote a similarly nonauthoritative education environment to that rejected under the values clarification model over a broader expanse of the curriculum, and one would expect it to produce similar controversy and dissatisfaction.

Further, liberal autonomy is likely unattainable. Thiessen writes,

> Far too often, the ideals of independence and authenticity are defined in the abstract and thus are set too high. The ideal of normal [i.e., traditional] autonomy recognizes that people cannot completely transcend the culture of their time and place. To aim to do so in educating children is foolish. (1993, p. 129)

In addition to being unsupported and likely unattainable, conceptions of liberal autonomy so limit the influence of educators in their efforts to nurture the moral and civic development of children that they undermine the efforts of public education to form moral citizens. Though Reich attempts to grant autonomy to children as a civil right, I argue that the public's interests regarding the nurture of common moral and civic commitments remains a valid and necessary concern of public education. Thus, these arguments toward the civic value of education for liberal autonomy are dubious. At best, they draw strength from traditional concerns regarding the nurture of independent and informed decision makers; however, they disable the public value of these concerns when they fail to guide the student toward the common moral and civic values considered vital to democratic society.

Liberal Autonomy, Civic Education, and State Power

Reich argues that parents and cultural groups subvert liberal autonomy when they fail "to cultivate the capacity for its exercise," attempt to pass on a sense of "servility" to particular elders, attempt to socialize children into an "unequal status in the community," or "shield them from interacting...with the values of other ways of life" (2002, p. 127). Not all parents willingly support autonomy-based education. It is controversial, but supporters argue that the interests of the child require state action.

According to this conception, the public's involvement in education should be to define, provide, and protect a space for the formation of autonomy. Thus, Reich argues, "Promoting the development of autonomy in children will mean supporting policies that sometimes go against the autonomous choices of parents and counsel intervention in cultural groups that wish to prevent or discourage the exercise of autonomy by children" (2002, p. 112). Dwyer (1998) also believes that the claims of liberal autonomy require the state to take control of religious schools for the sake of children. Thus, parents and groups with strong commitments to their ways of life will likely require the most state intervention and will likely feel the greatest injustice toward this use of state power.

Whereas civic formation has traditionally been linked with public education, Brighouse distances education from any narrow civic role while arguing for the educational formation of liberal autonomy. He writes, "Arguments for civic education typically...justify civic education by its functionality for maintaining justice." He then faults these arguments for "not taking seriously enough the interests of children in the justification of educational policy" (1998, p. 745). Subsequently, he makes civic education compatible with the rights of autonomy through critique. Brighouse writes, "Civic education is permissible *only if* it includes elements that direct the critical scrutiny of children to the very values they are taught" (1998, p. 720, emphasis in the original).

Within this paradigm, the nurture and protection of autonomy effectively replace many of the traditional concerns that parents hold regarding their children's education. Whereas public education has sought to remain noncontroversial by limiting the philosophical claims of the state and by maintaining structures of public accountability, the claims of liberal autonomy would necessarily expand state authority over family concerns. This, however, is justified by the perceived good of children and the public good; thus, Reich writes, "The state *can*...set as a fundamental aim of education the development of autonomy" (2002, p. 112, emphasis in the original).

Rebuttal From Democratic Philosophy

Aspects of this argument overlap the first. According to their perceptions of liberal interests, these scholars call upon the state to preserve a place for the growth of an autonomy that distances many of the desires that parents hold for their children.

Arguments driven by a concern for the child may actually be patriarchal impositions of interest upon the child grounded in particular and controversial perspectives and values regarding autonomy; the liberal state is not to impose controversial views. Though Reich (2002) accurately notes that one's view of the good determines one's view of the best interest of the child, he uses this insight to limit the influence of parents and the state rather than to limit his own claim that education for autonomy reflects the child's best interest.

Surely the public has a right to assess the best interest of the child. However, lacking a comprehensive base from which to assess this interest, state assessments patrol the limits of acceptability based upon common and traditionally accepted norms rather than enforcing controversial claims. In defense of a greater role for parental perspective in education, Stephen Gilles reasons that if both parents and the state reasonably define the "best interest" of a child, parents, reflecting a greater concern for their children, are most likely to provide for that education. He writes,

> The decisive question . . . should be which educational decision maker will more faithfully act in accord with its definition of the child's best interest. I argue that parents have better incentives to act in their children's perceived best interests than do the state and its delegates, and will consequently be, on average, more faithful educational guardians. (1996, p. 940)

In addition, scholar Stanley Haurwas (1991, p. 98) argues that adolescents are too young in their knowledge, experience, and reasoning to make many consequential decisions. Thus, they are under the legal authority of responsible others to guide and to educate them. It would be not just a moral, but also a legal breach of parental duty to fail to give them this guidance.

Though proponents of liberal autonomy claim that children have a right to be exposed to diverse ways of life, this exposure is biased against exposure to traditional religious faiths because an educational environment that exposes children to a plethora of perspectives necessarily minimizes student association with ideas that claim long-term and in-depth exposure. Additionally, since people can criticize a tradition only to the degree they have entered it, expecting young people to make significant life choices without adequately exposing them to deep alternatives not only presumes that all choices are superficial, but it also deprives them of these deeper choices.

Further, one can accuse those who would require children to receive an education consistent with the claims of liberal autonomy of depriving many of these children *of their autonomy.* How do we know that most children desire autonomy from the values and beliefs of their parents? Adages such as "Like father like son" and "The apple doesn't fall far from the tree" seem to reflect the opposite. Children love their parents and trust them to prepare them to live a full and good life in accordance with their more expansive experience. Thus, a state-imposed education for liberal autonomy violates a child's autonomy by interfering with its desire to receive the best from its parents.

Education supportive of liberal autonomy leaves children to wander without wise counsel, which is neither good for the child nor for the state. Rather than providing for children's liberty, liberal autonomy "may foster persons who are slaves to their own appetites, rather than self-governing individuals" (Gilles, 1996, p. 950). Scholar Mitchell Stevens (2001) raises a related concern. He finds that within settings intended to provide children with autonomy, often a peer dependency that greatly influences their moral development has grown. Thus, instead of imposing liberal autonomy on dependent children, Gilles offers the traditional path to autonomy: "Many people think a child gradually achieves true autonomy by making choices and acting well within a belief system that the child's parents adhere to and instruct the child to accept as true" (1996, p. 949).

Thus, the broad use of state power to support claims of liberal autonomy fails to provide for the child's best interest, fails to address adequately the obligations of parents regarding the developmental needs of children, undermines the autonomous choices of children regarding their natural attachment to parental values, and fails to nurture the healthy development of self-governing individuals.

Liberal Autonomy, Regulation, and Traditional Religious Schools

Religious schools often attempt to propagate particularistic traditions and thus raise concerns among advocates of liberal autonomy. Reich (2002) argues that neither private nor public schools should teach unquestioned obedience to authority or shield children from other ways of life. Dwyer (1998) argues that the largest sectors of religious schooling—Catholic and fundamentalist—both use authoritarian and oppressive schooling. He claims that they harm children as they infringe on their intellectual and physical freedoms, foster the repression of desires, discourage the capacity for independent and informed critical thinking, foster dogmatic thought and expression, and promote intolerance.

However, as in the area of civic education, adequate presentations of other views within the religious school setting may alleviate autonomy concerns. Thus, Brighouse (2004a) does not oppose religious schools as long as the state strongly regulates them to provide an education for liberal autonomy. The key to the development of liberal autonomy is state regulation that limits the influence of parents/teachers and insures the use of multicultural curricula to provide children with optional ways of life.

Similarly, Reich does not claim that liberal autonomy is directly associated with either secular or religious schooling, but "it suggests...greater suspicion of educational arrangements that tend to reproduce the home environment of the child in the school, shielding students from exposure to and engagement with diversity" (2002, p. 141). In his vision, he potentially accepts the indirect public funding of religious schools that reconstitute their programs, but "schools that seek to inculcate a servility to parents or a particular worldview...would be disallowed, reconstituted, or closed by public authorities" (2002, p. 194). To further insure that autonomy is protected within the school setting, Levinson argues that parents should not be able to influence school "curricula, ethos, or aims" (1999, p. 144).

Claims associated with liberal autonomy oppose many of the traditional ways in which communities pass their visions of life to the next generation, but this does not imply an opposition to community life. Reich (2002) argues that autonomy is compatible with, and may even require, close communities. Without communities, ways of life are not visible as life options. However, as Brighouse and Swift claim, this does not imply "that parents have … extensive rights in transmitting their values to their children" (2006, p. 81). Thus, religious and ethnic communities are not a concern in themselves, just the manner and extent to which they attempt to pass on their ways of life.

Proponents of liberal autonomy argue for strong regulation of religious schools to prevent presumed negative outcomes and to insure the positive address of presumably neglected concerns. Though these scholars make provisions for the continuance of religious schools, their proposed regulations would critically undermine the nature and mission of religious schools, which would surely lead to the broad discontent of attending families and the closure of many schools.

Rebuttal: Claims Overstated and Divisive

I first rebut the claims against religious schools. Though certainly, *some* religious schools inadequately support or even oppose public educational values (by failing to teach history, teaching against a democratic form of government, opposing human equality, etc.), but studies overwhelmingly show that religious schools cannot be characterized in this general manner. For example, an examination of studies regarding civic values conducted by Patrick Wolf (2005) shows that private schools tend to equal or exceed common schools in their ability to advance the values and qualities of political tolerance, voluntarism, political knowledge, social capital, political participation, civic skills, and patriotism. Other researchers, including James Coleman and James Davidson Hunter, find similar evidence regarding the generally positive moral and civic contributions associated with religious schools. Coleman (J. S. Coleman & Hoffer, 1987) finds that Catholic schools have strong moral and academic outcomes; Hunter (2000) finds that those with theistic worldviews are less likely to lie, cheat, or steal; and other scholars find other social benefits associated with religious schools (see also J. S. Coleman, 1992; Fritch, 1999, 2001; Gimpel, Lay, & Schuknecht, 2003; Hunter, 2000).

The evidence these studies provide refutes claims that religious schools promote intolerance, division, and narrow thought, but they do not serve to counter claims that they infringe on intellectual and physical freedoms, foster the repression of desires, and the like. However, a liberal autonomous view of the good that conflicts with the religious views of individual schools provides the grounds for these claims. Below, I will more fully address why critiques of this nature cannot serve to justify state action. Here, I note that religious groups generally view the infringement of certain student "freedoms" and "desires" to be supportive of the good of both the child and the public, and thus, the restraint of these is a matter of responsible adult action.

Above, I noted that proponents of liberal autonomy confidently trust that children will become good citizens apart from authoritative moral and civic advocacy within schools. These advocates neglect not only public concerns regarding these moral and civic values, but they neglect traditional educational concerns about public unity as well. Reich's limits of parental educational authority, for example, are surely divisive. He claims, "Parental authority must end when . . . it disables or retards the development of minimalist autonomy in children" (2002, p. 160). His claim requires not only the acceptance of the deeply controversial tenets of minimalist autonomy, but it would intrude into what has heretofore been a personal and valued realm of family values. Rather than promoting goodwill between the state and already fractionally alienated religious families who have to pay private school tuitions, his claim intends to undermine the private schools they value. The implementation of claims regarding liberal autonomy relies heavily upon the state's power to regulate, and this reliance upon power implies the expectation of deep resistance. To alienate not only the deeply religious, but also even those good citizens who oppose the tenets of liberal autonomy runs counter to concerns of public unity.

Thus, scholarly research refutes the broad claim that religious schools require strong regulation to prevent the promotion of intolerance and dogmatic thought. Further, the long-standing concern of public education toward the nurture of morality, civic commitment, and unity also opposes the strong regulation of religious schools that already serve these concerns. Lastly, strong regulation itself is an unjustified source of disunity.

Liberal Autonomy as a Right

Scholar Charles Bailey writes, "A general liberal education is characterized most centrally by its liberating aspect indicated by the word 'liberal.' . . . What it liberates the person from is the limitations of the present and the particular" (1984, p. 20). Though the concept of liberal education as a pathway to greater autonomy is not new, those in this sector argue for a liberal view of autonomy that opposes the moral and civic formation of children.

Conceptions of liberal autonomy require the recognition of the state. Reich writes, "When a person is autonomous, governments and persons must... respect his autonomy. Respect for the autonomy of persons can be (and is often) understood as a right that protects people from external interference" (2002, p. 107).

Reich argues for a "minimalist conception of autonomy" that he defines as

> a person's ability to reflect independently and critically upon basic commitments, values, desires, and beliefs, be they chosen or unchosen, and to enjoy a range of meaningful life options from which to choose, upon which to act, and around which to orient and pursue one's life projects. (2002, p. 92)

Thus, minimalist autonomy requires broad exposure to alternative life choices apart from authoritative direction and "is necessary for persons... in order to lead a good life" (2002, p. 92).

Dwyer (1998) reasons that the educational requirements of liberal autonomy are reasonable in that neither the state nor parents have exclusive rights regarding the education of children. Education should serve the rights of children; rights that obligate others and call upon the state as a protector. Some parents may oppose autonomy-producing education, but this opposition reflects a sense of parental rights associated with the upbringing of children. Dwyer argues, however, that "an appropriate analytical framework would accord rights in connection with childrearing only to children themselves, who alone have fundamental interests at stake" (1998, p. 178).

Brighouse and Swift temper this with the affirmation that parents have rights relevant to their children's education, but that they are not as broad as generally supposed. They write, "Although parents' rights are, indeed, fundamental, they are conditional and limited" (2006, p. 81). One cannot conceive parental rights to override the right of children to liberal autonomy.

─────

Rebuttal: A Contested View of the Good Life

These arguments for liberal autonomy describe autonomy as a human right with little concern regarding the age of the child. Since this is a relatively new and controversial claim, proponents seek to justify it. Reich argues that "minimal autonomy" is necessary for a sense of self-respect and independence, and Levinson (2002) justifies it as a civic goal of public education. I addressed these arguments above, but I have deferred addressing the core tenet of liberal autonomy until last.

According to Nicholas Wolterstorff, proponents who claim that liberal autonomy is a human right require that "we should accept only autonomous principles, and that all our acceptance of principles should be autonomous" (1980, p. 108). If this proposition is accepted, it compels the use of state power to protect children from parents who would seek to nurture their children exclusively within a particular worldview. It also mandates that the state modify its curricula and its educational setting to provide a "noninfluencing" zone of self-development rather than a place to nurture moral and civic virtue.

This is an unacceptably narrow prerequisite for public education policy built upon a controversial view of the "good life." Liberal autonomy is not a "good" supported by unbiased research or common public support; rather its advocates hold it as a key component of their religious vision. Education scholar Maria Costa argues that liberal democratic government cannot favor autonomy with the comprehensive development manner of Immanuel Kant or John Stuart Mill, who link it with their view of the good. According to Rawls' concept of political liberalism, she writes,

> The education of children should not be focused on promoting autonomy or individuality as ideals of the good life. Rather, their education should focus on their roles as future citizens. Thus, the justification of civic education relies only on its role in ensuring the stability of a just society. (2004, p. 6)

Further, descriptions of liberal education can be sources of concern. Bailey's assertion that a liberal education "liberates the person from . . . the limitations of the present and the particular" (1984, p. 20) is problematic; why must the "present and the particular" be viewed as oppressive when religious exposure not only seems to contain so much good for so many individuals but also can leave children with growing maturity? Thiessen also questions the validity of Bailey's view: "This negative view of a narrow upbringing is entirely unwarranted. Indeed, as various authors have argued, a 'primary culture' is essential to becoming an individual, and it is also essential as a foundation for growth towards autonomy" (2007, p. 38).

Finally, concerns regarding liberal autonomy provide evidence that their supporters inconsistently oppose the teaching of certain *kinds* of values. They oppose the teaching of religious values, whereas they accept the teaching of many other values that parents may hold as beneficial to their children. Education scholar Steven Vryhof writes,

Some have suggested, that "imposing" a set of beliefs on children . . . is oppressive and unfair. Children, they think, should be allowed to choose their belief system. . . . But often such thinking usually only applies as a knee-jerk reaction to *religion*. We will teach hygiene and basketball and piano and manners and fair play and a host of other practices, often in the face of the child's resistance, never questioning whether equipping the child with those skills or practices or values is helpful or fair or life enhancing. And we don't expect the children in later years to resent having a preference for cleanliness or the ability to play the piano; indeed, many look back and are grateful to their parents for supplying such training. In the same way, children can look back with gratitude for parents who equipped them with a religious faith that later in life enabled them to stand the light of day and endure the dark of night. (2004, p. 6, emphasis in the original)

Thus, claiming liberal autonomy as a "right" calls upon the state to protect children from the religious influence of their parents by providing an autonomy-producing education. However, this claim is unsubstantiated and contested. Educating for liberal autonomy exceeds legitimate state educational interests; it inappropriately reflects a particular view of the good life, it disconnects children from an "essential foundation" for healthy development, and it inconsistently filters certain kinds of values as inappropriate for parents to pass to their children. Therefore, the state cannot enforce liberal autonomy as a right around which it should structure public education.

Scholar Walter Feinberg provides a clear example of one who claims neutrality but clearly exemplifies many of the concerns of liberal autonomy addressed above. Feinberg claims to write from a secular position (2006, p. xiii), but his analysis indicates that he is more of a philosophic liberal. While appearing to merely provide analysis of the public concerns regarding religious schools, his presumptions often seem illiberal; and to those of other faiths, his conclusions heavy handed.

Building upon claims that liberalism and pluralism demand that our democracy regulate *all* schools (public and private) to insure they comply with concerns of personal security, safety, autonomy, intellectual growth, and a respect for human difference, Feinberg stretches these generally acceptable claims to extremes that paint religious schools as fearful entities. For example, he writes that parents are negligent regarding the public's concern for safety when religious schools teach against homosexuality or when children are not taught "safe" sex (2006, pp. 117, 121). Also, he aligns with the proposition that religious schools be monitored to insure they are places where children can be "authentic" and experiment outside rigid bounds of "moral slavery" (2006, pp. 125–126). Though he writes with an apparent gracious concern for religion and religious schools, he strikes at their conceptions of human dignity and morality and calls upon government to regulate them when they oppose his controversial views, which he claims reflect the public interests of our nation. In concluding, he subtly warns against allowing religious schooling to expand. He writes, "[Secular] public schools, when working as they should, can provide the trust and understanding that can allow single-tradition religious schools to flourish *at the educational margins*" (2006, p. 214; emphasis added). Though surely we can imagine school practices that government should not support or should even prohibit, Feinberg paints religious parents with a distrustful brush that colors them as those who are negligent and abusive.

Many of the liberal arguments against religious schooling follow the examples above. Their proponents claim to speak from a neutral secular perspective, but the particulars of their concerns, though likely commonplace in their academic circles, do not necessarily reflect common public beliefs or values. While attempting to provide the philosophic foundations for a "common education system," they end with advocating for an educational system that conforms with their religious views of the good life.

Summary Conclusion

Whereas laws prohibit liberal states from narrowly defining the qualities of "the good," they may legislate and teach the parameters of healthy public morality and citizenship that support the polity. Proponents of liberal autonomy tend to disregard these limits when they conflate their contested claims regarding the nature of human flourishing with the more pragmatic and procedural concerns of the state regarding moral and civic health.

Reich (2002) rightly notes that children need exposure outside their home culture to choose autonomously their vision of the good life, but his view of autonomy assumes that self-direction is either fragile or alien to human nature. I argue that a healthy and less controversial view of autonomy allows for parenting in which children gain exposure to other views of the good through the media, interaction in public, and intentional presentations within the classroom. Instead of requiring the absence of religious advocacy to satisfy those favoring liberal autonomy, we should devise state regulations that insure religious schools present a minimal and age-appropriate exposure to our nation's diversity.

Rather than attempting to claim exclusive public support for their educational ideology that neglects the traditional concerns of education, proponents of liberal autonomy would better serve the public by placing their vision of the autonomous life alongside the plurality of other beliefs that provide frameworks for moral and civic education. This would not only provide for the formation of autonomy-seeking communities that could be evaluated as to their effectiveness in support of public moral and civic values, but it would also provide others with the opportunity to choose an autonomous life apart from authoritarian state intervention.

In concluding, perhaps the most damaging argument against those opposing plural public education from a liberal autonomous perspective is the internal inconsistence of their position. Proponents claim to support human dignity by asserting that *children* have both the human right and intellectual/emotional capacity to make autonomous choices, but they deny that most *adults* have these same rights and capacities, for most adults would have to be forcibly prevented from raising their children according to their understanding of what is true and valuable. This view of human "dignity" would have to be enforced against the judgment of most citizens. Policies that step between loving parents and their children do not reflect liberty; rather, this proposal (claimed to be liberal) supports an elitist (or at least a religious) oppression of the masses.

Democratic Concerns Regarding School Choice

Philosopher Dwight Allman identifies the growing concern for moral and civic nurture that has directed many discussions regarding the mission of public education away from the concerns of liberal autonomy. He writes,

> Recently...the age-old problem of cultivating citizens has attained new prominence. Contemporary political theory has increasingly focused attention on the qualities and capacities that the exercise of self-government, not to mention the practice of justice, necessarily presumes. In the past decade, what some call "citizenship theory" has emerged out of a roaring debate between the partisans of rights-based, self-directing individualism and the partisans of a civic existence grounded in the formative experience of community. (Allman & Beaty, 2002, p. x)

While my argument regarding the public value of religious schools clearly falls within this discussion, this next set of arguments opposing the public funding of religious schools also claim to serve the moral and civic interests of the nation.

The second (and larger) subdivision of school choice opponents believes secular public schools have a positive civic influence upon children that private or religious schools will not have. Public education leaders have long believed that government-operated schools hold a unique advantage regarding the nurture of moral and civic qualities valued by the democratic public. In this vein, Patrick Wolf notes that scholars have advocated the importance of free neighborhood schools to the inculcation of civic values. Summarily, he writes,

> Public schools make an important statement about equality, a fundamental democratic value. Because all students in a particular community tradition- ally are assigned to a specific school, public schools are "common schools," where children from diverse backgrounds gather to learn about social coop- eration and the toleration of differences. (2005, p. 210)

With a confidence in the public common education model, the schol- ars within this division argue that public education should keep its distance from religious schools due to their perceived failure to accommodate pub- lic education concerns regarding the nurture of democratic autonomy.

Democratic Autonomy

Whereas those concerned with the development of *liberal* autonomy oppose traditional religious schooling based upon the perception that it violates the *rights of children* to autonomy-producing educations, those con- cerned with the nurture of *democratic* autonomy oppose traditional religious schooling based upon the perceived *civic needs* of our democratic system. They hold the belief that public common schools are superior for the nur- ture of citizens capable of independent and intelligent decision making.

This concern for a level of democratic autonomy is not new: accord- ing to historian Robert Healey, Thomas Jefferson believed that republican government relied on "general education to enable every man to judge for himself what would secure or endanger his freedom" (1962, p. 178). Jefferson wrote that autonomous citizens were the best safeguards to pre- vent civil and religious leaders from, "setting up their own opinions and modes of thinking as the only true and infallible [ones], and as such en- deavoring to impose them on others" (as cited in Hening, 1823, p. 84). Liberal democracies ostensibly represent the will of the people, but lacking an adequate autonomy, citizens from positions of fear or ignorance may reflect only the thoughts of their authorities. Thus, political science schol- ars Stephen Macedo and Yael Tamir (2002) argue that liberalism endorses and promotes autonomy, in part, because good citizens must judge laws through self-critical debate.

Political science scholar Eamonn Callan provides a working definition of autonomy:

> I am autonomous to the degree that I have developed powers of practical reason, a disposition to value those powers and use them in giving shape and direction to my own life, and a corresponding resistance to impulses or social pressures that might subvert wise self-direction. (1997, p. 148)

Though liberal and democratic autonomy are similar in their claim to support the public good, democratic autonomy is a subcategory of liberal autonomy, differing in its educational nurture and in its public relevance. Whereas the state is called upon to nurture the former as a human right that limits the moral influence of parents and the state in order to preserve the transcendent good of autonomy, the concerns of the state regarding the latter are less broad. The state nurtures democratic autonomy less by binding home influences than by insuring exposure to alternative perspectives, and it nurtures democratic autonomy for its utility as a necessary support to healthy democratic decision-making rather than as a right attached to a particular view of the "good life." Without the overburden associated with rights, democratic autonomy requires only (a) a character that is confident and able to make independent decisions, and (b) an adequate knowledge of options for informed decision making. Schools that foster a character of subservience to authorities undermine the nurture of democratic autonomy, as do schools that present a single view of truth with little recognition of other perspectives or ways of life.

Response to Concerns for Democratic Autonomy

As evidenced by Thomas Jefferson's educational plans (noted previously), a concern for democratic autonomy is a part of the American democratic tradition. In addressing this concern, I concur with the conventional linking of public education with the nurture of traditional democratic autonomy. However, I intend to refute claims that the common school setting is necessary or particularly favored over religious schools for its nurture.

Character Component

Callan supports common education as the best means of nurturing autonomous character, because it encourages students to interact with differing perspectives. "The essential demand is that schooling properly involves...sympathetic and critical engagement with beliefs and ways of life at odds with the culture of the family or religious or ethnic group into which the child is born" (1997, p. 133). Callan links democratic autonomy with the public good in that it serves to form "a character that would refuse to resort to domination or manipulation in dealing with fellow citizens and would resist these measures when others use them" (1997, p. 51).

Knowledge Component

Democratic autonomy requires not only the formation of an independent character, but it requires access to an adequate breadth of knowledge and perspective. Callan writes,

> To be denied a sympathetic understanding of ethical diversity by parents who seek to preserve unswerving identification with the primary culture of birth is to be denied the deliberative raw material for the independent thought . . . that a developed autonomy necessitates under the conditions of pluralism. (1997, p. 148)

From the above concerns, some educators question whether religious schools adequately prepare students to live in a pluralistic society. They believe that religious schools may oppose the formation of democratic autonomy by indoctrinating, fostering dogmatic discourse, or being closed to the broad knowledge, debate, and criticism associated with independent decision making.

Rebuttal: Religious Schools Can Nurture Democratic Character

With implications for character formation, Callan (1997) claimed above that "good education requires sympathetic and critical engagement with beliefs and ways of life at odds" with the child's upbringing. This requirement, which seems difficult to fulfill in religious school settings chosen by parents, casts doubt on whether these schools should be considered "public" schools.

However, Kenneth Strike argues that religious groups allow both diversity and choice within broad parameters. Though religious schools may require that children adhere to their basic tenets of faith, students will still meet children of other races, cultures, demographic backgrounds, and interests. Speaking of church-affiliated schools, Strike writes, "Congregations do not impose ways of life, tribes do. This may not make congregational schools into marketplaces of ideas, but it does mean that children who attend them are likely to encounter many forms of diversity" (2003, p. 179).

Graham Haydon (1995) affirms that religious schools can rightly affirm comprehensive moral formation as long as schools expose children to alternate views of the good. He notes that exposure to these alternate views may take place within the classroom, but the classroom is only one source of exposure to alternate views. They are also present in the culture through common exposure and the media. Thus, the concern that children will not be adequately exposed to diversity within religious schools seems to be overstated, Berger notes that a vast amount of choice exists even within "all embracing communities" (1992, p. 87). Further, religious schools do not necessarily lack material with which to develop the skills of heated, yet respectful, debate or the opportunity to exercise choice.

Additionally, Callan's (1997) concerns for autonomy fail to recognize that healthy autonomy can be viewed as developmental. Good parenting often recognizes that children should be given choices as they are mentally, emotionally, and intellectually prepared to make those choices. Thiessen (1993) notes that exposure to diversity must be balanced with children's need for stability and coherence during their growth toward autonomy. Unless student autonomy is viewed in terms of growth and process rather than as a state of being, students will likely make irresponsible decisions for which their educational authorities can rightly share blame. Thus, religious schools can fully embrace a democratic concern for autonomy while opposing the assertion that children must be treated as fully autonomous during the school day.

Finally, I argue that religious schools can nurture tolerance in a different and potentially stronger manner than can common schools. Common school settings, removed from comprehensive conceptions of the good, favor the nurture of a tolerance built upon deference to the relatively equal values and perspectives of diverse others. This paradigm of tolerance formation suggests that to grow deeper in one's convictions in a setting that advocates from a particular perspective is to become intolerant of those who hold other views. This need not necessarily be the case.

Deep belief can provide a ground for tolerance when tenets of faith support it. To draw a parallel, both schools that advocate a liberal view of autonomy and religious schools provide their students with an evaluative framework. Though the religious school may preference their doctrine, it is not the framework, but the doctrines of the framework that promote or oppose autonomy. Strike writes, "Autonomy has more to do with the character of the doctrine and of the virtues it encourages than it has to do with the mere fact that a doctrine is privileged" (2003, p. 171). Thus, I argue that whether a school promotes tolerance is similarly linked less with the fact that a school is religious than with the doctrines the particular school holds. Thus, one can alleviate concerns regarding religious schooling and the nurture of democratic autonomy and tolerance whenever a particular school's doctrines condone those particular qualities.

Christian faiths, for example, frequently hold that individuals are accountable before God for their actions and are to love diverse others, even enemies, while also condoning humility. References in the Holy Bible—Galatians 6:5–11, Mark 12:28–31, and 1 Peter 3:8—provide several such examples. Religious schools teach toward the development of healthy religious commitment that is distinct from fanaticism and intolerance, which Thiessen writes are "perversions of healthy commitment" (1993, p. 276). Budziszewski argues, "True tolerance is not forbearance from judgment, but the fruit of judgment" (1992, p. 5). If religious schools promote conviction-based qualities such as these, they may exceed the standards of common schools that provide for the building of autonomy and tolerance only upon mutual acceptance among equals. Examples of this religiously based tolerance are found in the lives of Christians like Corrie Ten Boom (1971), who, under Nazi rule, held that her faith mandated that she help Jews escape capture. It is evidenced contemporarily within countless religious ministries such as Teen Challenge, Catholic Charities, and Habitat for Humanity, which are dedicated to helping addicts, the poor, and the abused, regardless of race or belief.

Scholar Ian MacMullen (2004) finds that religious elementary schools provide stronger foundations for ethical autonomy than public common schools. He supports this conclusion based upon evidence affirming the importance of a primary culture, evidence that a "framework of provisional commitments" best supports the early nurture of ethical reasoning, and evidence from cognitive psychology that shows that children grow into autonomy in steps that begin with the development of a primary culture. MacMullen writes,

> Before children have the cognitive capacity to engage in authentically autonomous reflection, their long-run interest in developing autonomy is best served by consolidating their sense of identity within a coherent primary culture and beginning to teach the practice of ethical reasoning within the framework provided by that secure cultural identity. (2004, p. 613)

As an example of the exemplary personal and social character concerns that religious schools can support, I point to Catholic Canon Law regarding education:

> Education must pay regard to the formation of the whole person, so that all may attain their eternal destiny and at the same time promote the common good of society. Children and young persons are therefore to be cared for in such a way that their physical, moral and intellectual talents may develop in a harmonious manner, so that they may attain a greater sense of responsibil-

ity and a right use of freedom, and be formed to take an active part in social life. (Code of Canon Law: 795, 2007)

Thus, religious schools that teach toward deep commitments may also provide a secure groundwork to teach tolerance, and religiously based moral and character training provides a strong foundation for other ethical reasoning.

Religious Schooling as Indoctrination

Religion, once publicly affirmed to form appropriate democratic character, is now often considered an obstacle to its formation. Religious school opponents often express concerns regarding a limited or faulty presentation of information with the accusation that religious schools "indoctrinate." Educational indoctrination implies that teachers present inadequate or faulty information as representative and true. Scholar Michael Hand presents an argument for his belief that religious schools indoctrinate based on a syllogism. He claims, in part, that "Teaching for belief in not-known-to-be-true propositions is, when successful, indoctrinatory, except where teachers are perceived to be intellectual authorities on those propositions" (2004, p. 343). Thus, Hand argues that a nonindoctrinating education should teach only that which is considered true according to authorities. However, this makes little rational sense. "Authorities" have no more claim to know the "unknown" than do "nonauthorities." Further, if the public is required to strip the curriculum of all "unknowns" (save those taught by authorities), then it would virtually reduce the curriculum to "known facts." Without the "authority" to teach morality, math teachers could not teach that cheating is wrong; history teachers could not teach that slavery was wrong; and education would be largely stripped of interpretations of meaning, vision, purpose, and moral instruction (common or otherwise). Hand's attempt to link a good education with solid truth ends in a dry and meaningless assortment of data that few would associate with a good education.

Scholar James Arthur argues that since the Enlightenment, ideas that linked religion with morality and education have been attacked. He writes, "Education was about knowledge and was considered value-free, whilst religion was about dogma and was value-laden. These assumptions are ungrounded for they fail to examine the fundamental beliefs upon which education rests" (2003, p. 55). According to Thiessen, concerns regarding indoctrination and a lack of educational autonomy are derived from the "Enlightenment idea of liberal education... [which rules] out indoctrination because it violates the normative, the cognitive, and the procedural criteria which govern the concept of liberal education" (1993, p. 41). Indoctrinating efforts may manipulate children by failing to teach them to think, to require reasons for conclusions, or to evaluate their beliefs. I argue that whereas narrow indoctrination is opposed to liberal education, religious schools that nurture children in a particular faith do not necessarily indoctrinate.

From Hand's (2004) argument above, it is apparent that he presumes that an autonomous education should present only secular academic knowledge. However, as Thiessen notes, "It is necessary to give up the ideal of 'pure rationality' because our capacity to reason is finite" (1993, p. 129); postmodern scholarship has concluded that all knowledge is perspective laden. In this vein, scholar Robert Kunzman writes,

> Some theorists appear to equate *reasonable* with *secular*, and thus *religious* with *unreasonable*. From an epistemological standpoint, this is simply mistaken. Plenty of secular reasons are unreasonable, and many religious reasons are reasonable. As Richard Baer observes, "There are no reasonable epistemological standards that allow us to judge theological thinking as inherently inferior or less reliable than secular or non-theistic thinking. (2006, p. 109, emphasis in the original)

Thus, Hand's argument fails in a second point: "No religious proposition is known to be true" (2004, p. 343). He and others see religious thought as behind a wall that is impermeable to reason (Viteritti, 2007). But rather than asserting that academic knowledge is free of tradition and perspective or that religious thought reflects indoctrination, one should view them both as reflections of certain assumptions. Thiessen writes,

> Critical thinking...[is] necessarily tradition bound. Criticism always rests on some assumptions that are, for the time being, unquestioned....The choice and construction of beliefs is never the product of isolated, individual wills....Rationality is necessarily imbedded within a tradition to some extent. (1993, p. 130)

Thus, the religiously based moral and civic education of the past did not reflect the caricature of the religionist whose only concern was compliance. To the contrary, according to McClellan, the 19th-century concern was to create an inner-directed person who "is a person who when confronted with moral dilemma is less guided by tradition or opinion of others than by values internalized at an early age" (1992, p. 26).

With this said, public education is less concerned with the nature of truth than with how citizens relate with others regarding their diverse views. Does a deep (religious) commitment to a perspective prevent its holder from learning from or compromising with others in a peaceful manner?

Thiessen (2007) proposes that strong beliefs are not necessarily a problem. One can be committed to a view of truth but open to refutation with appropriate evidence. Commitment to certain views and openness to new ideas are necessary not only to a healthy individual, but for a healthy scientific mind. Thiessen writes,

> As Karl Popper has argued, a degree of closed-mindedness is necessary for a good scientist. Scientists should not give up a theory too soon in the face of contrary evidence. Of course, eventually the evidence becomes overwhelming and then one must be prepared to give up a theory. (2007, p. 43)

In the words of philosopher Richard John Neuhaus, one must give space for an "acknowledgement of the authoritative" (1995, p. 17) that will vary according to worldview. Thus, one can be open-minded while holding to a belief system as one recognizes one's own limitations and is open to revise one's beliefs (Adler, 2004).

Religious Foundations for Democratic Autonomy

Callan (1997) is also concerned that good citizens not utilize or succumb to either "domination or manipulation." Though social domination and manipulation may be difficult to define in our democratic and market-driven culture, I agree that one's use of and response to power is a public concern. As already noted, broad claims of this sort against religion fail due to a deficit of evidence. Thus, I choose to reevaluate the circumstances that direct the claims.

Many of the concerns that link religious schools with undemocratic qualities are perhaps attributed less to the religious nature of the schools than to the different educational styles they express. I argue that one can regard the worldviews at the heart of religious schools more constructively as publicly valuable sources of moral and civic nurture rather than as sources of authoritarian domination or manipulation. Religious schools allow children to start from a position of intellectual stability within a primary culture. Thiessen writes, "Exposing them to plurality and a Babel of beliefs and values too soon will in fact prevent the development of abilities which are a key to later functioning in a complex and pluralistic environment" (2001, p. 41). Even if children are to adopt worldviews different from their parents, they require an initiation into one culture to have a foundation from which to choose others (Thiessen, 2001).

Scholar Michael Merry argues that it is important for home and school to support one another. He writes, "An education for cultural coherence

tends to the child's well-being through identity construction and maintenance" (2005, p. 477). However, common schools avoid providing answers
to identity questions such as Kant's question of "Who am I?" that Peter
Berger claims can be answered only within a religious view of reality (1992,
p. 21). Thus, Brian Crittenden (1988) questions the educational abilities
of the state when it is legally bound to be incompetent regarding the epis-
temic, moral, and aesthetic standards that guide education in its formative role. Scholar Perry Glanzer thusly argues that in an educational choice
system, "Students could be formed by a narrative that gives a consistent
message about their identity and purpose, as well as clear guidance about
virtues, vices, principles, and moral models" (2003, p. 304).

Conclusion

The arguments above express the autonomy concerns that oppose the inclusion of religious schools within a system of public funding. Their proponents argue that either funding traditional religious schools will deprive
children of their right to an education for liberal autonomy, or it will deprive
them of a common education setting associated with the nurture of democratic autonomy. If one accepts the premises of the first liberal perspective,
then it seems that there should be clear evidence to support the case that an
education for liberal autonomy supports the well-being of the individual and
the public in a manner superior to education premised on more traditional
perspectives. However, I find little evidence that this position is little more
than a philosophic theory or a personal bias. Though enshrouded in expressions of goodwill and bolstered by a selective gathering of evidence, claims
that public education goals are tightly linked with educational autonomy
fall short. Rather than fitting neatly into an educational framework closely
aligned with the tenets of liberal democracy, these liberal conceptions of
autonomy more closely seem to reflect an attempt to use government educational power to impose a religious view of human flourishing on society
rather than to address the concerns of autonomy evenhandedly.

Regarding the claim that common education is vital to the nurture of
democratic autonomy, I have shown that arguments opposing the ability of
religious schools to form democratic autonomy fall short in several ways.
They fail to address the formative strengths of religious schooling, are not
backed by substantive evidence, and analyze religious school methodology only according to a secular paradigm of autonomy formation. Though
these autonomy concerns do not seem to override consideration of a plural
public education system, the next chapter will present other concerns that
some say should.

6

Religious Schools and Concerns Regarding Deliberation, Equity, Cohesion, and Religious Engagement

Though perhaps not as heated as issues of autonomy, scholars present other arguments that seem to oppose the move to a system of plural public education. Terry Moe summarily describes the opinions of many of these opponents:

> The real effect of vouchers would be to wreck the public schools by draining off resources for children. In the process, vouchers would undermine cherished values the public school system has long stood for—common schooling, equal opportunity, democratic control—and create a system driven by private interests. (as cited in Gimpel et al., 2003, pp. 122–123)

This chapter will define and counter the most prominent of these arguments that are weighty and worthy of address. Specifically, I will discuss the following:

Education Reform, pages 121–154
Copyright © 2013 by Information Age Publishing
All rights of reproduction in any form reserved.

- Arguments that the common classroom provides a superior setting for the nurture of the citizenship qualities associated with deliberative democracy.
- An argument that America's educational dilemmas could be solved with a robust national liberal arts curriculum.
- Arguments that religion can be adequately engaged in a common school setting.
- Arguments that parental choice in education would promote educational inequity.
- Arguments that religious schools promote division and Balkanization.

Educating for a Deliberative Democracy

Amy Gutmann, often writing with Dennis Thompson, defines her concerns for civic education in terms of deliberation. Together, they envision that our nation should operate with a political methodology of discourse and resolution rather than the methodology of majoritarian rule favored by democratic proceduralists. They fear that without greater philosophical resolution, growing diversity within our society will promote factional confrontations that will undermine national stability. Broadly, allowing more children to attend religious schools will hamper public dialogue and inflame the conflicts associated with our pluralistic society.

Deliberation and Its Civic Value

In her noted work, *Democratic Education* (1999), Gutmann establishes the qualities and outcomes that she believes are the priorities of democratic citizenship. While arguing that public deliberation best advances concerns for societal justice, she defines her view of democratic education, which aims to develop deliberative skills and character of school-age citizens. She writes, "Democratic education is best viewed as a shared trust, of parents, citizens, teachers, and public officials, the precise terms of which are to be democratically decided within the bounds of the principles of nondiscrimination and nonrepression" (1999, p. 288).

She and Thompson (1996) hold that public education is somehow "outside of government" and that it plays a vital role in advancing their civic vision to make democracy more deliberative. In preparing students to be good citizens, they write,

Schools must go beyond teaching literacy and numeracy.... Schools should aim to develop their students' capacities to understand differing perspectives, communicate their understanding to other people, and engage in the give and take of moral argument with a view of making mutually acceptable decisions. (1996, p. 359)

Gutmann and political scientist Benjamin Barber (2003) agree that democracy functions more smoothly and justly when children acquire the qualities necessary for peaceful deliberation and overcome a raw reliance upon self-interested power politics.

Schools are to instill in students a collective capacity to seek justice rather than just self-interest. Teaching communication skills lays a foundation for productive dialogue. Democratic character formation involves learning the "principle of reciprocity," which recognizes the value and equal citizenship of others. It encourages students to behave toward others as they would desire others to behave toward themselves. Citizens who reflect this character would be less likely to use political means to establish their views, thus, Gutmann and Thompson (2004) propose that this principle of reciprocity will replace the contentions surrounding the idea of "government neutrality."

Rebuttal: Real-World Experiences

I agree with Gutmann that moral and civic nurture is a key public concern, and a system of public education is vital to this end. However, Gutmann and I strongly disagree regarding the effectiveness of the common school's efforts in this area and the degree to which religious communities can be trusted toward the nurture of moral and civic values.

Gutmann (1999) builds her vision of democratic education around the claim that public deliberation is the best way to advance societal justice and to counter the adversarial nature of democracy. She, with those of like mind, support deliberative democracy and argue that it is superior to more adversarial forms of democracy (Levinson, 2003, p. 24). However, though teaching the skills of deliberation is valuable, it is difficult to justify Gutmann's call to align public education behind this one vision, a vision that can be reasonably accommodated within traditional religious schools in a modified form.

Levinson identifies two arguments that undermine the value of deliberative democracy. She argues that Gutmann presumes too much when she assumes that we can deeply communicate our concerns when using the language of public deliberation. Secondly, she argues, "It is likely to be harder to build the kind of trust that deliberative democrats correctly argue is required for deliberative democracy to function effectively and justly"

(2002, pp. 268–269). The two arguments share common ground; however, the common education setting does not naturally provide for the high degree of trust that Gutmann's vision of democracy requires, especially when yoked with the constraints of public reason (addressed below).

The vision of deliberative democracy is to build public decisions on consensus rather than on mere majority control. However, the possibility of consensus (the elimination of factions) was rejected long ago. Political scientist Gerald Gaus (2003, p. 210) argues that deliberative democracy overestimates the unity that deliberation will bring while underestimating our pluralism. Founder James Madison (Hamilton, Madison, & Jay, 1818, p. 504) spoke to this when he addressed the causes and "mischiefs" of pluralistic factions with the analysis that they are both rooted in liberty. To eliminate them would require the elimination of liberty, thus he supported controlling their effects. Gutmann (1999), on the other hand, heavily relies upon reducing factional tensions by attempting to create greater ideological uniformity within a common school setting and by decreasing the ideological liberties found in religious school settings.

Deliberative Democracy and Educational Authority

In tandem with concerns related to deliberation, Gutmann argues that democratic schools must reflect both public and individual interests. She writes,

> Democratic education grants democratic governments discretion over how to interpret the demands of civic education, provided the demands are not discriminatory or repressive. Parents do not have a general right to override otherwise legitimate democratic decisions concerning the schooling of their children. . . . Children are no more the mere creatures of their parents than they are the mere creatures of the state. (2002, p. 29)

Thus, Gutmann maintains that democratic procedures should govern "how citizens should be educated" (1999, p. 68).

From Gutmann's (1999, p. 31) analysis, parents pass on their own prejudices and beliefs to the general detriment of our diverse society. Thus, when schools are accountable to parents alone, those schools tend to undermine the deliberative processes associated with social stability. She argues, "History suggests that without state provision or regulation of education, children will be taught neither mutual respect among persons nor rational deliberation among ways of life" (1999, p. 31).

Gutmann (1999, p. 117) sees a public danger in the move of many citizens to religious schools and advocates for greater "democratic" control over them. She argues that allowing parents to choose schools according to their personal ideologies merely provides a means to propagate prejudice and disrespect toward those of other religious faiths between generations. She muses that if the Catholic/Protestant tensions of the 19th century had not been mediated within the increasingly respectful public schools, "the religious prejudices of Protestant parents would have been visited on their children, and the social, economic, and political effects of those prejudices would have persisted, probably with considerably less public protest, to this very day" (1999, p. 31).

Thus, religious schools grossly oppose the public's interests and require the intervention of the state to insure the propagation of democratic values. In the words of Gutmann, "The civic arm of democratic education is not minimal. Neither is it optional from a moral perspective" (1999, p. 316). Gutmann (1999, pp. 117–123) does not propose to abolish all religious schools. However, the "democratic" controls she places upon these schools would go far toward modifying their traditional missions and practices.

Although differing curricula can incorporate deliberative concerns, Gutmann (1999, p. 95) maintains that not all educational visions support them. Parental education choice, liberal autonomy, and conservative virtue education all undermine the values of democratic education. Whereas plural public education transfers too much educational authority to parents, and liberal autonomy places too much moral education authority in children, virtue education rightly supports moral deliberation rather than the moral authoritarianism common to religious schools. Thus, she argues that deliberative democratic education is a formative concept around which the state must regulate other educational visions.

Rebuttal: Fears Unsubstantiated

Gutmann argues for expansive public authority over education based upon fears regarding the interests and beliefs of parents. As previously noted, I support the public regulation of education, but I argue that Gutmann's fears are largely unsubstantiated and lead to excessive and detrimental regulations. Light regulation can address reasonable concerns as it has in Canada and some other Western nations.

Macedo (2000, p. 265) expresses the concern that those who trust communities take too much for granted. Similarly, Gutmann fears giving parents and religion too great a role in education. She writes,

> To save their children from future pain, especially the pain of eternal damnation, parents have historically shielded their children from diverse asso-

ciations, convinced them that all other ways of life are sinful, and implicitly fostered (if not explicitly taught them) disrespect for people who are different. (1999, p. 31)

However, such claims seem to rely on the assumption that respect implies the acceptance of other ways of life as equally valid. Thiessen (1995, p. 7) brings greater reasonableness to this accusation when he defines intolerance as a disrespectful manner rather than a favorable acceptance of other views. Civic respect for others can grow even in an environment that rejects certain views; it is not dependent upon a common education setting.

Though good surely comes from broad exposure to people of diverse backgrounds, it is questionable whether the secular arena is the only or most effective setting for this exposure. Supported by studies by Joe Coleman (1998), Nancy Rosenblum states, "Pedagogy is as important for instilling democratic values and practices as curriculum, and private schools are as likely as public schools to implement participatory activities that foster cooperation over competition, deliberation, and so on" (2003, p. 84).

As mentioned in the previous chapter, the concern that religious schools generally lack the spectrum of social diversity to provide for the development of democratic discussion and reasoning skills is not without merit, but religious schools do not necessarily have homogeneous student bodies. Though greater public deliberation may be a worthy goal, Gutmann (1999) requires an unwarranted degree of state power to achieve her vision. She seeks to control the factionalizing tendencies of religious schooling, but she provides dubious evidence in support of the claim that they are a threat to democracy.

Concerns regarding the need to protect children from parents who would neglect the autonomy of their children are exaggerated. As Thiessen writes,

Children are seldom treated as property by parents. To object to religious schools by arguing that "children are not chattels of parents" . . . is essentially just rhetoric. No sincere religious parent views his or her child as a mere chattel. It is precisely because children are made in the image of God that Christian parents think it is important to have their children taught about the God who created them as unique and valuable individuals. (2001, p. 67)

Religious parents deeply care about their children, and the provision of religious schooling reflects their care according to their view of the good. Though some religious schools may grossly violate public standards, these schools are exceptions. Religious schools in general do not reflect abusive parental interests.

Gutmann (1999) calls upon and justifies the use of extensive state power to implement her plan of democratic education. However, I have shown that the fears she portrays lack substance, thus, her appeal to utilize public force lacks the necessary justification to deprive citizens of their liberties.

Concerns Regarding Civic Deliberation

Central to Gutmann and Thompson's conception of deliberation is its reasonableness. They write, "Most fundamentally, deliberative democracy affirms the need to justify decisions made by citizens and their representatives.... Its first and most important characteristic, then, is its *reason-giving* requirement" (2004, p. 3). However, these justifications reflect a secular orientation that religious schools may reject or be ill-equipped to nurture.

Gutmann and Thompson argue that public deliberation requires the exchange of reasons that "appeal to principles that individuals who are trying to find fair terms of cooperation cannot reasonably reject... reasons that should be accepted by free and equal persons seeking fair terms of cooperation" (2004, p. 3). Thus, they conclude these reasons "should be *accessible* to all the citizens to whom they are addressed.... A deliberative justification does not even get started if those to whom it is addressed cannot understand its essential content. It would not be acceptable, for example, to appeal only to the authority of revelation" (Gutmann & Thompson, 2004, p. 4, emphasis in the original).

Gutmann and Thompson's (2004) concern regarding the secular nature of public justifications is not unique. Political scholars Stephen Macedo, Robert Audi, and others also maintain that political discussion in public should be free of religious grounding. Robert Audi (2000) argues that within a pluralistic society, publicly accessible reasons should support legal coercion. Society's laws should coerce only in areas in which the rational person would act if properly informed (Audi, 1993). Thus, civic education should insure that students be taught to use public secular reasoning and to advance coercive measures on the public only when one's secular motivations are high enough to move other citizens (Audi, 1993, p. 691).

This manner of reasoning fits well within secular schools, but religious schools may focus on religious reasons and motivations that are inaccessible to others. Thus, the interests of the public toward the civic development of students regarding public deliberation seems to be better served in common schools rather than in religious schools.

Rebuttal: Secular Public Reason is Untenable

Gutmann and Thompson fail to provide evidence that religious schools are averse or unsuited to teach secular deliberative skills even though they are surely able to teach their students discursive skills. However, my greater concern regards the claim made by Gutmann and Thompson (2004) that public reason giving *should* be secular. These concerns regarding the nature of public speech reflect the ideas of Rawls and others on the topic.

Gerald Gaus (2003, p. 210) argues that this kind of speech is difficult to define and to achieve. It requires that one presumes to know what is acceptable to others and seems to limit society from aspiring to higher-than-common ideals. Thiessen rejects concepts of public reason for their unreasonable constraints upon the individual. He writes,

> Liberal theorists like John Rawls and Stephen Macedo would ask students and teachers within a common school to adopt, to "bracket" their ultimate commitments when liberal/democratic values are being discussed, and to limit themselves to a "public reasonableness." It is very difficult, however, to achieve a neutral public rationality; indeed, various writers today maintain that there simply is no such a thing. Civic education based only on public reasonableness further requires a kind of intellectual schizophrenia from students and teachers. It forces them to leave behind their most cherished beliefs in public discussions. (1995, p. 5)

Scholar Christopher Eberle (2002, pp. 331–332) also rejects the claim that good citizens should censor religious reasons in public discussion. The doctrine of restraint burdens the religious and is arbitrary in that it assumes secular reasons are more "right" than religious ones. Further, the tenets of public reason rely on the possibility that people can reach a neutral public reason that is empirical and free from "irrational beliefs" (Eberle, 2002, p. 14).

Scholar Paul Weithman (2002) notes that the requirement of public reason is a point of alienation for those who do not accept the tenet; and scholar Kent Greenawalt (1995) argues that liberalism allows for different viewpoints, and only individuals can weigh the value of their reasons (religious or otherwise) regarding their public concerns.

Political scientist William Galston (2002) affirms that Gutmann and Thompson's (2004) deliberative democracy is not compatible with pluralism. Rooted in the reciprocity of public reasons, it unjustly alienates many by requiring religious people to filter out their core beliefs. Gutmann (1999) presumes that a democratically controlled system of public education would reflect her secular deliberative model; she fails to acknowledge that our diverse and religiously concerned public might choose a system of educational choice that includes religious schools. Galston argues that our democracy should not oppose our diversity: "[A] liberal pluralist society will organize itself around principles of maximum feasible accommodation of diverse legitimate ways of life, limited only by the minimum requirements of civic unity" (2002, p. 119).

Thus, one of the core concerns of proponents of deliberative democracy is toward the nurture of a type of public deliberation that requires the exchange of secular reasons. However, sufficient evidence has not been given to justify the priority of this nurture, especially in light of arguments that the tenets of public reason require one to attempt to disassociate from one's value system, discriminate against the religious, endorse a "right" way of thinking, alienate dissenters, and oppose pluralism. Therefore, I argue that concerns regarding the nurture of public reason are insufficient to oppose the benefits found in a plural public education system.

Summary: Religious Schooling for Reason and Exposure

Gutmann (1999, p. 33) considers diversity to be of "political value" when children are exposed to it within the common school setting with the opportunity to learn from it, and she considers it to have merely "ornamental value" when it is reflected by individual communities and religious schools. She further argues that public justice and peace are indebted to formative experiences of deliberation within common school settings that use the shallow language of public reason. I counter these claims by providing greater evidence of religion's public value and by showing that concerns of justice and peace have other, more traditional religious roots.

I propose a radically different perspective. I argue that religion is substantive and that children *deprived* of the educational time needed to develop a worldview have *less* to contribute publicly. Deliberative skills develop slowly from a firm cultural foundation (Thiessen, 2001, p. 238). Children nurtured in a secular education environment reflect little intellectual understanding of their traditions and thus reflect only shallow diversity, have little ability to communicate their ideological positions to others, and have little from their religious culture with which to evaluate and contribute substantively to our diverse society. This philosophical shallowness reduces the value of religion as both an individual and a public source of meaning, perspective, and community.

The educational setting was the traditional forum in which cultures reproduced themselves (Vryhof, 2004, p. 181). Gutmann (1999) opposes religious school settings (because of fear of faction and intolerance) in favor of education settings that teach democratic deliberation. However, Gutmann's list of "democratic" concerns is value laden and controversial (Gilles, 1996, p. 938). Her concerns may be valid if one can prove that nurturing citizens with only shallow educational values and understanding best serves the moral and civic needs of democracy and deliberation. However, my argument throughout this book has been that it does not.

Robust Common Schools vs. Diverse Religious Schools

While Gutmann (1999) attempts to capture state power towards the goal of "democratic education," others may claim that their educational vision—rather than the diverse visions of religious families—deserves this power and will bring meaning and depth to public education. With broad scholarly and policy leadership experience, Diane Ravitch (2010) argues that both high-stakes testing and school choice are undermining education in America. In particular, she criticizes the moral, civic, and intellectual shallowness of contemporary public education and argues that current broadscale educational efforts are leading public education down the wrong path. I support her general analysis of public education's problems, but I find her final solution remarkably untenable.

Ravitch's vision is to "restore the historic tradition of public schools as places where students learn good behavior, good citizenship, and the habits of mind that promote thoughtfulness and learning" (2010, p. 241). To accomplish this, she proposes the implementation of a comprehensive, nationwide, liberal arts curriculum, which would be determined after public deliberation by duly authorized scholars and professional educators. As a complement to this curriculum, Ravitch proposes supporting the classroom by giving teachers greater professional authority and autonomy by distancing politicians from education, eliminating much educational bureaucracy, and disbanding school choice initiatives save those that attempt to serve children that local public schools were unable to reach.

Why is Ravitch's proposal so untenable? Because it is so like mine! She too sees the moral, civic, and intellectual decline of America and believes the goal of education is to "educate children to become responsible people with well-developed minds and good character" (2010, p. 228). She too is concerned that schools should prepare children not just to pass tests or get jobs, but to live meaningful and satisfying lives. She too believes that schools should be meaningful parts of the communities they serve. And finally, Ravitch similarly holds a meaningful view of a good education and thus disdains the lack of philosophic consideration among those who endorse surrendering the public's educational interests to an unregulated educational market. While our visions are similar, our proposals are diametrically opposed.

Ravitch (2010) optimistically hopes that families will *further surrender* their child's education to state or national education scholars and secular teachers, while I argue that to gain this vision of increased educational depth, the state must entrust parents with *greater* authority over their child's education. Whereas Ravitch maintains her vision is secular and fits within the common education paradigm, I argue that her vision is controversial and steps into religious realms better supported by a plural public education paradigm. Acknowledging the likelihood of conflict over a *robust* national moral, civic, and academic curriculum, Ravitch (2010, p. 232) notes that up to the end of the first half of the 20th century, American public school curricula were so similar to one another that it was as if the nation had a national curriculum. She is optimistic that today's society can follow suit. But here, Ravitch seems to either gloss over the deep differences that divide Americans over issues of truth and value, or she seriously underestimates the depth of the ideological soil necessary for the flourishing of the curriculum she proposes.

Ravitch (2010), displaying a naïveté incompatible with her experience, hopes that our curricular and culture wars are over. Further, she seems blind to the legal and historical struggle associated with attempts to include moral and ideological depth within the common public school curricula. I have traced some of this conflict above, and anticipate having Ravitch join me in support of a plural public education system. Though she would lose her national curriculum, she could help open the doors to see depth, breadth, and meaning restored to our "great American school system."

Curriculum scholar Wesley Null (2011) also finds American public education curricula to lack depth and substance. He blames curriculum writers, in part, for this problem, as they tend to view and write curriculum as merely a systematic covering of ideas, a pragmatic way to solve society's immediate problems, a means of existential nurture, or a tool for culture-shaping radicalism. He argues that curriculum must have a philosophic end or *telos*; "curriculum and philosophy both rely upon reason and logic, but both also can be tied loosely to matters of religion and faith" (2011, p. 7).

Null advances his solution to the problem of curricular shallowness through a proposal that teachers and curriculum writers adopt a deliberative approach to curriculum. Rather than merely viewing curricula as "organized subject-matter," writers, teachers, and administrators should view curricula as a response to the questions: "What should be taught, to whom, under what circumstances, how, and with what end in mind?" (2011, p. 5).

The deliberative process incorporates the concerns of the community, students, and state standards and integrates them with their philosophic, virtuous, and holistic ends. Thus, the fulfillment of American educational goals relies largely upon education professionals who are knowledgeable and virtuous themselves.

Null obviously recognizes the religious nature of his proposal—even giving examples of what deliberation might look like in religious schools— thus I anticipate that he would support a plural public education system. However, I include his proposal here, alongside Ravitch's, as another false hope under the common education model. Though Null is careful to contextualize his deliberative proposal to the differing circumstances of secular and religious schools, he too fails to address realistically the constraints the secular education paradigm places upon his educational vision. Whereas he claims, "Curriculum deliberation has the potential to revive liberal education in its richest sense" (2011, p. 263), one need just imagine the outcry that would likely surround a Christian teacher's effort to address the *telos* of sexuality in the liberal atmosphere of a San Francisco high school. Though wisdom would surely constrain the teacher's discussion, the problem is clear: under a common education paradigm, liberal education *cannot* be revived with any sense of "richness" save for those with a secular view of the world.

Many other scholars, such as A. G. Rud (2011), see the need for public schools to access and promote higher ideals. While Rud, gleaning inspiration from the life of Albert Schweitzer, proposes integrating public education with a "reverence for life," it is likely that virtually every other scholar, teacher, parent, and politician has their own ideals that they believe would inspire America's young people toward more whole, meaningful, and socially supportive lives. However, the legal, social, and bureaucratic constraints surrounding the common education paradigm constrain most of this wisdom and goodwill. Ravitch, Null, Rud—most of us—recognize the ideological hollowness of public education, but too few see either its cause or the paradigmatic shift necessary for its remedy.

Engaging Religious Identities in the Common School

Robert Kunzman insightfully argues that the personal faith of each student is relevant to the education day. He argues in favor of the engagement of student religious beliefs within the common school classroom in what he terms "Ethical Dialogue" (Kunzman, 2006, p. 6). Though Kunzman *does not* claim that secular schools can adequately engage the religious nature of education, others may use his ideas to oppose the formation of a plural public education system. If they can successfully do so utilizing Kunzman's teaching strategies, this would effectively neutralize my arguments regarding the need to include religious schools in a system of school choice. Though no one has attempted to criticize plural public education from this perspective, I will attempt to do so in order to show the weaknesses of the proposal.

Kunzman writes, "Schools' continued avoidance of ethical controversy bodes ill for our civic capacity for informed and respectful discourse" (2006, p. 5). From here, he advocates for deep ethical engagement while "guarding against the dogmatic imposition of religiously informed policies that affect all of us" (2006, p. 5). He notes the shallow, ungrounded flavor of common school discussions:

> Something deeply important is missing from most of these [moral education and character education] conceptual and curricular approaches, both in terms of depth and breadth. The current focus on a-contextual, prescriptive virtues typical of much character education curricula lacks the complexity inherent in most ethical challenges we face. Even those approaches that push students to wrestle with greater complexity do not generally provide sufficient opportunity for them to engage with the deeper ethical sources (religion and otherwise) that often inform our lives outside the classroom. (2006, p. 6)

Currently, ethical discussions within common schools not only tend to be shallow, but they intentionally seem to be so. Kunzman writes,

> Whether the controversy focuses on stem cell research, gender roles, or our responsibility to others in our community, teachers and schools frequently avoid or downplay the ethical issues involved, particularly when they are informed by religious perspectives. The educational result, I contend, is a citizenry with little skill in discussing ethical controversies, particularly as they relate to religion, and thus even less sense of how to make decisions about living together in respectful and reasonable disagreement. (2006, p. 6)

Thus, Kunzman's civic goal is to assist diverse students to develop the "capacity to reach either consensus or reasonable disagreement, to recognize the reasonableness in positions with which we (even strongly) disagree" (2006, p. 78).

Kunzman's (2006) methodology, in part, maintains the relative neutrality of the teacher among student views. The teacher then facilitates respectful discussion regarding civic concerns. His philosophy and methodology diverge from Gutmann's and others who frequently support the need to develop the skills of public deliberation in that Kunzman's "deliberative reason" allows for the address of religious beliefs, whereas "public reason" does not. Hence, his trajectory enters and draws from the deeper identities and beliefs of students when the others deem this realm (as discussed above) to be inappropriate and a source of misunderstanding.

Though common education leaders avoid controversy, and Kunzman's proposals provide opportunity for conflict to arise over how common school teachers address deep ethical issues, I support Kunzman's proposal for the reasons that he offers. Strong citizens need to be able to discuss deep ethical issues in accord with their deepest beliefs.

With minimal additional analysis, educators can apply Kunzman's proposal for ethical dialogue to the broader civic curriculum where not only are deliberative skills engaged from within deep perspectives, but where moral formation and democratic commitments are formed within contexts that encourage students to draw from their religious identities. When scholars address this broader civic engagement, it appears to accommodate my concerns for deep civic engagement within the common school setting, and thus, it seems to invalidate the argument that capitalizing upon the formative qualities of religion requires the public move toward a plural public education system.

Rebuttal: Common Education Inadequately Engages Religious Beliefs

Moral education scholar Robert Kunzman argues that even the field of moral psychology recognizes that concerns regarding moral education need to address the broader moral frameworks in which individuals reside. He argues that "it is oftentimes misguided to discuss questions of right and wrong without also discussing beliefs about human flourishing, what some psychologists are now calling one's broader 'moral identity'" (2006, p. 3). And this identity cannot but draw in discussions of comprehensive beliefs.

As noted above, I support Kunzman's proposal as well as its broader moral and civic application within the common school realm, but I reject the argument that it markedly duplicates what I have held to be the public value of religious schooling. Whereas common schools may facilitate the development of ethical dialogue, and whereas they may encourage students to draw from their particular religious views within broader moral and civic curricula, the practical and legal constraints under which they must operate limit what they can accomplish.

Where Kunzman focuses his work toward an engagement with religion within common schools, I argue that the value of religious engagement will increase when the public engages it within supportive religious schools. I build this argument on one of Kunzman's comments. Reflecting on how his students would respond to the question of how religion should shape our society, Kunzman writes, "On the one hand, this is a complex question. On the other hand, I find that students almost always have opinions about it" (2006, p. 108). From this, I note that children's immature beliefs are often conceived of as lacking substance, to be mere "opinions," and common school educators cannot provide them with the religious knowledge resources with which to discourse from positions of deeper understanding.

In common schools settings, children can "grapple" with the good, but they leave class ignorant of a greater understanding regarding the grounds and implications attached to their views of the good. Kunzman recognizes the deep roles that core beliefs play in the lives of students and citizens, yet, while focusing on the need to prepare students for reasonable and peaceful dialogue, his concerns fail to provide for the greater ethical preparation that would undergird both deliberation and civic nurture. An extension of his ideas in the broader moral and civic curriculum faces the same critique. Students may bring and engage religious ideas, but this presumes either that children require little authoritative moral and religious instruction or that they can receive adequate instruction at home or church. However, this presumption is either illiberal or it places an unrealistic expectation upon the home and church.

Regarding the first, to align public education with a controversial view of human flourishing that minimizes or opposes the role of moral authorities violates the concerns of conscience that our founders established liberal democratic government to protect (as previously discussed in my rebuttal of liberal autonomy). Regarding the second, parents are often as ill-equipped to prepare their children with a depth of understanding related to the faith they support, as they are to teach geometry, composition, or history, and church settings only provide an hour or two per week to address topics that demand more time.

When common schools attempt to engage religious beliefs, they can do little more than engage them as mere opinion rather than the "profound religious-cum-ethical commitments" (Callan in Kymlicka & Norman, 2000, p. 57) that they can be. It is difficult for them to draw upon religion as a source of meaning, understanding, motivation, and order because these qualities are in a process of formation, and secular educators have no authority to facilitate this process. Whereas common schools can ask students to bring their immature beliefs to bear on moral and civic concerns, religious schools can nurture these beliefs within every aspect of the curriculum in a manner that facilitates their engagement with public concerns. Within private religious schools, the state may allow for the incorporation of public moral and civic values into religious systems of meaning, understanding, and order, which provides them with greater motivational meaning. Additionally, religious schools are generally a part of broader communities and social networks that build social capital (J. S. Coleman & Hoffer, 1987; Putnam, 2000). Thus, the light engagement that Kunzman rightfully argues for the common school setting fails as an adequate substitute for the public value of religious schools.

However, I do not argue against Kunzman; he appears to be aware of the concerns I have raised. Kunzman acknowledges that the ethical diversity and the legal constraints faced by common schools are a challenge to his proposal, and he sees greater potential for his concerns within religious schools interested in "thoughtful engagement with ethical difference" (2006, p. 8).

School Choice and the Concerns of Equity

Scholars have frequently opposed the inclusion of private schools within a system of public funding by arguing that their inclusion would increase educational inequities. These opponents do not direct their concerns specifically at religious schools, but they oppose this type of proposal because most private schools are religious. I will identify these concerns through, in particular, the writings of education scholars Jerry Paquette, Thomas M. Shapiro, and Heather Beth Johnson.

Do Equity Concerns Compel School Choice?

Paquette holds that the compelling interest of public education is that it be the great leveler and enabler of society's least advantaged. He argues that social justice supports the provision of greater educational opportunities for these children, and educational change must not further disadvantage them. Paquette notes that the belief that private "schools better fulfill their vision of what schools ought to do for the young" (Paquette, 2005, p. 572) motivates private school parents. Parents believe these schools foster higher academic achievement, better character development, better opportunities for social networking, and integration into a higher cultural life.

For Paquette, the equity concern begins with the question as to whether private schools are superior to government-run schools. If private schools are "more efficient and effective than their public school counterparts, equal treatment of equals (horizontal equity) would require that all students have access to them, not merely those whose families can afford to pay" (2005, p. 575).

Utilizing test scores, graduation rates, and university attendance, Paquette concludes that the studies of other education researchers show that private schools are not clearly superior to their government-run counterparts. Thus, Paquette (2005, p. 575) concludes that equity does not demand the opening of private schools to all through government funding.

Rebuttal: Equity Concerns are not Merely Academic

Though education funding in liberal societies embraces the equity question, eviscerated standards need not evaluate educational quality. A filter that imposes a narrow secular definition of educational value upon the public distorts Paquette's conclusion. Concerned parents as well as public officials evaluate a "better education" according to more criteria than those used by Paquette. Evaluations of education may include concerns regarding school safety, philosophy, student-teacher ratio, moral climate, and even theology.

When scholars more broadly consider the question as to whether equity concerns propel greater school choice, their conclusions may be different. Scholar Joseph Viteritti writes,

> I understood school choice primarily as a matter of social justice. Education has always been an essential part of the American dream, so much so that every state constitution defines it as both an individual right and a parental obligation. As long as middle-class parents have the means to remove their children from undesirable schools—either by selecting private schools or by moving to high-priced communities with better public schools—we owe poor parents similar opportunities to control the education of their children. It is morally indefensible to confine poor students to schools that middle-class families would never consider for their own children. (2007, p. 2)

Thus, Viteritti calls on the state to respect parents, even poor parents, enough to dignify them with the choice of their children's schools.

Equity concerns are more directly opposed by districting in which parents must choose a "better education" according to their ability to pay private school tuition or to live in neighborhoods reflecting their educational choice. Because they typically filter children according to belief rather than by socioeconomic culture, race, or ethnicity, religious schools already achieve greater racial diversity than public common schools (Greene & Mellow, 1998). If brought within a system of public funding, religious schools could help decrease current educational inequities (Greene, 2005).

Thus, even if academic equity does not compel the state to endorse school choice, other equity concerns do. Families reflect varieties of educational values regarding school size, academic offerings, religious orientation, location, the quality of facilities, educational philosophy, school safety, and so on. Educational equity supports enabling low-income families to choose schools according to their educational values in a manner similar to higher-income families.

Do Equity Concerns Oppose School Choice?

Paquette (2005) also considers whether equity concerns *oppose* greater school choice. He reasons that private schools would accept fewer poor, minority, and special-needs students, thus these students would become increasingly concentrated within government schools. Often called skimming or creaming, this phenomenon describes the disproportionate move of successful and privileged students to available private schools.

Paquette (2005) notes that the tendency of private school administrators to select for the brightest and easiest to educate to uphold their schools' reputations produces skimming. The greater probability that already successful families will have the social and intellectual preparation to be most successful at securing a place for their children in the school of their choice reinforces it. With the growth of disparity and stigmatization, the indirect public funding of private schools would breach equity standards by failing the least advantaged. Supporting his prediction, Paquette says that, "Overwhelmingly, experience to date with private school choice programs suggests that those who choose tend to be more than a few rungs up from the bottom of the socioeconomic ladder and tend to be reasonably well educated" (2005, p. 576).

Thomas M. Shapiro and Heather Beth Johnson (2005) also studied school choice with the question of whether it would further or hinder equity. They interviewed families to determine the ways in which they currently choose or determine the quality of a "good school." They found that parents do not always look first at academics but often at characteristics of the school's atmosphere and community. They found that regardless of motives, parents choose schools that reflect their community and values. Shapiro and Johnson see a danger in this; they write,

> Whites often resegregate themselves and their children in schools and communities that look like them, and pass inequality along. If we, as a society, make this easier for them and even subsidize these actions, then we facilitate the reproduction of class and race inequality. (2005, p. 256)

From this analysis, they oppose unregulated school choice programs.

Thus, those arguments that oppose broader school choice maintain that the least advantaged are worse off under greater school choice and that parental choices tend to pass on generational inequities.

Rebuttal: Fears of Skimming and Inequity Propagation Are not Definitive

In opposing school choice, Paquette (2005, p. 576) notes that studies support the conclusion that the more well off are more likely to take advantage of educational choice in the private school sector, but he fails to do more than hypothesize that the remaining students will be worse off. Schools ordinarily form their educational programs around the needs and abilities of their students, thus, the hypothesized effects of skimming need not be counted as a disadvantage to the already least advantaged.

Contradicting the fear of public common schools acquiring a suspect reputation as a function of unregulated skimming, neither private nor public schools now carry universal reputations of quality. Parents make generalizations regarding school quality, but schools seem to reflect their unique identities and reputations. Since many families have little interest in religious schooling, it is unlikely that secular common schools will become the schools of last choice.

Further, reflecting a concern for proportionality, Paquette's analysis fails to address a more pronounced skimming or stratification that occurs in public schools and is clearly opposed to public education goals (J. S. Coleman, 1992, pp. 260–262). Parents choose "better" schools by their choice of public school districts, and internal skimming occurs in common schools through the offering of advanced courses for children with the "social and intellectual preparation" that sets them apart from the least advantaged. These forms of skimming, necessary to provide a meaningful education for both the advantaged and the disadvantaged, present far greater equity concerns than those hypothesized under school choice.

Above I noted that equity concerns must consider the broad values that education represents, and schools represent these values in differing measures. Paquette's (2005) analysis of skimming is premised, in part, upon the belief that private school administrators select only students that will further their reputations. I argue that *if* this perception is real, current funding arrangements negatively influence it by forcing private schools to appeal to financially successful families who can afford to pay tuition, and thus, the reduction of funding pressures will enable schools to become more equitable in their enrollment practices. Counter to Paquette's presumption regarding future choices of administrators, the social welfare movements of history indicate that religious groups tend to place a high value on caring for the poor and the disadvantaged. Thus, if school choice incorporates religious schools and thereby reduces the need to appeal to the wealthy, many of these schools may act from their faith values to select *for* the disadvantaged and difficult to teach.

Shapiro and Johnson's (2005) argument holds the fatal flaw of presuming that parents *should* choose schools according to academic outcomes, which implies that other educational values are misguided. Certainly the liberal state represents values concerning equity that it should not set aside in providing for the school choice intrinsic to a plural public education system, but this argument paints with a broad brush all parental concerns that may propagate inequity. Within our pluralistic culture, equity concerns call for greater recognition of diversity within our educational values. Whereas public education currently favors those who support secular education, a plural public education system would allow families to choose schools utilizing broader criteria such as religious beliefs and education philosophy.

Summary Analysis

Paquette (2005) analyzes school choice propositions through the lens of equity following the Rawlsian concept that justice demands that any disparity be of benefit to the least advantaged. Though this concern has merit, the arguments of Paquette as well as Shapiro and Johnson (2005) provide ample evidence as to how ideas regarding educational equity are value laden and risk becoming illiberal impositions when defined too narrowly.

Further, in ways that are seldom considered, the current common education paradigm promotes inequity for those conscientiously opposed to secular education. Not only does public education only provide religious school choices to those with the greatest financial advantage, but it also serves to support other educational inequities. Little curricula is written for students in religious schools, and few universities offer degrees in religious school teaching/administration due to the relatively small market of religious schools, which is due, in part, to the monopolistic nature of public education. Additionally, the budgets of privately funded religious schools are rarely able to provide for the special education needs of their students. Thus, a plural public education system would conceivably provide a broader foundation upon which religious schools would flourish, which would in turn provide larger markets to draw the attention of publishers and institutions of higher education while also providing resources for those with special needs to receive equitable educations within religious school settings.

Equity has an honorable place within the range of democratic educational concerns; however, its discussion neglects certain liberal ideals when its evaluation reflects only secular academic achievement. A broader evaluation of equity favors permitting families to choose schools according to educational values rather than their ability to pay tuition. Concerns about inequity do not fully support or oppose school choice, thus, these concerns should be addressed by government regulations that are bordered on one side by legitimate public interests and on the other side by liberalism's high regard for individual liberty.

Public Unity and the Need to Sustain Order

Following concerns regarding autonomy, perhaps the greatest concern opposing plural public education relates to the claim that common schools serve as our nation's primary source of national unity by providing "common attitudes, loyalties, and values...under the central direction of the state" (C. L. Glenn, 1988, p. 4). Thiessen reflects this assessment in writing, "Opposition to parochial schooling in the United States is also rooted in a deeply entrenched vision of seeing public education as playing a key role in creating national cohesion" (1993, p. 20). Both positive assertions regarding common education and negative assertions regarding religious schooling support this claim.

Common Education as a Vital Force for Unity

Political scientist Benjamin Barber claims that public schools are

the very foundation of our democratic civic culture...institutions where we learn what it means to be a public and start down the road toward common national and civic identity. They are the forges of our citizenship and the bedrock of our democracy. (1997, p. 22)

Macedo (2000) notes that in a pluralistic society, shared civic ends cannot be achieved without offending someone's religion (p. 85). He argues that with a focus on diversity alone, our nation will falter; thus, public common schools must propagate a shared moral and civic culture in spite of their offense to some (p. 134).

While Macedo (2000, p. 268) acknowledges that religion plays a role in the formation of civic values, he is apprehensive to place public trust in religious schools and fails to see enough common school shortcomings (outside of depressed urban areas) to embark upon broad educational change. He further refutes the public support of private schools in favor of a common education system based on the civic needs of liberal democracy. He proposes a reform of the secular common school to provide greater degrees of choice, the formation of school communities, and a greater emphasis upon our shared civic concerns.

Though America reflects deep ideological diversity, Macedo (2000, pp. 3–6) argues that liberal democratic society is not required to accept diversity uncritically. It is the role of public education, in part, to build unity and to shape diversity for civic purposes. Religious groups may call for certain educational freedoms, but the needs of public order must balance these freedoms.

Gutmann (1999) argues that public common schools are a source of moral capital that is necessary to overcome the disunity generated by religion. She first argues that public schools played a vital role in national character formation that reduced the once great prejudice against Catholics. She then argues, "Moral capital is just now being created for blacks and Hispanics, and even more well-established minorities might reasonably fear that returning to a state of families would eventually squander the moral capital created by public schooling" (p. 32). Thus, Gutmann argues that schools that strongly reflect the interests of families weaken public moral standards, and schools responsive to broader public controls raise the standards of public morality.

Common school proponents often fear that religious schools promote "Balkanization" and the "danger of a rupture of the delicate social fabric that binds society together" (Paquette, 2005, p. 580). For instance, Callan (1997, p. 223) argues that common schooling is to be preferred through public funding even while pragmatic reasons allow privately funded schools to remain. His fear is that separate schooling that divides children according to their ideologies will lead to political division. Callan writes, "The pluralism of free societies makes urgent the task of creating citizens who share a sufficiently cohesive political identity" (p. 221).

Paquette holds that private school support would promote Balkanization. He argues that the presence of

> "sectoral" private schools suggest that unfettered voucher or tax credit schemes might encourage the proliferation of boutique schools that would cater increasingly only to those who shared commonalities of culture, moral

priorities, ethnicity, race, and worldview. Concentrations of more and more students, especially bright and capable students, in schools that represent narrow constituencies with particularistic interests is worrisome indeed while trying to preserve and shore up liberal democratic principle. . . . The problem is that inadequately regulated public funding of private schools leaves the way open to public funding of schools that indoctrinate students into conviction that the particular social reference group the school serves has some unique claim to moral or political authority and ought to dominate access to resources and political decision making. One can easily envision sadder but wiser politicians awakening one morning to discover (probably on the front page of a tabloid) that voucher money is flowing to the Ernst Zundel School of Racial Purity. (2005, pp. 580–581)

Education scholar Nel Noddings also opposes the public funding of religious schools. She considers it a "dangerous move" because it would imply the support of all religious schools, and "many religious schools endorse ideas and practices that reject or weaken the social agenda of liberal democracies" (2007, p. 74). As noted above, Gutmann (1999, p. 31) also fears giving parents and religion too great a role in education. She sees them as a source of social disrespect as well as other destructive qualities.

Thus, scholars from multiple perspectives argue that common education is a vital and necessary force for building civic morality and unity, and that the public support of religious schools would likely breed intolerance, antidemocratic sentiments, and social division.

Response to Concerns for Public Unity and Order

Except during the Civil War and in spite a numerous periods of social unrest, America has experienced a relatively strong unity through most of its history, and scholars (as exemplified above) frequently claim that common public education is a primary source for its nurture. However, they generally give little evidence in support of this claim or the correlated claim that religious schooling promotes division. The claim that the public promotion of a common set of democratic values and ideals through a system of public education contributes to our unity seems reasonable, but I dispute the claim that common schools provide the necessary and exclusive settings in which to nurture a common civic identity and strengthen social cohesion.

It is not my intent to argue that common education has no unifying qualities, nor to argue that all religious schools promote unity. Rather, my intent is to oppose the claims of religious school opponents by presenting the following arguments:

- Common education is frequently a cause of disunity.
- Religious schooling is not proven to be divisive.
- Religious schools can advance public efforts toward unity.

Common Education as a Cause of Disunity

Historically, public education reflects concerns regarding the nurture of moral and civic values that support public order and unity. I noted that these two concerns have perennially conflicted within educational settings that were both committed to a respect for private conscience and committed to bringing students together in a common classroom. Public commitments to both values determined that, within public education, the nurture of not only America's civic identity, but also America's youth, would reflect fewer and shallower values.

Common school supporters underestimated the importance that people placed on their religious views. Though common education was conceived to create harmony among diverse groups of people, historically, it created conflict whenever educators taught values that some families opposed or when they neglected values that some families considered vital to the nurture of their children. McClellan writes that common school supporters

> failed to find a ground common enough even to unite all Protestants. They did much to spread their own faith, but by trying to turn their particular world view into a kind of civic religion, they deepened divisions in society, driving embittered dissenters to create their own schools. (1992, p. 47)

In 1943, following a century of educational secularization, Supreme Court Justice Robert Jackson identified the difficulty that continued to be associated with common education: "As governmental pressure toward unity becomes greater, so strife becomes more bitter as to whose unity it shall be" (*West Virginia v. Barnette*, 1943). Contemporary conceptions of liberal democracy have served to alleviate some educational tensions stemming from valid accusations that public schools aligned with a set of "common values" and a "civic identity" that were too comprehensively based. However, tensions remain. Which values do we consider common? What are appropriate ways to nurture them? And what should we do when families conceive that responsible education requires the nurture of values considered uncommon?

Analysts have written about the struggles caused by the conflicts arising from the preferred place of common schooling through our history. Arons notes several of these with the issues they address:

> The histories have titles like *The Great School Wars, Schooled to Order, Conflict of Interests, Education as Cultural Imperialism.* They chronicle struggles between Protestants and Catholics; among Americans who trace their heritage to northern Europe, the Mediterranean, Latin America, North America, Asia, or Africa; between scientific reasoning and spiritual faith; between the needs of industry and the idiosyncrasies of individuals; between a bewildering, exhilarating diversity and a sometimes oppressive nationalism; between entrenched racism and the struggle for equality. (1997, p. 2)

Others have compiled similar lists. Education Scholar Myron Lieberman (2007, p. 316) catalogues 14 public school issues ranging from sex education to grading policy that draw parental support away from public school classrooms. The most damaging conflicts regard concerns over family values (McCluskey, 2007). That nearly 13% of U.S. children currently attend private and home schools demonstrates the gravity of these reasons. Families leave common schools for many reasons, but the type of education they choose indicates, in part, the nature of their discontents; about 83% of private school attendees choose religious schools. To this number, one must add an unknown number of those who find conflict with common education but who remain in secular public schools for financial or other reasons.

Thus, the key public institution for the promotion of public cohesion is also a source of division. Many religious families view the exclusive public funding of common education as an unreasonable repression of their values. "The problem for society at large is that by repressing dissenting values, seeds of future consensus and social cohesion are destroyed" (Arons, 1983, p. 196).

Lieberman links much of the cause of these conflicts with the yoking of public education with common education. "How much or how many of these controversies would there be if parents could choose the schools, public or private, that educate their children? To be sure, some conflict would remain, but most of it would lose its raison d'être in a full-fledged school choice plan" (2007, p. 114).

Arons finds it ironic that although founded upon a concern for conscience, our democracy singularly supports an education system that opposes many concerns of conscience:

Most of these school conflicts originate when knowledge or matters of private conscience are subjected to governmental decision making, or when the definition and preservation of communities become politicized and subject to the will of the political majority. This pattern seems all the more disheartening and dangerous when one considers that constitutional democracy was designed to prevent just this kind of government involvement in matters of belief and opinion. (1997, p. 43)

Education scholar Peter H. Schuck adds that a lack of educational choice deepens the intensity of these conflicts. "The ferocity of [these ideological conflicts], in many cases, is due to the monopolistic nature of the existing public school systems in these communities. This monopoly raises the stakes by mandating a single, one-size-fits-all curriculum" (2006, p. 121).

If definitive evidence exists that common schooling is vital to unity, then one can accept these tensions as the necessary cost of unity. However, supporters of common education have not produced this evidence. Rather, the prevalence of discussions regarding citizenship formation reflects the concern that, in spite of common public education, society is fragmenting (Isin & Wood, 1999, p. 6).

These tensions produced by common education weaken the social fabric, and a system of school choice seems adequate to remove many of them. Schuck writes,

A society that relies on decentralized choice gains an incalculable value—political conflict reduction—that goes well beyond the efficiency and autonomy values enjoyed by those who exercise it. This muting of political conflict is essential to the survival of a polity as diverse and competitive as twenty-first-century America. (2006, p. 120)

Thus, claims regarding the vital nature of common education to public unity stand opposed, in part, by evidence regarding the conflicts common education engenders.

Unsupported Claims of Divisiveness and Domination

The claims that religious schools foster divisiveness and that common schools foster social cohesion should have supportive evidence. Thiessen writes, "But these claims are most often made without any concern for empirical backing" (2001, p. 37).

Instead, proponents garner support by discrediting noncommon education. As noted in Chapter 2, public education leaders have accused "sectarian schools" of being sources of public division since common education began. The fear of Balkanization and of the "danger of a rupture of the delicate social fabric that binds society together" (Paquette, 2005, p. 580) are still linked to religious schooling even though it seems that the "wars of religion" have been effectively ended by the conception of liberal democratic government. Religious schools are a part of American history, and millions of American children have attended these schools with no substantively divisive effect (Glenn, 1987). Additionally, there are currently about 27 private school "choice" programs accessing religious schools across the United States (M. Glenn & Gininger, 2012). These complement the many private voucher programs, yet neither these experiments with school choice nor the century-and-a-half of religious private schooling have proven to disrupt the public peace or generally fail to nurture citizens with adequate moral and civic qualities. To the contrary, studies (Campbell, 2008; J. Coleman, 1998; J. S. Coleman, 1992; Kleitz, 2005; Wolf, 2005) affirm that religious schools promote high moral standards, and generally equal or exceed public schools in promoting civic values. Thus, although religious schools nurture the deep beliefs and values of faith that some associate with public division, these beliefs and values seem to provide good foundations for civic unity because religious school students have joined in public debate with little apparent social tension. When there have been instances of aggression regarding religious schools, such as in mid-18th-century New York, this aggression was generally against religious groups who opposed common public education.

Religious school opponents may point to the common school conflicts discussed above as evidence of the divisive nature of religion; however, in light of a liberal concern for conscience, they do so wrongly. The founders established our government, in part, to protect conscience; public education is similarly committed to this concern as a government entity. The conflicts above reflect the conscientious opposition of religious people to common school impositions. Thus, one more accurately places the claim of divisiveness upon the common schools that violate conscience rather than upon the religion that forms the conscience. Within a liberal democracy, the public response to conscientious conflicts is to seek alternate ways to achieve public ends with minimal infringement upon conscience rather than, directly or indirectly, to oppose its formation.

Finally, in seeking to discredit religious schools as divisive, opponents argue that religious schools lack adequate diversity to build the tolerance our pluralistic society requires. However, studies of current religious schools show that they attract students according to ideological concerns that often transcend issues of race, income, or ethnicity. Thus, reflecting upon the broad implementation of school choice, education scholar Terry

Moe concludes that "under reasonable assumptions... the new private sector winds up being more ethnically diverse than the public sector does" (2001, p. 164). Thiessen (2001) more extensively cites studies that find that religious schools have similar commitments to tolerance and lack evidence of being divisive either by what they teach or by their prevalent existence as an educational option.

Fear of Sectarian Political Domination

Opponents of religious schooling have raised the fear that religious schools undermine public unity because they teach children to force their views on the public. However, scholar Christopher Eberle (2002) believes these fears are out of touch with contemporary realities. Religious groups have a stake in maintaining religious freedom. Studies show that most American Evangelicals favor religious liberty and oppose propositions to revise a religious establishment.

Rather than attempting to impose an authoritarian form of government, a study finds that those who leave public schools to receive private and home school educations are *more* likely to be involved within the democratic process, especially in grassroots activism (Stevens, 2001). Viteritti writes, "The existing evidence indicates that people who attend religious schools exhibit high levels of civic and political participation, which should not be surprising given the role that religious institutions play in promoting civil society" (2007, p. 231).

Political domination by religious groups seems to be a distant threat as long as the First Amendment prevents government alignment with a particular worldview. Richard Rorty illuminates the reality that a plurality of communities has proven manageable in our nation. They check the power of one another and prevent totalitarian control by any one in accord with James Madison's prediction in *The Federalist* (Hamilton et al., 1818, p. 504).

Religious Schools as Sources of Democratic Unity

Glenn notes that the claim that public schools supported assimilation and were necessary for public unity was the greatest "myth" of the 19th-century common school. He writes that this myth "has persisted with undiminished force in the twentieth [century], despite all evidence that public schools are in no sense 'common' and that the assimilating forces of modern life itself create more uniformity than may be good for us" (1987, p. 261).

Common school supporters often claim that religious schools serve to maintain the values and culture of immigrants with the effect of hindering their civic growth, but the desire to propagate one's faith and culture to one's children is not necessarily antithetical to the desire to assimilate. Evidence from the 19th century opposes this fear. Glenn writes,

> [A] difficulty with the "resistance to assimilation" thesis is that virtually every immigrant group was in fact eager to fit into American life and to assure that its children would not suffer under the stigma of being a foreign element. In some respects, in fact, parochial schools rivaled the public schools in their commitment to "Americanization." German and Irish Catholic immigrants were eager to embrace virtually everything about contemporary American life while providing an alternative educational system for their children. (1987, p. 204)

Those who oppose the inclusion of religious schools in a system of public funding on grounds of disunity also seem to reflect the fear that the beliefs of religious people are too narrow and rigid to accommodate the needs of our society. However, Alan Wolfe argues, "Religion is a dynamic force constantly adapting itself to new situations" and that "there is no reason why this process of adaption cannot include the building of bridges" (2005, p. 106).

Rather than approaching religious schools in search of arguments as to how they might promote division, one can approach them as potential sources of unity. They help to bring together diverse people and they form social capital. Following expansive studies of Christian schooling, Vryhof commented on this unifying quality. He writes of one school: "Families representing a fantastic variety of ethnic, cultural, and racial backgrounds have gathered around a common faith vision" (2004, p. 112). Though religious schools come together around a common vision, this need not imply that the vision will be civically divisive. To the contrary, Christian visions that embrace Biblical commands to seek peace, to love even one's enemies, and to acknowledge the legitimacy of public authorities seem conducive to the strengthening of commitments to public unity (for Biblical examples, see Hebrews 12:4, 1 Peter 3:11, James 3:17, Matthew 5:44, Romans 13:6).

Many other religions also demonstrate a concern for compassion and peace. Thus, this evidence suggests that religious schools are generally unlikely to be sources of public division, and they may even represent valuable sources of public unity.

Where Would Catholics be Today?

Both Gutmann and Macedo utilize the experience of Catholics in America as evidence for the civic efficacy of common education. As noted in a previous chapter, anti-Catholic prejudice found root in claims that Catholics were unsupportive of "American" ways. Further, prejudice was rooted in different Catholic moral standards and their general opposition to the common school. As noted above, Gutmann (1999, p. 31) presumes that if not for public common education, prejudice against Catholics would likely be as strong today as it was in the 19th century, and she believes that giving parents too much educational authority will undermine social stability. Similarly, Macedo (2000, p. 7) credits common education, in part, for the theological changes within Catholicism that promoted a greater doctrinal acceptance of liberal democratic government. There may be some truth to these claims, but historical analysis finds evidence that both these changes were more greatly influenced by forces outside the common school. A strong historical case can even be made that the common school *hindered* the acceptance of Catholics and *slowed* their approval of democratic polity.

First, I note that Gutmann (1999, p. 31) minimizes the nature of the prejudice against Catholics by referring to it as "religious prejudice." Surely, there was some competition regarding the proper path to God, but the deeper roots of prejudice regarded the preservation of American democracy, as well as ethnic and lifestyle issues. These claims were not baseless. Before the 20th century, the Catholic Church supported a unified church and state. This tenet opposes the American conception of democracy that placed authority in the people rather than in the ecclesia. Thus, the prejudice was not merely "religious," and it continued until the public majority viewed them as being morally, economically, and politically supportive citizens.

Rarely did more than half of Catholic children attend parochial schools (Carper & Hunt, 2007, p. 67). Although public schools may have provided an influence against prejudice and toward Catholic Americanization, other forces acting from outside the common school appear to have had greater influence. Catholics most probably became strong American citizens because of certain cultural predispositions with which they immigrated, because of their church community resources, because of their economic attainments, and because of their acceptance of democratic claims *from within their faith.*

Irish Catholics came with a particular cultural predisposition for American citizenship. Though they were not the first Catholics to come, they shaped America's Catholic experience. "Due to the predominant Irish influence, Catholicism in America soon acquired a special character. . . . It was

English-speaking, 'puritanical,' democratic, popular and activistic" (Herberg, 1960, p. 145). It also fused religion and nationalism, which "enabled the Irish Catholic to become a passionately patriotic American.... The Irish Catholic newcomer...adopted this country as his own and transferred his deeply emotional nationalism to his adopted land" (Herberg, 1960, p. 146). With this commitment, parochial textbooks came to support a strong civic identity, though it is "Catholicism rather than Protestantism that is the foundation of civilization and American independence" (Elson, 1964, p. 55).

Additionally, the "fairly rapid advancement in social and cultural status of...Catholic ethnic groups" (Herberg, 1960, p. 148) accelerated the Americanization and acceptance of Catholics. The church supported this advancement economically, socially, and even politically. It gave each member the "effective means and instruments for his advancement. Catholic schools were particularly effective at providing the tools and opportunities needed for the advancement of Catholic children" (Herberg, 1960). The church enabled Catholics to Americanize, not by leaving the church but by becoming more active within the church.

The acceptance of the democratic philosophy was perhaps the most important transformation that supported the Americanization of Catholics. This too took place outside the common school and served to decrease prejudice against them. Catholic thinkers provided early arguments supporting the compatibility of their faith with democratic polity. In the mid-1850s, Orestes Brownson, an influential Catholic intellectual of the 19th century (and *not* a product of the common schools), became part of a liberalizing movement with others who "shared a devotion to political liberty, and an uneasiness with the direction taken by Vatican authorities in the years after 1848" (McGreevy, 2003, p. 45).

In the 1890s, John Ireland, Archbishop of St. Paul, Minnesota, supported the Americanization of Catholics by praising both common and parochial schools (Carper & Hunt, 2007). The experiences of the Catholic Church in America cumulatively led to its pragmatic, if not theological, acceptance of democracy. In 1916, Cardinal Gibbons declared, Catholics

> accept the Constitution without reserve, with no desire as Catholics to see it changed in any feature. The separation of church and state in this country seems to them the natural, inevitable, and best conceivable plan... both for the good of religion and of the state. (1916, p. 210)

By 1944, Pope Pius XII proclaimed a relative acceptance of democracy in his Christmas message, and Catholic theologian John Courtney Murray had undertaken a systematic reexamination of Catholic teaching on church and state. According to Herberg, Murray "soon developed a viewpoint and approach capable of relating Catholic doctrine to American democracy in a way that would do violence to neither" (1960, p. 151).

Thus, prejudice against Catholics waned as they took ownership of American liberty, as they found their place in the economy with the help of a supportive community, as they found support for democracy from within their faith, and finally, as they supported the efforts of World War II and opposed communism. The common school surely supported the Americanization of some Catholics and encouraged Protestants to view Catholics without prejudice. However, common schools also served to create prejudice by branding dissenters as un-American. Thus, counter to the claims of Gutmann and Macedo, it is apparent that the deepest transformations that brought Catholics into equal and supportive citizenship took place within their communities of faith—within a "state of families" that Gutmann disdains.

International Evidence

In addition to philosophical arguments and studies from America's limited experience with religious schooling, other nations provide evidence regarding the effects of plural public education systems upon social cohesion. Thiessen argues that the countries of Denmark, The Netherlands, and parts of Canada have pluralized education systems, and they "are not noted for divisiveness, racism, or intolerance" (2001, p. 38). Regarding his own nation, he writes, "After over a century of dualism in Canadian education, we find Catholics and non-Catholics coexisting in a peaceable manner. A dual system of education has not fostered divisiveness and intolerance in Canadian society." (2001, p. 39).

Following a study of the school choice systems in France, Belgium, Britain, Canada, West Germany, and The Netherlands, Glenn wrote, "No real evidence exists, after all, that confessional schooling has a socially divisive effect" (1989, p. 210). Thus, while many American education scholars still assert that national unity is dependent upon common education, the experiences of other nations oppose this conclusion.

Summary Conclusion

The question of public unity must be put into perspective. How much is necessary, especially if it reflects government intervention? Thiessen responds,

> Clearly, for a society to exist there must be some unity. But how unified does a society have to be? There is always the danger of going too far in demanding unity. Unity, carried to the extreme, entails complete assimilation and homogeneity. (2001, p. 32)

A broader recognition of religious schooling supports the diversity of our society. Stephen Carter (1994) even argues that one can view the conflicts that arise around the interface of public policy and religion to be socially valuable sources of new ideas.

In discussing concerns regarding unity within a pluralistic setting, liberal theorist Richard Rorty (1991) advanced the idea that the public may unify more around shared hopes than around shared beliefs. These shared hopes of peace, prosperity, and personal liberty provide the ground for the trust that underlies social cohesion. While narrower beliefs (including the belief that public education must be common) encourages social division, broad hopes seem likely to transcend the belief systems of most religious schools to direct curricular attention to our shared concerns as a people.

Sociologist Will Herberg held that one could find common American beliefs and commitments within diverse religious schools. He wrote,

> However severe the tensions, however deep the suspicions, that divide Protestant, Catholic and Jew, there are limits beyond which they cannot go. In the last analysis, Protestant and Catholic and Jew stand united through their common anchorage in, and common allegiance to, the American Way of Life. The "unifying" function of education is not annulled because Catholics have their own schools and Jews attempt to inculcate their children with a loyalty to their "people." The same basic values and ideals, the same underlying commitment to the American Way of Life, are promoted by parochial school and public school, by Catholic, Protestant, and Jew, despite the diversity of formal religious creed. (1960, p. 242)

Thus, these scholars not only argue that religious schooling is separate from fears of division, but they argue that one may view it as a public asset that undergirds our democratic society.

Chapter Conclusion

This chapter identified a second set of scholarly concerns opposing the move from a common to a plural public education system. I addressed concerns associated with deliberative democracy, hopes associated with robust visions of common education, possibilities linked with additional religious engagement within a secular setting, concerns implied by assumptions regarding equity, and fears regarding religious schools and public unity. Though each of these areas reflects valid concerns that public educators and involved citizens should consider, I do not find any of them to prohibit the move to a plural public education system. Surely certain religious schools do and will arise that oppose one or more of these public concerns, but in light of the public value of religious schooling, it is best for the public to deal with these schools individually through a process of selection, oversight, and regulation.

Looking forward (although in previous chapters, I attempted to tease out the roles religion has played under the common education model), many readers may not yet be clear as to how a religious educational paradigm would advance the public's educational interests. With this in mind, in the next chapter, I will describe a number of key educational interest that common schools may address only weakly, but that flow naturally from within a religious school's paradigm of character, truth, value, and community. Once more I hope that the following discussion will help educators to comprehend the magnitude of the educational loss that has followed in the wake of the common education model. Rather than merely seeking to find religion "hiding in the corners" of the common school, I will illuminate the potential of plural public education.

7

Religious Schooling as a Valuable Public Asset

In the proceeding, I have written more to confront the secular education ideal than to illuminate the potential strengths that religious schools within a plural system of public education would bring to America. Vryhof sees the potential of these schools: He writes, "Faith-based schools are not the enemy of the republic; they are perhaps more 'public' than public schools in that they express and represent the aspirations and desired freedoms of their citizen parents" (2004, p. 146). While earlier chapters argued that education leaders once agreed with this, I showed that their attempts to capitalize on the religious source of the "American identity" through common public education ultimately undermined their efforts. Legal support for rights of conscience left public education with an educational framework separated from the core beliefs and values of children and families.

Secular methods and philosophies have displaced many of religion's educational roles, but as of this writing, the educational establishment is

Education Reform, pages 155–184
Copyright © 2013 by Information Age Publishing
155

generally relying on computerized tracking and accountability to motivate educational success, while many civic and political leaders are insistent that valued improvement will come from school choice and competition without deeper philosophic reflection. Though the latter movement tends to enable the public's educational interests to be engaged in religious school settings, the regulations placed upon these schools and the relative rarity of religious school inclusion make it apparent that these schools are disfavored by the education establishment.

Religious schools have a long history in America and have survived in spite of the competition of a "free" public education system (Jones, 2008), and making the resources of religious schooling available to the public requires not just "school choice" but a more comprehensive reform of our public educational paradigm. In this chapter, I build on the previous arguments associated with the religious nature of education to demonstrate specifically how education with religious foundations can contribute to the public's educational interests. In other words, this chapter will describe how religious schools might predictably support particular public interests when common schools have proven to be less than satisfactory.

In the following pages, I will present how religious schools, within a plural public education system, may provide the state with the following:

- Superior settings for "traditional" education.
- Superior sources of grounded moral education.
- Means to nurture strong civic character.
- Resources to close the achievement gap and revitalize impoverished communities.
- Resources to build social capital and restore public meaning.
- Secure ideological foundations.
- Resources to advance public unity.

National Civic Health and Common Education

If this book argued that access to religious schooling was a religious right, or if I argued that education was primarily about academic success and that school choice advanced this success, then a consideration of our nation's civic health would not be in order. However, I have argued that the public's concern toward the nurture of moral and civic values *is equal to* its concern toward academic nurture. Thus, one may assess trends in public moral and civic health as potential indicators of the success of our public system of common education.

I do not assess this health to be good. As evidence of America's moral and civic well-being, I note that crime rates dramatically began to rise in the 1960s. This trend continued into the 1990s when it began a decline that remains well above 1960s levels. In addition to unlawful activity, civic participation has decreased. Political philosopher William Galston writes, "During the last decade, many scholars have argued that civic membership, both formal and informal, is weaker than it once was" (Galston in Garfinkle & Yankelovich, 2006, p. 198). Scholar Michael Sandel (2002) finds evidence of declining civic spirit in the growing financial disparity between the rich and the poor as well as in the increased isolation of the wealthy from public places and services. Additionally, the National Commission on Civic Renewal (Bennett & Nunn, 1998) concluded that recent decades have witnessed a decline in civic involvement, a growing distrust of government, and even disillusionment with the ideals of civic progress.

Glenn argues that due to secularization, "the public school has largely abandoned the role that was of such central importance for Horace Mann and his contemporaries: developing character and conveying moral principles for which there was a societal consensus" (1987, p. 287). Thus, some of the blame for these declines may reasonably fall on our system of public education, which places less emphasis on the development of character and morality than it did when morality could be taught with its traditional religious roots.

The past decade has witnessed shooting rampages in schools, theaters, and public events, but moral decline is not evidenced only by open violence. Scholar Daniel Yankelovich (Garfinkle & Yankelovich, 2006) notes that moral decline has played a central role in costly corporate ethical scandals, and manifests itself in public rudeness, crudeness, obscenity, harshness, aggression, and excessive sex and violence in the popular media. Summarily, he states, "In general, Americans are unhappy about the decline in social morality, and opinion polls consistently register a public desire for a restoration of moral values in American life" (Garfinkle & Yankelovich, 2006, p. 23). The decline of civic behavior also affects the public as standards of justice become more bureaucratized and impersonal, as volunteerism and the higher values it represents decreases, and as social cohesion wanes with the decay of public spirit.

Some scholars, such as David Purpel (as cited in Molnar, 1997, p. 147), deny the need to fear these trends. He notes that moral change is not necessarily bad. Others attempt to quell concern by noting that previous generations have also decried social declines that would not necessarily concern us today (see McKown, 1935, pp. 18–34). Though comments such as these may serve to slow judgment regarding fashion and moral norms, they cannot serve to dismiss concerns such as rape, assault, and auto theft, which I will address later.

Other scholars defer blame for these declines from the public education system. Although it is unreasonable to blame or credit public education for every civic weakness or health, one may overly disconnect public education from the social product to which it contributes. Gutmann (1999, p. 302) commits this error when she defends the failure of many inner-city schools by arguing that we must first eliminate poverty and unemployment for public education to be successful. Macedo (2000, pp. 255–258) also commits this error when he argues that communities themselves, rather than public schools, are to blame for the breakdown of community life in America. Macedo offers a list of social factors (including consumerism, family disintegration, etc.) that reasonably contribute to the recognized failures associated with the public education system. However, both Gutmann and Macedo neglect to address the fact that educational leaders have historically linked the educational process with personal and social formation to *prevent* the social diseases they blame for school decline.

Scholars cannot concurrently claim that public education is vital to democratic moral and civic health while asking that it be absolved from responsibility when that health fails. Surely, social health and educational health are mutually supporting, but successful childhood education (at home and school) has traditionally been viewed as the precursor of healthy society. In other words, Gutmann and Macedo's propositions attempt to absolve the public education system, whereas they may serve to reveal its weakness. Diversity hampers the common education model in its mission to nurture personally and socially healthy children *in loco parentis*; nonetheless, it attempts to do so. Thus, since public education represents perhaps the public's greatest investment in the current and future health of our society, it carries a large measure of responsibility for its failures.

Public education leaders have responded to these social concerns with greater advocacy of common morality through character and virtue curricula reminiscent of the first decades of the 20th century (see Chapter 4). Surely, new character education curricula have contributed to the decade-and-a-half improvement reflected by crime statistics; however, the moral and civic needs of our society remain high. According too the Bureau of Justice, federal crime statistics as of 2010 show that violent crimes (including murder, rape, robbery, and assault) continue at a rate two-and-a-half times that of 1960, and property crimes (including burglary, larceny, and auto theft) continue at a rate nearly double that of 1960. If previous chapters have sufficiently alleviated the generalized fears associated with religious schooling, then the qualities religious schools offer to the public become valid considerations that challenge arguments supporting the common education paradigm as preeminently suited to nurture public moral and civic values. If families and communities (rather than state institutions) are recognized as premier sources of moral and ideological nurture, then the public should facilitate ways to support their efforts. The best way is to give them a meaningful role in the education of their children through a plural public education system.

Superior Settings for "Traditional" Education

Though this book gives little focus to the academic merits of religious schools, research confirms that even if religious schools provide no other public benefits, they remain a key support to the public's interests in promoting higher levels of academic achievement.

Studies have demonstrated that religious schools strengthen the standard academic achievement of children. Jeynes' sociological work, *Religion, Education, and Academic Success* (2003), draws together the research of many scholars that ultimately provides evidence that religious schooling increases the probability of student academic success. As rationales, Jeynes points to empowering factors such as religious concern for a strong work ethic, the advocacy of moral priorities that complement educational diligence, increased family support toward academic success, and the community atmosphere of schools (2003). Research by Chang-Ho Ji (2010) further discerns the nature of religion's influence on academic achievement and concludes that its greatest effect is to motivate the student and to increase the cultural capital of parents that in turn influences children to greater achievement.

In further attempting to discern the connections between religion and academic performance, Ji (2010) found little to indicate that the personal faith of parochial school teachers and administrators led them to excel in their academic teaching skills or school leadership. He interpreted this finding to result from the developmental stability that individuals reach in adulthood. Whereas young people draw from their faith as they continually face value-laden decisions as to who they are to be and what they are to do, upon settling into their chosen roles as educational professionals in religious schools, teachers and administrators draw more from their professional training than their faith. Taken at face value, this finding seems to counter my thesis that religion will inform and inspire *all* members of a school community to greater excellence. However, rather than countering my claim, I believe this conclusion serves to illuminate an additional educational concern.

Ji's (2010) results likely reflect the pervasive influence of the secular education paradigm that predominates at higher education levels. For generations, colleges have trained teachers and administrators to teach and lead in secular public schools. Even religious colleges tend to prepare students according to the standards and methods of the secular public schools where most will gain employment. Thus, it is not surprising that religious schools whose faculty and administration have been trained to view their subject matter through secular lenses would display no more religious inspiration than their counterparts in secular schools who are likely staffed by professionals of similar faith and training. As long as the secular education paradigm holds sway over the training of most education professionals, it will be difficult for religion to demonstrate its motivational force through teachers and administrative leadership in the religious primary and secondary schools. If the "religious school effect" gains our attention even with the secular training of education leaders, it is likely that its positive influences will multiply as religious thinking infuses educational approaches.

Grounded Moral Education

Education historian Carl Kaestle accurately identifies the dilemma of contemporary public education: "How do you conduct moral education in the schools of a pluralistic country, with no established church and with protected dissent, when almost everyone believes that moral principles must be rooted in some cultural tradition and some transcendent values?" (1984, p. 101). Similarly, but more directly, scholar James Leming asks,

> How can we successfully teach children to be good in public schools where we cannot teach a religious-based morality? . . . [Especially if] as most Americans believe, the motivation for goodness is predicated upon a belief in a transcendent being and subordinating one's individual will to God's will. (2001, p. 62)

Many believe that public morality requires foundations deeper than common schools can establish, and they understand our public moral health and decline in terms of moral capital. Increasingly, social analysts are claiming that American society has been living on the moral investments of previous generations and that these investments are diminishing. Though not all religions are the same, religion plays "a substantial part in placing an emphasis on the dignity of human beings. It can be an important stimulus for the conscience and will to do the right thing" (Arthur, 2003, p. 148).

The separation of morality from its traditional formative sources makes the common school's task of moral formation more difficult, as does the tendency of democracies toward socially corrosive individualism, which scholar Peter Berkowitz (2003, p. 161) argues has been counterproductively encouraged by common school moral and civic curricula. The common school paradigm hampers moral educators who must rely upon exposing children to common morals in an atmosphere of shallow advocacy within a social environment representing diverse perspectives. Though the education day provides valuable opportunities to integrate moral teaching, the restraints of common education require that much of a child's character is left untouched (Hauerwas & Westerhoff, 1992, p. 7). Within this moral education setting, educators hope that children will perceive and adopt publicly supportive values into the core of their lives.

However, while John Dewey held that religious communities hindered the moral development of children, the attempted separation of moral education from all religious perspective begun in the 1960s seems to provide evidence to question that assumption. Dewey believed that reasoning from broad experience would lead to moral behavior, but having viewed the effects of moral education based on autonomous reason alone, Hunter argues that "so much of what we think of as 'innate' in our moral sensibilities . . . derives mainly from cultural resources" (2000, p. 226).

Whereas prior to modernity, and more particularly, prior to common schooling, educational settings actively passed on religious traditions and worldviews as vital aspects of a good education, secular common education displaced these religious resources. Hunter (2000) finds evidence that this shift has ramifications regarding the moral climate of our nation. He surveyed the relationship between students' worldviews and the moral qualities they exhibited. He termed those who based their moral views on their religious commitments to be "theistic," those who based their moral views on social practices and conventions to be "conventionalists," those who based their moral views on the perceived interests of the community to be "humanists," those who based their moral views on self-interest to be "utilitarians," and those who based their moral views on personal emotions and felt needs to be "expressivists." Of relevance to moral education, he found that students orient their "moral compasses" according to their worldviews. Hunter writes,

> The pattern is a clear and consistent continuum ranging from expressivist and utilitarian at one end to theist at the other. In general, the students least likely to say they would cheat, lie, or steal, and the most likely to show restraint in sexual matters, were those operating within a theistic moral orientation . . . followed by those working within a conventionalist moral framework. Conversely, the students most likely to cheat, lie, steal and least likely

to express restraint in sexual matters were the expressivists and utilitarians. Humanists were in between in every case. (2000, p. 164)

These findings may provide some insight into America's crime rates, mentioned above. Though surely affected by many other complex factors, it is interesting to note that rates increased most dramatically at a time when the educational context swung from mildly religious to supportive of expressivist and utilitarian views under autonomous, reason-based moral education. Then, crime rates somewhat declined with the wide-scale implementation of character education programs that provided moral instruction from humanistic and conventionalistic perspectives. Thus, Hunter's research may strongly support the public value of religious schooling that can nurture theistic moral perspectives.

From an analysis of the status of our nation's social health, public common education is not meeting the moral and civic needs of our society. This failure should not be surprising if one believes the nurture of these qualities to be most effective in private and religious settings. Religious schools provide these settings, and thus one can consider them a public resource.

Religious Schooling Morally Nurtures the Whole Person

Vryhof writes, "Public school educators still only offer lowest common denominator education, devoid of larger concerns of religion and worldview and life purpose and functional community" (2005, p. 152). Other scholars argue that nearly all teaching in all its contexts involves morals and moral judgments (Strike as cited in Goodlad & McMannon, 1997, p. 19) and that the teaching of values must address religion (Doyle, 1997). Whereas religious schools may embrace these concerns and provide for a more meaningful education of the whole person, common schools largely separate these concerns from the educational day.

However, the social effects of this must be considered when, according to educational scholar S. Alexander Rippa, "In some communities the public high school has assumed to an amazing extent almost all the responsibilities of personal development—individual and social tasks at one time performed by the family, the church or synagogue, and the community" (1992, p. 263). The school setting is increasingly becoming a source of nutrition, childcare, entertainment, counseling, and health care. It actively or passively effects the formation of their moral values, their sense of truth, their interests, their goals, and their academic abilities. Schools may not be able to back out of the roles they have assumed, but within a religious context, they can more faithfully provide the broad nurture that many parents and civic leaders believe children need.

Macedo (2000, p. 11) argues that liberal government requires a distinctive, but not a comprehensive, morality, teachable within the public schools. His guidelines may be appropriate within the constraints of the common education setting, but one must ask how strong that "distinctive" morality can be apart from deeper religious support. Scholar Nathan Tarcov argues, "The public should not consider cultivating good citizens apart from cultivating good humans" (as cited in Allman & Beaty, 2002, p. 67). This argument implies assisting students with finding the answers to deep questions; sociologist Peter Berger (1992, p. 21) notes that only within a religious view of reality can one find the answers to these questions. Similarly, scholar Richard John Neuhaus describes religion as in the "meaning business" (1995, p. 60). Thus, religious moral education attempts to nurture the whole person and extend deep meaning not only to life, but also to every subject of the curriculum.

Additionally, deep nurture of the whole person serves the community in which the individual resides as well as the individual. Our society often depends upon religious communities to form "reasons, norms, and moral convictions" (Macedo, 2000, p. 38). When common education avoids teaching deep values, it may serve to lower the energy of social disagreements, but it may also lower the values associated with our nation and public life. Human equality, religious liberty, democratic government, the preservation of nature, and other ideals have won acceptance in society. However, they have represented (and often required) not only the extrapolation of comprehensive beliefs into the social realm, but the accompanying motivations to pay the price of change, which, as the founding fathers famously wrote in the Declaration of Independence, often occur at the expense of "lives, fortunes and sacred honor."

Central to an education that deeply nurtures the whole person is the development of the conscience. Where the contemporary paradigm of public education allows for only the nurture of shallow moral ideals in accord with what is publicly common, religious schools seek to form a deep moral conscience. Arons argues that this latter approach is vital to our national health.

> In spite of all the debates, disagreements, and struggles that have surrounded the exercise of conscience, the centrality of conscience to the structure of a democratic society is also undeniable: democracy in America is based upon deeply held beliefs about the role of individual conscience in a system of self-government. The freedom of individual intellect and spirit at the

core of conscience is central to achieving a just consent of the governed. It is the cornerstone of a political system based on popular sovereignty. It secures the sanctity of the individual person against the power of the state. It is the most reliable protection against majority rule becoming a tyranny of the majority. And it is an essential condition for sustaining community life in a constitutional democracy. (1997, pp. 8–9)

As religious schools help children answer the big questions of life, provide for the development of their comprehensive views, and actively aid in the formation of their consciences, they help students with the formation of healthy identities. The religious school contributes to the individual's sense of stability and growth toward autonomy. From his study of Catholic schools, Bryk, Lee, and Holland (1993) conclude that from a gradually developing sense of deep identity within a religious school community, a child can grow to tolerate the differences of others with less of a sense of fear.

Similarly, education philosopher Terence McLaughlin (1984) finds that children need uniformity within their learning environment and a primary culture in which to grow. Too early an exposure to a diversity of beliefs will inhibit the development of abilities later necessary for their functioning within ideologically diverse settings. Thiessen, as quoted previously, argues, "Exposing [children] to plurality and a Babel of beliefs and values too soon will in fact prevent the development of abilities which are a key to later functioning in a complex and pluralistic environment" (2001, p. 41). Thus, the nurture of the whole person aids the child in the formation of a set of beliefs and values that provide an ideological platform for the rest of their learning.

Some scholars fear that as religious schools propagate systems of meaning and belief, they become sources of division. I addressed many of these fears in Chapter 6 as exaggerated and unsubstantiated. However, here I argue that those who fear religious meaning must also consider the social effects when meaning is lacking. As Arons (1997) previously addressed the importance of conscience, so political science scholar William Galston argues for the value of meaning. He writes, "The greatest threat to children in modern liberal societies is not that they will believe in something too deeply, but that they will believe in nothing very deeply at all" (1991, p. 255).

Thus, although the needs of society increasingly draw common schools into the role of child rearing, they are limited in their ability to nurture children in a deeply meaningful way. Religious schools, on the other hand, offer the public the opportunity to deeply nurture the whole "citizen" in areas of value, belief, conscience, and identity.

Sources of Strong Civic Character and Understanding

Paralleling the constraints the paradigm of common education places upon moral education, the paradigm places similar constraints upon curricula designed to nurture civic character and philosophic understanding. Public educational interests support the formation of citizens with strong civic character who uphold the rule of law, support our democratic institutions, are altruistic, and have "bought-in" to our plural union. Kevin Ryan writes, "Government is highly invested in promoting a citizenry of character as opposed to a citizenry of moral disasters and weaklings. A citizenry without character leads to two inevitable alternatives: social chaos or a policeman at every corner" (Ryan & Bohlin, 1999, p. 21). However, common schools can nurture character only with secular curricular resources.

This difficulty of nurturing civic qualities is accentuated by the common school, where every attempt to define a moral consensus is attacked by some group as "narrow, sectarian and not inclusive" (Hunter, 2000, p. 77). Though multiculturalists like Will Kymlicka claim that no common civic culture is needed (Reich, 2002), Thomas Lickona (1991, p. 20) claims that a common ground exists in valuing pluralism, honesty, justice, civility, the democratic process, and respect for truth. The issue relates less to the particular qualities of the common culture than to the government's role in its definition and propagation.

If some minimal set of common qualities exist, as I believe they do, then providing the most effective means for their propagation is fundamental. Charles Taylor writes, "As long as we're united around the norms...the issue is what sources can support our far-reaching moral commitments to benevolence and justice" (1989, p. 515). Thus, the question of how best to nurture civic character entails a concern for our diversity as well as a concern for its most effective nurture. I will examine how a concern for our deep diversity favors a plural system of civic education later; but here, I will cite evidence regarding the quality of religious school character education that indicates its effectiveness.

Whereas common schools focus on secular means of improving their moral and civic nurture, such as character-education programs that draw attention to reasonable social and civic norms, religious schools have access to alternate resources that have been traditionally effective. Vryhof writes that secular schools focus reform options on "fancier technology and longer days, newer textbooks and higher pay, smaller classes and better teacher training" (2004, p. xiii). We have since added competition, school/teacher evaluation, and "testing," but Vryhof's argument is likely unchanged: "Children grow into responsible adults through their engagement with communities of meaning" (p. xiii). The foundations of many of these communities are religious views, which Robert Kunzman argues provide strength for civic commitments. He writes, "The civic and political realms have necessary and important boundaries, but must be informed by the private realm's deep ethical frameworks if they are to have any purchase and power in our lives together" (2006, p. 142).

Research concerning civic outcomes supports these claims regarding religious schools. An examination of studies regarding civic values conducted by Patrick Wolf (2005) shows that private schools tend to equal or exceed public schools in their ability to impart values considered beneficial to the public. They exceed public schools due to their access to transcendent perspectives. Vryhof writes,

> Although all schools advocate civic values—honesty, respect for individuals, respect for property, do your best, and the like—faith based schools try to raise the bar, upholding higher standards of conduct by grounding them in a religious context that requires commitment, the essence of social capital. (2012, pp. 53–54)

For example, whereas public schools may argue that respect is necessary for life in civilized society, religious schools may provide deeper meaning and motivation by teaching that respect is necessary because all people are created in the image of God. Vryhof argues,

> Virtues need to be grounded in a more complex world view that gives a fuller account of human experience, that resonates more fully with reality in all its many corners, and that, to a significant extent, offers an explanation for the unexplainable. (2004, p. 8)

Closing the Gap and Nurturing Impoverished Communities

The U.S. poverty rate in 2011 was 15.9% (Bishaw, 2012). In most areas, poverty is not merely a monetary concern but a self-propagating cultural concern with many ideological roots and effects. Academically, poverty is closely associated with the achievement gap, one of the most pervasive concerns of public education leaders. Unfortunately, decades of research and effort have shown little success toward narrowing this gap (Barton & Coley, 2010). However, even to the casual classroom observer, it is obvious that the roots of the achievement gap go far deeper than traditional secular education can reach. They are largely religious in nature and extend beyond material needs into the values and beliefs of individuals, families, and communities. Even though many religious schools only weakly integrate their faith with their curricula, their religious orientation and community concern remains influential. Thus, it should not be surprising that religious schools have demonstrated an unexpected success in helping to close the achievement gap (Jeynes, 2003, 2007a). In fact, the academic successes of religious schools in urban areas have been one of the most publicly influential arguments for school choice.

However, the public value associated with religious schooling goes beyond the academic. Religion not only offers powerful and unique opportunities to influence the thinking, emotions, and behaviors of individuals, but it provides communities with new compelling visions and cultural values around which groups mobilize their resources and grow (Maton & Wells, 1995). Whereas secular public school personnel must remain distant from religious advocacy, religious schools teachers can ideologically nurture children, their families, and the communities in which they live. In this nurture, which they link with churches or synagogues, stands the best hope of being the nuclei around which impoverished communities grow toward health. Yet public schools currently create a "secular space" that is permissive to many of the moral and ideological concerns that the religious communities prohibit. In other words, secular schools inadvertently compete with and diminish the nascent influence of religious communities. Religious schools, on the other hand, complement the concerns and efforts of religious communities. Working together around a common and powerful life vision, families, churches, and religious schools can provide the moral, intellectual, spiritual, interpersonal, and communal resources to revitalize impoverished communities in ways that secular governmental efforts have proven to be feeble.

Religious Schooling Builds and Accesses the Strengths of Community

From his numerous studies of Catholic schools, sociologist James Coleman (1991; Coleman & Hoffer, 1987) found that religious schools produced beneficial moral and academic effects. He associated these effects largely with the climate of these schools and concluded that "religious sector schools supply something that is deficient in many single-parent families, something that is not supplied by schools outside the religious sector, whether public or private" (1991, p. 163). What sets them apart is their deep sense of community. "These voluntary institutions benefit from a network of social relations that is characterized by mutuality and trust" (Viteritti, 1999, p. 86).

Education leaders consolidated public schools in the latter part of the 20th century with the intent of forming larger and more ideologically diverse communities (Macedo, 2000). However, their attempts have not succeeded, because as the research of Coleman suggests, "The capacity of people to associate depends on the degree to which communities share norms and values that enable them to subordinate individual interests to larger group or societal interests" (Viteritti, 1999, p. 191). Thus, public attempts to address civic concerns hinder community formation and the educational benefits associated with community.

Cohesive communities of shared trust and belief are coupled with what researchers refer to as the "Catholic school effect" (Benson et al., 1984; Bryk & Schneider, 2002; Coleman & Hoffer, 1987), which elevates moral and academic outcomes of urban children. The effect seems to find its source in the "spirit of community, the sense of caring, the assumption that all children are capable of learning at the highest level of comprehension" (Viteritti, 1999, p. 84).

Additionally, the benefits of community found in religious schools extend beyond the schools themselves. A study of religious schools in urban areas found that they "not only provided quality education for the students who attended them, but were, in the eyes of many, a stabilizing force in their neighborhoods" (Edelmann, 1997, p. 54).

Hunter's review of community research supports the effectiveness of moral education conducted within moral communities wherein faculty and students agree upon and live out their shared convictions (2000, pp. 157–175). Community settings recognize that "the transmission of values need not be explicit, and often isn't. . . . Children absorb *many* of their values" (Vryhof, 2004, p. 5, emphasis in the original). Effective moral nurture depends upon cultivating a sense of conscience consistent with the conscience embodied within the school community. However, Arons argues that contemporary public education opposes this interdependent relationship. He writes,

> The bureaucratic culture of education has become hostile . . . to the growth of community, behaving as if each were a threat to successful schooling. Conscience—its exercise by teachers, its development in children, and its place in our primary institution for transmitting culture—has been rendered nearly irrelevant. Community—its maintenance within schools as a necessary context for learning, and its support by schooling as an essential part of a free and meaningful life—has been subverted. (1997, p. 123)

Though Arons interprets the ongoing reticence of the education community to allow public dollars to reach religious schools as an opposition to community formation, public school leaders desire to deepen the sense of community within common schools. However, the best schools form natural communities (Viteritti, 1999, p. 217). Thus, religious schools, due to their intrinsic qualities associated with community formation, offer the public the opportunity to form valuable educational communities.

Religious Schooling Builds Social Capital

Whereas the previous section demonstrated that religious schools form and have greater access to the strengths of community, this section will address the publicly valuable social capital frequently associated with these religious communities. Specifically, it will demonstrate that religious schools, due to qualities largely inaccessible to common schools, provide the public with strong sources of social capital. Political scientist Robert Putnam notes that social capital "refers to connections among individuals—social networks and the norms of reciprocity and trustworthiness that arise from them," and it is strengthened when civic virtues become "embedded in a dense network of reciprocal social relations" (2000, p. 19).

Relationships of trust are a key ingredient of social capital, and new sources of social trust need to be found (Marty, 2010). Scholar Christopher Beem describes the vital nature of social capital that serves to highlight it as a fundamental public educational interest. He writes,

> Trust between individuals thus becomes trust between strangers and trust of a broad fabric of social institutions; ultimately, it becomes a shared set of values, virtues, and expectations within society as a whole. Without this interaction, on the other hand, trust decays; at a certain point, this decay begins to manifest itself in serious social problems. (1999, p. 20)

The increase of social ills listed above may serve to indicate the public need to support the development of more social capital. Putnam argues that although new sources must develop, "religion is today, as it has traditionally been, a central fount of American community life and health" (2000, p. 79). Thus, while surely common schools successfully build some social capital, schools that tie into and maintain a religious community vision hold a particular advantage toward its nurture.

Putnam's (2000) own research, along with that of others, support his strong conclusion regarding religion as one of social capital's richest sources. This research finds that religion contributes to public life, in part, by the following:

- Teaching "moral virtues such as self-sacrifice and altruism" (Gimpel et al., 2003, pp. 122–123).
- Increasing acts of charity in support of the common good (Wuthnow, 1991, p. 334).
- Promoting greater civic engagement than any other social resources than education (Viteritti, 2007, p. 176).
- Organizing more than half of all those who volunteer (Marty & Moore, 2000, p. 152).
- Helping those in need (Viteritti, 2007, pp. 102–104).
- "Instilling a valuable moral resource that contributes to participatory attitudes" (Gimpel et al., 2003, pp. 122–123).
- Nurturing others in the values, skills, and character needed for social stability (Arthur, 2003, p. 44).

In summary, Putnam (2000) finds that religious people are generally strong citizens. They are more likely to visit friends, entertain at home, attend club meetings, and belong to societies, sports groups, youth groups, service clubs, hobby clubs, literature groups, art groups, and study groups.

One may question whether the religious qualities that make church settings strong sources of social capital carry over into religious school settings. However, Gimpel and colleagues find that "religious instruction is associated with the formation of social capital" (2003, p. 122), Putnam (2000, p. 363) finds that school age children need to bond at a small community level, and studies by Fritch (1999, 2001) find that small and religious schools produce more social capital than large and secular schools. Thus, it appears that religious schools are indeed advantaged over common schools to form social capital.

However, as political scientist Michael Woolcock (2001, pp. 13–14) notes, social capital can be bonding, bridging, or linking with the first becoming potentially divisive or separatist if not accompanied by the second and third, which serves to "link" one with dissimilar others. Surely, religious schools can be identified that do not build linking capital, but as previous discussions regarding unity have demonstrated, most religious schools seem to reflect a healthy balance of all three types of capital. They operate on higher educational visions than those of public schools, which might seem to imply divisive exclusiveness; but their higher visions generally encompass the visions of the latter. American religious groups share the concerns of social existence within a pluralized setting and reasonably address them from within their worldviews to provide education that is academic, moral, and civic.

Though some scholars and education leaders remain suspicious of religious organizations, Viteritti (2007, p. 204) notes that they represent a minority of the populace; studies indicate that more Americans fear that religion has been given too narrow, rather than too broad, a place in American public life. Reflecting on this point, Viteritti writes,

> There is a basic intelligence to the American disposition towards religion. Generations of social science research has informed us of the positive effect that religion has on civic and political life. It is indispensable to both spheres. It has always served as a source of strength for those who are otherwise disadvantaged. The same religious convictions that incline people toward moral judgment (which is not necessarily bad) incline them to do good deeds. (2007, p. 204)

From his reading of Putnam's research, Viteritti concludes that there has been "an erosion of civil society during the latter half of the twentieth century, and a 'hollowing out' of the institutions that compose it" (2007, p. 176). The public needs new sources of social capital, and religious schools seem to be ideally suited to be one of these sources. Grounded in community and shared beliefs, they provide the public with strong sources of social capital due to qualities inaccessible to public schools exclusively operating on a common paradigm of education.

Religious Schooling is a Source of Public Meaning

One of public education's goals has been the propagation of the nation's cultural traditions, symbols, commitments, and ideals that provide a sense of unity and shared destiny (Bellah, 1985, p. 27). However, many of these treasured national resources are religious, and the concerns of pluralism within a common school setting have worked against their meaningful propagation. Whether their origins were prior to, coexistent with, or subsequent to America's founding, these have been removed or stripped of the public advocacy of their deep meaning. The Mayflower Compact, the Declaration of Independence, early state constitutions, engravings on public buildings, historic patriotic art, coinage, prominent speeches of founders and presidents, early historical analysis and teaching, inspirational stories, and public symbols such as crosses, plaques, and mottos frequently reflect religious meaning. Under the influence of the common school model, these have been removed or stripped of much of their deep meaning; though common schools are permitted to teach *about* these civic treasures, they cannot *advocate* the meaning they hold. At best, they can only advocate the "common" meanings of these symbols and ideas. Thus, once meaningful and inspiring civic stories such as the Providential protection of George Washington during the American Revolution and Benjamin Franklin's call to prayer at the Constitutional Convention that brought peace and inspiration, and the Declaration of Independence's recognition of God are eviscerated of meaning. They are either neglected as controversial or irrelevant, or they are taught as factual and merely representative of the beliefs of the day.

Conscientious liberal political theory may have necessitated this "de-meaning" process, but it has come at the expense of both alienating those for whom the symbols had great meaning and disconnecting many national ideals of their deep meaning. Some of the (often disparaged) efforts of the "religious right" have been in response to the arguably accurate perception that America is stepping away from the values it once represented. Though the public cannot directly restore the deeper meaning of these symbols, it can more equitably allow the private sector to do so within religious schools. This falls short of a public endorsement of meaning, but a public *recognition* of the value of religious meaning expressed through the provision of alternate schooling is less alienating than what currently appears to be a tacit, yet public, *denial* of meaning.

Shared symbols provide us a sense of cohesion, but when stripped of deep meaning, they lose not only much of their power to bond but also their power to motivate, to provide national direction, and to provide focal points of value and intellectual reflection. A plural public education system provides the public with the greater opportunity to allow communities to reinstate, reinterpret, or to create meaning associated with public life and symbols. One might expect that Christians would revive many of the deep traditional meanings associated with our nation's symbols and history within their schools. However, once-foreign or outsider faiths might also write meaningful narratives of their own religious journey in America upon new and old symbols.

The founders conceived many of the ideas and institutions associated with our civic identity within religious contexts. Religious schools offer the public an opportunity to have deep meaning woven back into the American heritage. Though aspects of symbols and their histories may remain common, their meanings need not become shallow within individual hearts. "In God We Trust" is the national motto of the United States. While once a weighty statement, it now officially reflects more tradition than meaning. However, within Christian schools, educators may restore its meaning to reflect the corporate trust that our founders placed in the God of the Bible, or they may modify it to reflect the trust that other faiths conceive toward their gods.

One may argue that since the liberal public cannot endorse the particular religious meanings that private schools may teach surrounding our nation that they are therefore without public value. This conclusion, however, is quite wrong. The liberal state is rarely a source of meaning; it reflects only the meaning conceived by its citizens and made public through democratic and Constitutional means. Thus, the source and meaning of diverse public conceptions such as justice, Lincoln's Gettysburg Address, democracy, human equality, the rightful role of government, and our national motto can (and I argue *must*) be given a place of prominent discussion and teaching within religious settings. Although surely, different perspectives of meaning will arise, and high degrees of character will be needed to insure orderly public debate, apart from meaning, public life tends toward procedures driven by shallow opinion. Religious schools, however, provide academic forums to restore and communicate meaning regarding our shared public life.

Providing the State With Secure Ideological Foundations

Plural Public Education Prevents an Establishment of Religion

In 1963, religious historian Sidney E. Mead published *The Lively Experiment: The Shaping of Christianity in America*. He was one of the first to claim that American public schools functioned as a state church by intentionally and preferentially attempting to shape the morality, character, and views of the populace. He claimed that compulsory attendance was to "guarantee the dissemination and inculcation among the embryo citizens of the beliefs essential to the existence and well-being of the democratic society." According to Mead, these beliefs were essentially religious. He said, "In other words, the public schools in the United States took over one of the basic responsibilities that traditionally was always assumed by an established church. In this sense, the public school system of the United States is an established church" (pp. 67–68).

Some scholars argue that even following the educational disestablishment of the 1960s, the worldview promoted within this "established church" is not neutral toward religion. Warren Nord writes,

> The underlying worldview of modern education divorces humankind from dependence on God; it replaces religious answers to many of the ultimate questions of human existence with secular answers; and, most striking, public education conveys its secular understanding of reality essentially as a matter of faith. Indeed, I will argue that at least in its textbooks and formal curriculum students are *indoctrinated* into the modern (secular) worldview and against religion. (1995, p. 159, emphasis in the original)

Similarly, scholars James Carper and Thomas Hunt write, "We contend that the public school is the functional equivalent of an established church, buttressed with religious language, expected to embrace all people, legitimating and transmitting an orthodoxy or worldview, and underwritten by compulsory taxation" (2007, p. 4). When the state preferentially funds this view to the exclusion of other views that hold deep claims within the realm of education, the concern that public education has become a secular religious establishment is not without merit.

Educators often avoid religious themes in accordance with the common school's intent to avoid controversy (Glenn, 1988, p. 177). Legal scholar Michael McConnell also argues that defining schools as places where faith is virtually irrelevant can serve as a religious view. He insightfully writes,

> Secular schools may well refrain from overt anti-religious teaching. But the worldview presented to the children will be one in which religion plays no significant role. Such a curriculum may not necessarily produce atheists, but it will tend to produce young adults who think of religion as something separate and distinct from the real world of knowledge, if they think of religion at all. (2002, p. 117)

Thus, a plural system of education can protect the public, in accord with the best intentions of liberal democratic philosophy, from the real or perceived claim that common schools continue to represent a state religious establishment.

Religious Schooling Guards Against "Official Knowledge"

The above unease is not just "religious," it regards a concern for liberal political philosophy that limits the power of the state to control knowledge. Chester Finn Jr. writes, "Because we cherish freedom as a core value and insist that the state is the creature of its citizens, we are loath to allow state-run institutions to instruct tomorrow's citizens in how to think, how to behave, and what to believe" (2005, p. 188). Stephen Arons argues that at its core, the Constitution not only protects the individual from the imposition of a state religion, but from ideological interference in general. He writes,

> The Constitution as a whole embodies the view that, unless the wellspring of intellectual and cultural diversity is thus protected, the "consent of the governed" will be rendered hollow, democracy will become a "tyranny of the majority," and the individual risks becoming "the mere creature of the state." (1997, p. 78)

Official standardized knowledge is dangerous. "Consciously or not, the institutional arrangement [of common public education], sanctioned by state power, implicitly carries the assumption that those in charge have a real grip on what society needs in order to advance" (Viteritti, 2007, p. 85). With a similar concern, Arons writes,

> When the sphere of intellect and spirit is subjected to political regulation, freedom of thought and belief and the individual mind are shoved aside by political power. As schooling and knowledge are politicized, a pall of orthodoxy is cast not only upon the classroom, but upon both conscience and community as well. (1997, p. 85)

It is difficult to protect the state from accusations that it is manipulating public opinion when it allows public funds to reach only schools reflecting common secular perspectives. Thus, religious schools are an asset to the public as they provide for the propagation of educational perspectives apart from the secular perspectives of the state.

Religious Schooling Intellectually Resources the Public

Further, when the state limits the breadth of intellectual discussion, it also limits the intellectual resource pool from which the public may draw. All religions see life differently—they are "not just about spirituality" (Carter, 2000, p. 28), and these different perspectives resource the public with new visions, ideals, and solutions to shared problems. In America, Christianity has provided a powerful critique of government surrounding issues of national concerns such as the ideology surrounding the Constitution, slavery, civil rights, and many other contemporary ethical concerns. The state needs this varied and often transcendent input that it has difficulty nurturing within the paradigm of common education. Scholar Stephen Carter (2000, p. 31) even goes as far as to say that democracy will not survive without religion's concern and transcendence.

Thus, common education alone is a poor intellectual resource for the public for at least three reasons: (a) it preferentially supports a view of knowledge, a selective body of information, and a particular set of moral values as a functional religion; (b) it unwisely links state power with a broad and preferred intellectual formation; and (c) it obstructs the formation of alternate deep perspectives that serve to support and critique the state.

These objections have traditionally been countered with the acknowledged right of children to attend private schools as supported by the *Pierce* (1925) decision; however, tuition expenses serve to limit or prohibit this freedom for many. This reality raises an issue of proportionality. Government can limit and regulate rights when strong public interests are at stake; for example, the right of free speech does not allow one to yell "Fire!" in a crowded theater. Thus, although freedoms are not arbitrarily limited, the concern for public order can legitimately serve to limit them (Macedo, 2000). However, previous chapters have argued that public order has not been decisively shown to require common education, nor has religious schooling been demonstrated to oppose public order. Therefore, the exclusive funding of common schools does not proportionally reflect the realistic concerns of the state regarding public order.

Galston supports the right of the state to educate for citizenship, but he qualifies it. He writes,

> The state must be parsimonious in defining the realm in which uniformity must be secured through coercion. An educational program based on an expansive and contestable definition of good citizenship or civic unity will not ordinarily justify the forcible suppression of expressive liberty. (2002, p. 109)

Therefore, since common education is a definitive religious offense to those termed by Charles Glenn as "cognitive minorities" (1988, p. 11), and since common education is a potentially cogent source of state imposed ideology, it serves the public interest to provide an equal educational alternative more commensurate with the conscientious interests of citizens and the justifiable needs of public order.

In this vein, McConnell argues, "A liberal pluralistic society committed to non-establishment of religion should organize education along pluralistic lines" (McConnell in Macedo & Tamir, 2002, p. 87). Similarly, political science scholar Jason Scorza argues for a plural system of public education, because "preserving the possibility for citizens to choose different reasonable, decent, or acceptable ways of being a good citizen respects the autonomy of individuals, guards against civic education becoming an instrument of mass conformity and docility, and helps provide civic diversity" (2001). Thus, removing the tuition barrier associated with religious schooling under a plural public education system will serve the public by insuring that the state remains truly neutral regarding comprehensive views.

Understanding in a Religious World

Religious schools are vital to the postmodern American public that is slowly coming to grips with the reality that much of the world cannot be accurately defined or understood by secular understanding. Enlightenment science has not moved "religious thought" to the margins of relevance, nationally or internationally. As discussed in Chapter 3, the philosophy of the modern public school grew during a time when it was presumed that "scientific" thought would both displace religious belief and provide adequate moral foundations for society. This presumption did not become reality. The nations of the world (the West included) remain expressions of their ideological foundations as they address and defend national and global issues.

Books such as James Davidson Hunter's, *Culture Wars: The Struggle to Define America* (1991), Samuel Huntington's *The Clash of Civilizations and the Remaking of the World Order* (1996), and more recently, Darrow L. Miller's *Emancipating the World: A Christian Response to Radical Islam and Fundamentalist Atheism* (2012) captured public attention because, in part, they challenge a paradigm that most were taught at school. Secular schools seemed to teach us that all people are basically good, rational, and merely desirous of material security and liberty—that healthy civilizations could be built upon "reason" irrespective of their religious foundations. Unexpectedly, these books counter or amend this truism. They directly or indirectly imply that our goodness, rationality, and values are the *secondary* effects of our ideological foundations. Yet it was not the discussion of this idea that captured the public's attention; our attention was captured by the fact that modern events seem to verify that it is true.

Today's secular education, built upon many refuted modern premises, fails to prepare Americans to either anticipate or provide solutions for the conflicts of a *religious* world. We were taken unaware by the attacks of September 11, and we entered the battlefields of Iraq and Afghanistan and supported the uprisings of the "Arab Spring" believing that we merely needed to free their peoples from oppression, and democracy would flourish. Instead, we found the case was not so simple. Our leaders had not been taught to "think religiously." We did not account for the religious nature of our own standards and values, thus we failed to understand why our Western and "secular" offerings were largely rejected by nations long shaped by other moral and ideological foundations.

A good public education should prepare children to be understanding participants in a religiously diverse nation and world. Whereas secular school philosophy was predicated upon the presumption that religion would fade in a technological world, this has not proven to be the case. Equipped with a religious understanding, religious schools help children to understand the ideological components of society and the necessity of winning ideological "buy-in" to ideas before social transformation can follow. Though I may yet be proven wrong, I was convinced the "Arab Spring" would not reflect shortcuts from tyranny to liberty because I knew the moral and ideological foundations for liberty had not been laid. Whereas secular schools are more likely to reflexively "support the innocent in their battles against oppression," or to send aid to impoverished countries, religious schools might more wisely teach children to understand cultures and social problems largely as reflections of complex ideological beliefs. They would likely teach that *human* problems are not solved through military or material aid alone, but by the long-term philosophic rebuilding of the society more akin to evangelism and education.

The realm of " the secular" is created when diverse religious people make an effort to live, work, and make decisions together. It is a ground of agreeable peace in the midst of disagreement. Though secular philosophy has proven to be a valuable ground for government, it is a limited ground for human understanding. Religious schools, where communities understand what it is to be "religious," best support the public's educational interests by preparing future citizens to deeply understand the costs, benefits, nature, and possibilities of a secular space *within the midst of deeply held religious views*. While secular schools may expose students to some of the diversity of our religious world, their philosophy and methodologies aimed at supporting secular society tend merely to teach religious children to hold their views lightly for the sake of compromise.

Though compromise is necessary in a diverse society, America also needs citizens who strongly hold to certain of their ideals. Centrally, how does one teach children to discern the degree or even the advisability of compromise in schools that do not identify with, understand, or address the implications of religious beliefs? How can schools that treat religion as generally irrelevant to the subjects of the curriculum help children identify with the ideological attachments of others? The place of compromise between "saving the snail darter" and "saving babies" is not simply a proposal to "save the whales" and can best be discussed in schools where the philosophic framework discusses the value of life from ultimate reference points.

Though I claim that religious schools engage the issues of society and the world, some may fear that they are merely inward looking or unconcerned with civic issues. However, religious schools commonly address social life from comprehensive perspectives. It is natural for religious schools to recognize and teach moral obligations. James Arthur writes,

> For them, there is a clear and intimate relationship between the character of a person and the religious faith they practice. This belief in God affects the choices they make, the relationships they forge, the lifestyles they adopt and the attitudes and behaviors they exhibit. (2003, p. 44)

Thus, although civic concerns may not be the first concerns of religious schools, they address civic concerns within a deep and broad frame of reference and meaning justified by their proven value.

The world's great religions are great, in part, because they have successfully provided moral, intellectual, and civic foundations that have advanced the civilizations with which they are associated. They have each succeeded in providing a foundation for meaningful life, value, and moral order in a manner reasonably consistent with the realities of individual and community life. In spite of their different conceptions of truth, one should expect that the external moral standards of the differing faiths are similar; each has wrestled for generations with the needs of community life and come to advocate most firmly those moral standards found to be most important to their shared existence. Whereas the progressive thinkers of the 20th century associated tradition and religion with moral bondage (Marsden, 1994; Westbrook, 1991), in a free society, these norms may more accurately reflect the accumulated and evolving moral wisdom that is satisfying to the individual and beneficial for society.

Thus, religious schools offer the public the opportunity for deep civic nurture that imparts higher moral standards, engages deeper academic motivations, provides insight and understanding of others, supports secular government, and draws upon accumulated social experience.

Advancing Public Unity

Previously, I argued that supporters of common education fail both to provide credible evidence supporting the unifying nature of common schooling and to provide evidence that religious schools are a source of disunity. Opposing these claims, in this section, I will argue that if religious schools are included within a system of public funding, they can serve to advance public unity.

Religious Schooling as an Alternative to "Offense and Disaffection"

Macedo (2000, p. 100) rightly notes that in a pluralistic society, the public cannot achieve shared civic ends without offending someone's religion; however, a unifying public goal is to minimize offense in the pursuit of those ends. Religious school opponents have not successfully argued that the contributions of common education are vital to public unity nor have they successfully argued that religious schooling is necessarily more divisive than common education; thus, it seems reasonable that many of the concerns of religious dissenters should be accommodated within the public education system. To this end, Macedo (p. 253) also concedes the value of school choice as a means to bring outsider groups into the civic process.

Educational values run deep. Thiessen argues that both parental love and parental maturity seem to justify a broad place for parental discernment regarding the education of their children. He writes,

> Parents are self-governing adults entitled to choose and pursue their own conception of the good life. . . . Thus, parents should have the authority and primary (though not exclusive) responsibility to educate their children in accord with their own conceptions of the good life. (1995, p. 2)

However, when the state acts to counter the loving intentions or the judgments of parents regarding the education of their children, the conflicts can serve to undermine much public good will.

Many common school dissenters experience coercion within the current public system. Those who cannot afford the tuition expenses of private education feel coerced to attend the local common school, and those who can afford private school tuitions are required to pay education expenses twice: once through taxation, then again through private tuition. Arons notes that this is a counterproductive situation for the state attempting to build unity, because "coercion yields only conformity, disaffection, or at its most extreme, rebellion" (1997, p. 6). Further, he writes,

> Schooling is a crucible out of which community cohesion may be formed and strengthened, or melted down and made useless. When voluntary compromise and reorientation come out of these struggles, community cohesion is strengthened, as is the quality of education taking place within that community. But sometimes an individual's conscience or a minority's deeply held beliefs prevent compromise. If such dissenters are nevertheless forced to accept the majority's will, polarization increases, community cohesion is weakened, and another round of the zero-sum conflict predicted by the Supreme Court becomes inevitable. (p. 5)

Similarly, it may be argued that when groups perceive that the state is suppressing or "neutralizing" their religion, it encourages them to further distance themselves from the values of the public. When this happens, the public education system has not only failed to draw in certain citizens, but it has served to distance them further from the shared values of the polity. Though not a supporter of religious schooling, Macedo (2000, p. 102) speaks to this situation. He advises that it is better to draw parents into contact with state interests than to force those interests on them and to ward off their support.

Scholar James Skillen (1994) argues that just as the separation of state power from the church brought unity, so will a separation of state power from expansive educational control. Thus, a plural public education system built around common public interests rather than common public schools can serve to remove the offense of common education and draw in those who have felt marginalized by the state because of their beliefs. Through a system of plural public education, the public can replace many experiences of offense and coercion among those who feel marginalized with increased gratitude and trust that they are indeed free and equal citizens.

Religious Schooling Provides an Alternate Paradigm of Unity

I argue that our national unity is only as strong as the beliefs and commitments of citizens in support of that unity. The paradigm of common education allows for the formation of a national unity based upon an affirmed equality, a common heritage, shared symbols, a shallow set of shared values, and reflection upon shared civic concerns. This leads to a degree of mutual acceptance among citizens. Classrooms, as claimed by Walter Parker, are to be "places where multiple social perspectives and personal values are brought into face-to-face contact around matters that 'are relevant to the problems of living together.' Such matters are mutual, collective concerns, not mine or yours, but ours" (2005, p. 3).

Though these common school strategies surely provide some grounds for unity, they provide little ideological depth or meaning. Since these strategies presume a commitment to equality and unity without providing deep support for either, I argue that the unity they build tends to rely on the beliefs and values that each student brings into the classroom. It seems apparent that common schools have difficulty presenting civic values that trump the appeals associated with self-gratification and materialism. It also seems reasonable that those deeply committed to the value of others will generally support a stronger unity than those committed to the fulfillment of their own pleasures.

Yet this is how it should be in a liberal state wherein the state is not to be the moral guide or teacher (Linder & Pierard, 1978), at least in a deeply formative manner. Thus, the state is more rightly dependent upon the nonpublic realm to provide the "transcendent ethical principles" that undergird commitments to public unity. I argue that religious schools, in which deep values and beliefs can be taught and drawn from, can provide the public with a stronger source of unity than is available to common education curricula.

Some may counter that the state cannot depend upon religious schools to nurture the common ideals of our nation. However, I argue that religious schools provide for an alternate paradigm of national unity. Whereas the common school model of unity relies upon forming cohesion through common civic education and mutual experiences that serve to subordinate social differences, the religious school model of unity relies upon the nurture of both deep and pragmatic values that support our unity even in the midst of our ideological differences. Thus, while differences alone often become sources of public division, they can be sources of "linking capital" and unity when those differences include influential beliefs that place a high value on peace, hospitality, justice, individual freedom, and a concern for others (Woolcock, 2001).

One may also counter that some religions appear to lack adequate linking capital to support the unity interests of the state. This observation may be correct (I will address how the state can selectively support particular religious schools in a legal manner in the final chapter). However, the common education paradigm of unity relies upon the reasonableness of individuals to perceive and value the goods associated with our democratic system and, following these perceptions, to support the system that provides it. With the same confidence, religious school leaders should generally be trusted to perceive and value these same goods.

I argue that, when offenses are minimized, religious communities will tend to support our democratic system. Supreme Court Justice Robert H. Jackson reflected this confidence in 1943 when he wrote, "To believe that patriotism will not flourish if patriotic ceremonies are voluntary and spontaneous instead of a compulsory routine is to make an unflattering estimate of the appeal of our institutions to free minds" (*West Virginia State Board of Education v. Barnette*, 1943). I believe that the "appeal of our free institutions" is a powerful force that not only shapes the civic education programs of traditionally supportive faith schools but is also a force that reasonably inspires the buy-in of outsider groups toward the American polity.

Though some faith traditions may oppose aspects of the liberal democratic tradition, I argue the most effective means to encourage their buy-in is not the direct action of the state to "Americanize" its citizens in a secular environment, but to rely on the motivational appeals of democratic liberty. I argue that religious communities amalgamate and reorder their commitments within the settings and under the pressures in which they live. Catholics likely became "good Americans" not *because of*, but *in spite of* the common school.

As noted above, religious groups offended by common education battle perceptions that distance them from the public. The public may advance unity goals by placing the teaching of good citizenship in their hands as a sign of civic trust. Within lightly regulated settings (such as the school system I will propose in the next chapter), religious communities can wrestle with the claims and provisions of democracy within the deep contexts of their faiths. I believe the outcome would be a citizenship committed to both transcendent and pragmatic ideals of public unity. Thus, I anticipate that religious communities will tend to adapt their theological understanding to support the good they perceive in democratic institutions, and they are in a position to better transmit those values *through their own faith schools* to the next generation. Thiessen supports the idea that cultural/religious schools that teach democratic values will help strengthen the civic goals of society. He writes that these schools "will do much more to create harmony within a pluralistic society than the imposition of liberal values and multicultural programs within an environment that is alien to students from minority cultural or religious traditions" (2001, p. 244).

Thus, I argue that plural unity will find greater support through the deep support and buy-in of those attracted to our liberties and institutions than it will find through the shallow civic curricula of common schools that tend to gloss over and even offensively minimize our differences in their attempts to build unity.

Conclusion

Many scholars are concerned about the social health of our nation, which is an extension, in part, of the moral and civic health of the American citizenry. Public education represents our primary corporate effort to support this health. However, common schools, limited by the First Amendment and by philosophical diversity, lack the resources to adequately address the deep moral, ideological, and emotional concerns that are key to individual moral and civic health. The personal and ideological resources most strongly associated with human development are currently most available in the private school sector and contained within meaningful, stabilizing, and motivating ideologies and the communities they form. Religious schools can freely and deeply address the moral and civic concerns of the state in ways secular schools cannot. Religious schools are public assets that provide grounded moral educations, sources of strong civic character and understanding, resources to close the achievement gap and help impoverished communities, resources to build social capital and restore public meaning, secure ideological foundations for the state, and deep sources of public unity.

Though some narrowly argue that the move to a plural public education paradigm would oppose the public's educational interests, this chapter has turned this argument on its head; the common education paradigm has progressively squeezed the religious lifeblood from public education, leaving the state with but shallow foundations. The expansion of religious schooling promises to reinvigorate America's experiment with liberty, democracy, and diversity. In the following chapter, I propose some philosophic and structural foundations upon which a healthy plural public education system can grow.

8

Proposal and Conclusion

Thiessen succinctly captures the case that I have made thus far; the public's educational goals are more expansive than secular efforts can address. He writes,

> There is an incompleteness to any civic education that seeks to cultivate
> liberal/democratic values without their particular justifications. Common
> schools cannot deal adequately with this component of civic education.
> What are needed are schools that not only teach the civic virtues, but also
> teach the justification of these virtues within the context of a particular comprehensive supporting worldview. (2001, p. 236)

The subject of this chapter is to discern the qualities and structures of a healthy plural public education system.

The Dynamics of Religious Schools

Lack of religious school experience may leave many with the presumption that religious schools embrace fewer liberal educational ideals than is actu-

Education Reform, pages 185–207
Copyright © 2013 by Information Age Publishing
All rights of reproduction in any form reserved.

ally the case. Religious schools differ widely, but they offer the opportunity to do more than just add prayer, Scripture reading, theology, and authority to an otherwise standardized curriculum. While secular schools surely attempt to do more than teach basic knowledge and skills, testing and standardization force these to the top priority. With broader interests and academic freedoms, religious schools tend to have concerns such as to inspire a "love of learning," to promote the "pursuit of wisdom," or to "nurture of the child with the love of God." Such phrases begin to illuminate the potential richness of a religious education.

A religiously based education seeks to nurture the child's mind, heart, and character in accord with a coherent view of truth, value, and morality. Religious schools bring together a community of parents and educators representing a mutually trusted view of life and the world and then attempt to envelop and suffuse the curriculum with meaning, purpose, and inspiration (Engelhardt, 2009). Whereas secular school educators must generally keep private their deepest inspirations, understandings, and concerns related to the child and the curriculum, the religious schoolteacher *understands these things to be a vital aspect of the curriculum*. With a context that more naturally encourages interpersonal trust, promotes deep reflection, and inspires internal motivation, the religious paradigm of education likely affects all educational outcomes.

Philosophic liberals are right to express concern regarding the "imposition" of one's beliefs upon another. It seems to offend the dignity of the individual. However, in the case of children, they are born "undignified" and dependent. Their parents carry a moral obligation and a loving desire to wisely nourish, protect, teach, and guide their children toward the point of adulthood. The whole of this process is guided by the parents framework of truth and value. Law protects the dignity of the parent-child relationship from governmental intrusion except in the case of clear abuse or neglect. Far from being abusive or neglectful, the family- and school-based nurture of beliefs and values takes place in a context of love, responsibility, and goodwill. Rather, the public's greater concern should be toward settings designated for childhood nurture that *fail* to operate according to the wisdom, knowledge, and experience of responsible parents.

Religious-school teachers are generally aware that children enter the classroom with a high degree of individuality. They are fully aware of the independence of their students and know that they will reject or hold lightly those values and beliefs that the child perceives as wrong, superficial, or irrelevant. Thus, recognizing that students enter the classroom as reasoning, uniquely gifted individuals who will ultimately choose their own life paths, effective teachers present the convictions of their community in a context of options, experiences, and reasons that they hope will be convincing to reasonable students. Rather than denying a student choice, religious schools provide the child with an opportunity for deep insight into the comprehensive nature of life in a manner that is unattainable in a common school setting. Indeed, various scholars argue that the development of a "primary culture" is essential to becoming an individual and as a foundation for growth toward autonomy (McLaughlin, 1984).

As to the vital place of reason in liberal democratic society, my argument for religious schooling does not question the fact that people are reasonable, but to the contrary, it argues that people *are* reasonable and that *the comprehensive views of religious schools provide superior grounds for reason*. However, my proposal goes further; it argues that reason alone is insufficient to support public moral and civic interests. Meaning and value are also sources of human motivation, and religious views ground them within the communities within which religious schools revolve.

Religious schools also aid in the formation of strong stable civic identities. Common school founders viewed the religious grounding of American ideals as essential to the stability of the nation, and they believed they were preserving it in the common school. Perhaps they were correct to see the degree to which our polity was indebted to Protestant faiths for many of its seminal ideas; however, they were wrong to believe that those of other faiths would be unaffected by their experience with democratic liberty and intellectually closed to a reevaluation of their faith and civic values in its light. To this end, religious schools provide academic settings in which the claims of faith and the claims of our polity come together with the knowledge, cares, and experiences of life. With the guidance of trusted authorities, students assemble these diverse bits of data into a broad, meaningful whole. Reflecting broad concerns for the child, religious schools are generally not as foreign or illiberal as some perceive them to be.

Too Much Power to Religion?

Some may fully agree that the teaching of public moral and civic values in religious school contexts will strengthen attachments to these concerns, but they may fear this strength. In particular, they may fear the power of *traditional* religion while they trust the ideological power of their own belief systems. Feinberg (2006), discussed in Chapter 6, seems to fall into this category and reflects many others who seem to believe that traditional religious thought must be limited by the state as a danger to society.

Those who fear the formative power of traditional religious schools often express their fear in publicly supportive rhetoric, but perhaps their efforts depart little from those who attempt to align government power with their own ideological perspectives. Their fears are presented in different ways: while Feinberg (2006) focuses on preserving liberal autonomy and liberal morality from the indoctrination of religious schools, others fear that the linking of God and country will invariably lead to nationalism (Nussbaum, 1996) or that religious schools will produce robotic followers. Though certainly traditional religious schools *can* trample on human individuality, promote nationalism, or incite violence, the thing to be feared is not religion in general but the actions of particular ideologies that can be addressed individually. Religious schools are valuable to society, thus, rather than fearfully opposing all religious schools, we should look to our nation's ideological foundations for insight into to how both our liberties and "real fears" can be addressed.

The ideas and structures of liberal democracy should alleviate fears associated with religious schooling. Ideologically, liberalism advocates for the reason-based trustworthiness of other citizens. Though citizens may prove themselves unreasonable, liberal society allows them virtually unlimited liberty to conceive and teach their ideologies; it acts only to limit their *actions*, and then only when those actions clearly oppose the public good or the rights of others. Liberal democracy is not only founded upon a confidence in the average person's capacity for self-governance, but it also provides structural limits to control the abusive use of power. Of particular relevance are the Constitution's First Amendment religion clauses. They provide peace for all by insuring that public power cannot be wielded to impose or suppress any worldview. Thus, ideals and structures are in place to insure that all individuals and communities (religious and otherwise) can live in liberty.

Rather than fearing the expansion of religious schooling, I have shown that it should be valued. Benjamin Barber writes, "Our attachments start parochially and only then grow outward" (1996). Similarly, Michael Walzer (1996) argues that outer social circles derive their meaning from our inner social circles. Thus, our nation's communities give birth to meaningful ideas, and their associated schools help to distribute these ideas into all areas of society. Michael McConnell (1996) argues that religion is one of the most powerful tools for combating selfishness and narrow national self-interest. Thus, religious schools bolster public safety, economic prosperity, and even our international service by more effectively teaching morality. And further, under a wisely designed plural public education system, public education would become a constitutionally recognized open forum. With the transfer of ideological power from the state to its citizens, I believe a philosophic reawakening would follow that would holistically enrich both public and private life. Rather than narrowly fearing religious schools and the citizens who operate them, religious schooling should be engaged as the public resources that they have long demonstrated themselves to be.

Apprehensions Toward Religious Schooling

Having argued for broader state recognition and funding of religious schooling, it is important to note that religious schools rightly fear this closer relationship with the state. Much as the education leaders mentioned above fear the influence of religious schools, religious school leaders fear the regulation of the state. However, this reciprocated distrust should come as no surprise; public school leaders have long viewed religious schools as civically dangerous, while religious school leaders have viewed the public system as hegemonic or, at best, ungrateful.

For over a century, supporters of common education have believed that secular education represented the best education for the state, if not also for children. Until recently, secular public education enjoyed the exclusive support of First Amendment interpretation and utilized the public's vast educational resources to shape the general moral, ideological, and academic perspectives of the nation with little concern for religious schools. On the other hand, religious schools supporters, who often viewed public education as a philosophic and financial monopoly, have believed that their faiths propose superior educational standards, curricula, ideals, methods, and settings for the good not only of their children but also of the public. Though a plural public education system could markedly amend the educational power of the state, if improperly structured, a plural public education system could severely undermine the valued educational missions of both the public and religious schools. Thus, even though the school choice movement already blurs the line between public and private schooling, both the state and religious schools are wise to approach a plural public education system with caution.

With this said, I believe both the state and religious school communities have much more to gain than they do to lose when considering plural public education. The major part of this book has defended the value of plural public education to the state, but there is an equal defense to be made regarding the value of plural public education to religious communities. Though, under the proposed new system, current religious schools would lose a small degree of their educational freedoms, they must look beyond protecting the status quo in which many have found a comfortable niche. Not that they must accept every dictate of the state, but they must see the value of their educational contributions to their broader religious communities and the nation, *and they must be willing to work to defend the freedoms that undergird their private interests and their public contributions.*

Whereas surely a plural public education system would create some new obligations for religious schools, it would alleviate *many* funding concerns, which would allow them to dedicate more time to their educational missions. In a nation that is overwhelmingly religious, only about 12% of children have the opportunity to receive religious educations. Not only would a plural public education system enable existing religious schools to redirect their attention from fundraising to improving their programs, it would also allow every child the opportunity to receive a religious education regardless of their financial standings. Additionally, faith communities whose holistic dimensions have been narrowed under the incremental influence of secular education at all levels will be enabled to recapture the field of education and thus expand the ideological thinking of their communities. Under a plural public education paradigm, the day may soon come in which academics in all fields approach their subject matter holistically from within their faiths and contemplate its implications both for the faithful and democratic society. In turn, religious schools might not merely have administrators and teachers who bring a secular view of education to their jobs, but these schools might have leadership that has reconceived the educational realm from the perspectives of their faiths.

Though a further book must be written to convince some religious communities of the value of a plural public education system, I have briefly included these religious school fears to help educators steeped in secular education philosophy to see that they are not the only ones for whom plural public education poses risks. Religious school leaders face engaging a state bureaucracy that has shown little understanding or concern for their particular contributions, but for the good of their communities and the public, I hope religious families and communities will embrace plural public education.

Reviewing Education Models

America's educational needs are perhaps greater now than at any time in history. And these needs are not merely academic, but they relate more holistically to human identities, commitments, and foundations for reason. As Salomone writes, "The Supreme Court has repeatedly instructed the American public that the ultimate objective of publicly supported primary and secondary education is to prepare the young for democratic citizenship" (2000, p. 197). This book has sought to provide a compelling solution to this centuries-old American educational problem that has reached a level of critical concern. The development of moral and civic values compatible with liberty and supportive of our liberal democratic government is still the central mission bestowed on public education. However, as Glenn notes, our current system is intrinsically ill-equipped to fulfill its mission: "We may have set ourselves an impossible task in seeking to provide a single model of education that is to be at once capable of nurturing character and civic virtue and yet inoffensive to the convictions of any parent" (1988, p. 285).

This potential impossibility has forced common education to balance these concerns with the result that it remains weak in its nurture and offensive to many. Regarding nurture, either education leaders have ideologically supported this weakness in favor of a concern for liberal autonomy, or they have presumed that secular curricula would suffice to meet the public's moral and civic needs. I have argued that this weakness represents a failure of public education to serve the interests of the public.

Not only have the competing concerns of common education led to this weakness, but they have led to significant offense. It appears that most families have little conflict with "good" public schools. However, a significant number are dissatisfied, and their dissatisfaction reflects a strong religious component. Nearly 9% of U.S. children attend private schools, over 80% of which attend religious schools. Additionally, parents are removing their children from public schools at an increasing rate to school them at home where most receive religious educations (Stevens, 2001). About 1.7% of school-age children were homeschooled in 1999; by 2003, this number increased to 2.2%, and by 2010, it stood at 3.8% (Ray, 2011). To these numbers, one must add an unknown number of families who believe secular education is inadequate but who cannot attend private schools for financial or other reasons.

Thus, the "secular ideal" is currently offensive at least to 12% of school-age children, and this number is likely to grow. Modern scholars believe that religion would fade with growing scientific awareness and discovery; however, Francis Huntington, affirms that the secularization trend has reversed. The world is not only becoming more religious, but we are in the midst of a global religious revival (Berger, 1999; Huntington, 1996). Speaking of this sociological reality, Thiessen writes, "Particular identities seem to be growing in importance in our day. And we somehow need to learn to live with the importance of particular identities" (2007, p. 38). And, as discussed in Chapter 7, secular common schools do not adequately prepare citizens to understand the ideological roots and solutions to the problems of the world in which they live. Treating religion as educationally irrelevant has proven to be counterproductive.

For nearly two centuries, the pervading opinion among American civil and education leaders has been that the inclusion of religious schools of a variety of perspectives within a system of public funding was *not* in the best interest of society. But concurrently, secular public education has continued to fall short of its commitments to the public. I have argued that the common education model has maintained a preeminent status, not by its proven merits, but by a combination of presumptive claims, fears, deep secular beliefs, traditions, and legal entrenchments. A more even evaluation of claims, fears, and benefits places religious schooling in a more favorable light.

As the public increasingly comes to understand that public common schools cannot deliver the best education for all children, public education, as described by Cooper and colleagues (2012), is seeking a "golden mean." This golden mean diverts from polar conceptions of "public" and "private" schools and blends them to offer children a diverse array of schooling options that satisfy the educational concerns of the state and families. As an example, Cooper and colleagues propose the possibility of educational settings composed of public school teachers who travel to various local religious schools. The schools' "private" teachers teach doctrine, pray, and lead worship, while their "public" teachers teach "required secular subjects in English, mathematics, social studies, and science" (2012, p. 375).

Though Cooper and colleagues (2012) also support vouchers for publicly regulated self-contained schools, their latter concept illuminates the fundamental divergence point of this book. Due to the religious nature of both education and the public's educational interests, I maintain that there are no intrinsically "secular subjects!" *Every* subject is taught best when taught from a religious/philosophic perspective. Thus, although I fully support the availability of the option above for those whose faith find it acceptable, the public's educational interests push the paradigm further. As long as the public's investments in education (research, teacher training, curriculum selection, assessment, and teaching) remain narrowly captured within a secular paradigm, then the public's educational ventures will forever fall short of desired ends.

Pushing the concept of a "golden mean" beyond that in which the public remains aligned only with a secular educational perspective, a plural public education system would allow greater numbers of children to attend religious schools that not only holistically complement the identity and intellectual concerns of their families but are lightly regulated to align with the public's educational interests. Schools within this system would have greater freedom to discuss issues of public concern in contexts of deep meaning, build the social capital associated with ideological communities,

deeply inspire children to curricular achievement, and invigorate meaningful philosophic discussions. This system would allow those who dissent
from secular education perspectives to change schools without leaving the
umbrella of public education.

Finally, a plural system of public education would welcome schools that
broadly support the tenets of our liberal democracy from diverse perspectives. Whereas common education was initially built upon a general suspicion of the self-governing capacity of certain minority groups, and later
upon a presumptive confidence in "secular" rather than "religious" educational tenets and methods, plural public education expresses greater liberal
confidence in its citizenry to wisely educate their children. It reflects the
beliefs that a plurality of faiths can embrace the tenets of liberal democracy,
that a plurality of religious schools can support our national unity, and that
the state should not narrowly preference or oppose any ideological perspective that lays claim to educational ground.

Designing a Plural Public Education System

Several key philosophic and legal ideals shape our current common education system. Philosophically, common education generally aligns with
these beliefs:

- The public should support education to insure that all children
  have an opportunity to succeed according to their ability.
- The public has a particular interest to nurture the basic moral,
  civic, and academic understanding associated with good American citizenship.
- The contents of a good public education should be determined
  primarily by education professionals and elected representatives.
- The divisive influences of philosophic diversity are stronger than
  the unifying influences of our shared American ideals.
- Human nature, intuition, and other youthful capacities (after
  instruction in the art of reason) are adequate foundations for
  public morality and character.
- Religion is a private matter that offers little to a good education
  and less to public health.
- Public money should not support the religious program of private schools.

A plural public education system would share the first two ideals, but it
would reformulate the latter five. As to curricular content, under a plural
public education system, education professionals and elected representa-

tives would identify a general set of public interests, but the system would recognize that many diverse, privately chosen curricula could contain these interests. As to philosophic diversity, a plural public education system within our liberal democracy would reflect the belief that our shared American ideals provide a unifying influence stronger than the divisive influences of most of our diverse perspectives. As to human foundations, a plural public education system would reflect the belief that children and young people are generally nurtured toward fuller and more productive lives when they are holistically educated within settings that reflect the beliefs and values of their home. Lastly, regarding the relationship between public money and religious schools, a plural public education system would reflect the belief that both public and private life are indebted to religious beliefs for their moral, motivational, and ideological frameworks, thus, public money must enable willing families to attend publicly supportive religious schools. To facilitate this end, though the *Zelman* decision (2002) made provision for an indirectly funded plural public education system, in many states, Blaine Amendments must yet be circumvented. Taken together, the implications of these ideals shape the plural public education structures to reasonably accommodate the limited concerns of the state and the broader concerns of parents.

What structure should a healthy plural public education system take? A first response of the public education community might be to establish multiple layers of bureaucracy with some representative boards to regulate the "private" religious schools coming under the new public education umbrella. Though claims of "fairness" and "tradition" bolster this possibility, neither claim is necessarily relevant to our public education goals. Our goals are to insure that children have access to quality publicly supportive education, and we must admit that neither the fairness nor the bureaucratic efforts of our standardized common education system have proven to be of any greater success than that achieved by private schools. Just as I challenge public education with a pivotal philosophic shift, I challenge it to a vital structural shift.

If the wellsprings of meaningful philosophic perspectives are to re-source our educational efforts, trust in broad secular public controls must be replaced by broad trust of parents and educators to discern and implement the curricula, philosophies, and methodologies they deem best for their children. Though this radically alters the role of the state in education, it is not unreasonable. The First Amendment severely limits the liberal state from taking a position on foundational truths, thus it cannot continue in a heavy bureaucratic role, nor can representative bodies accommodate the individualized concerns associated with family beliefs. Further, parental discernment expressed through educational choice has maintained a high level of validated educational quality in both home and classroom settings. Even when parents are not trained as education professionals, they appear willing and capable of insuring that America's children receive a good education. Thus, in proportion to the choices made by parents, the structure of a plural public education system should reflect government-run common schools, privately operated public charter schools, and privately operated "joint venture" religious public schools.

With parental choice operating upon a liberal trust in the mature and loving discernment of parents toward the good of their children and society established as the primary source of regulation, the public must still have policies and procedures to insure that public money is not misappropriated or used in schools *clearly* opposed to our democratic society. Thus, a plural public education system should be structured to facilitate parental choice while patrolling the extremes for abuse or neglect of their public trust, such as by opposing basic democratic values or, as Putnam (2000) reminds us, producing out-group antagonism or forming social capital bent on evil.

This book is primarily a philosophic treatise on the nature of a good public education. However, this philosophy implies action, and this action to shape a new education reality faces obstacles from the start. I am fully aware that like oil and water, many proponents of both public secular and private religious schools resist "tainting" themselves with the other. If religious education is valuable to the public, then our society in which the public *funds* education, yet can directly *deliver* only a secular education, *must* see public and private concerns and efforts come closer together. I wrote the major part of this book to convince public educators of the value of religious schooling; here, I speak to private religious school proponents to convince them of the value of identifying with public educational interests and standing with diverse other schools under the public education umbrella. I do not propose this as a submission to current secular paradigms of control, education philosophy, or conceptions of the public good. Rather, I propose a greater identification with the "public" in the spirit of bringing diverse religious perspectives into discussions of education and societal good—discussions that have long been dominated by perspectives only from within the secular ideal.

My challenge to religious education leaders is not to submit to the entrenched secular education rubric, but to redefine a new one along "plural" lines. Without this redefinition, the secular ideal will continue to utilize the power and resources of government to shape American education (and thus the nation) apart from overt religious concepts and ideals. I hope the arguments of this book make it clear that I believe virtually every private religious school *already* supports the public's educational interests by nurturing children with the knowledge, skills, understanding, and character needed for a healthy, productive, and involved life in our democratic society. Those resisting the school choice movement frequently (and pejoratively) proclaim that private schools merely serve private interests while only the public schools serve public interests. This vague generalization seems to give the moral "high ground" to secular public schools, and it must be thoroughly rejected by education leaders through the redefinition of several words and concepts. I argue that both private and current "public" schools serve the public's educational interests. Thus, under a plural public education system, the current (though waning) concept of public education as "publically *controlled* schools" must be replaced with the concept of "publicly *supportive* schools that (directly or indirectly) receive public funds." Thus, the receipt of public funds *must not* imply absolute submission to public control, but rather the commitment to teach with philosophic reflection from within one's faith perspective toward the good of our shared society. All schools under the plural public education umbrella should be considered (by themselves and others) to be "public schools."

There are many reasons private religious schools may balk at assuming, at least in part, this public identity. They may associate "public" with secular, state control, and the loss of religious identity and mission. But I argue that to the degree they distance themselves from the word "public," they continue down the path of marginalization by allowing secular educational concepts to be aligned with public interests—*they allow the secular ideal to continue to dominate public educational efforts.* As this book claims, healthy society relies on religiously held ideals, thus, religious school leaders and supporters must speak to public educational interests as "insiders" rather than merely "fringe interests." Some suggest that religious schools could more safely call themselves "publically supportive" schools without being considered "public schools," but I believe this is like taking a backseat in an auditorium: one can claim to be present while attending more freely to one's own business, but at the expense of leaving the discussion to those close to the microphone. A true plural public education system *must not* favor secular perspectives over religious ones, but this reconceptualization of public education will take place only if religious school leaders enter the public education arena and assert the unique "goods" that they offer society.

I align with the school choice movement, but I believe much of its current vision falls short. It supports a *type* of plural public education, but it does not yet articulate a vision of plural *public* education. All public "choice" schools are secular, while the relatively few religious schools within school choice systems are considered "private." This surely implies a realm of freedom: the freedom of families to attend religious schools with public money and the freedom of those schools to avoid some government scrutiny, but it is a limited freedom. As long as "public" schools must be secular, all government efforts (through research, higher education training, regulation, etc.) need only align with the secular ideal while providing parents an opt-out choice of a "private" religious school. If government's educational efforts were minimal, this might pose little concern, but they are not; they influentially shape society (and religious schools) toward secular perspectives. I am after bigger game than merely securing "choice" for families; as a citizen and a religious school proponent, I aim to capture the field of education from the governmentally supported hegemony of secularism. While rejecting the identity of "public" seems to protect religious schools from public encroachment, I claim that it merely erects a "golden cage" that provides safety but accepts the belief that religious thought merely belongs within private circles. I reject this semantic cage. I encourage parents and religious school leaders to not just fight for their own school of choice, but for the good of our nation. And I believe that requires identification with a plural *public* education system.

Fear of state power is justified, but staying removed from this power merely entrusts it to others perhaps less wise or trustworthy. America's religious school community can learn how to associate with power from the victories and failures of sister schools in other nations. Glenn (2000) gives valuable advice toward this end and encourages schools to firmly grasp their "non-negotiables" and protect them. Perhaps the strongest advice I have for religious schools willing to more closely engage public power is to recognize and build upon their strengths. Australia offers an encouraging story from 1962 (Engelhardt, 2012), and as with many landmark events, the precipitating issue was dwarfed by the issues at stake. At that time, local health authorities imposed the requirement that Our Lady of Mercy Preparatory School, a Catholic school in Goulburn, New South Wales, add additional bathrooms. Lacking money for the addition and frustrated by governmental interference into the financial priorities of the school, the bishop decided to close the school until the government funded its mandate.

The state refused, but this drew other Goulburn Catholics who also suffered from what they perceived as a long-standing injustice associated with the allocation of public education money that neglected their schools. In solidarity, they joined in protest by closing their schools. As a result, the public schools were inundated with new students and had room to enroll only about half of them. National media covered the situation from a perspective critical of the Catholic position. After a week, and without state concessions, concern for their children moved parents to vote to reopen their schools. Though further public funding did not immediately follow, this event brought the education justice issues to the public's attention, highlighted the public service Catholics schools provided, and planted seeds of civic involvement that led to the founding of the Australian Parents Council, an influential organization representing parents of private school students. From these beginnings, recognition of both the private and the public value of Catholic schools have grown and is reflected by greater public funding and areas of educational freedom.

So how do these reflections inform the design of a plural public education system? First, public education must be redefined and built upon a greater trust of citizens to discern the qualities of a good public education; they must be the primary regulators of the schools they choose to attend. Second, to bring the strengths of religious education into the public sphere, religious schools should fully identify with public education efforts to nurture the good of society. Gutmann (1999) argued that democratic principles should shape our schools, but her ideas distance education from parents and ideals. A strong plural public education system will restore educational authority to the ideological seedbeds of families and communities.

Regulation

As noted, parents will function as the primary regulators of the schools their children attend through both the pressure of their choices and school involvement, but the state will still need to regulate the extremes of acceptability. Here, I deepen my argument for minimal regulation.

Numerous regulatory conceptions have been proposed to protect the public's educaitonal interests. Viteritti, for example, maintains that the appropriate regulation of religious schools would merely uphold a concern for academic standards similar to those of the public schools and the assurance that funded schools do not undermine the "fundamental principles of American democracy" (2007, p. 234). James Dwyer, on the other hand, sees the public funding of religious schools as an opportunity to take control of religious schools for the sake of the autonomy rights of children (1998, p. 181). Still others may accommodate public funding proposals as a means of broadening the arm of the state into religious schools to insure the discharge of other narrow concerns.

Though the spectrum of regulatory philosophies is broad, public regulation has the power to destroy religious schools (Glenn, 2000). Thus, the public must choose the regulatory philosophy surrounding a plural public education system with utmost care. I argue that burdensome or philosophically narrow regulation opposes the public's education goals, invites legal challenge, and opposes the principals of liberal democracy. First (and centrally), narrow philosophic regulation will destroy the religious qualities that make plural public education valuable to the public. The thesis of this book argues toward the public value of religious schools, *but this value is in proportion to the vitality of the faith and community within each school.* The more narrowly one defines the public's interests, the more it will force religious schools to conform to the image of common schools with a corresponding loss of religious identity—a danger that often affects religious schools that become dependent upon secular governments (Glenn, 2011).

The research of both Putnam (2000; Putnam & Feldstein, 2003) and Stark (2004) support this conclusion that the control of faith leads to its decline. Religious schools are highly valued and influential in the lives of their attending families because they align with their conscientiously held views. To the degree that religious schools are perceived to compromise their views, they lose their position of familial and community trust and thus, their deep influence. Viteritti's (1999) "minimal" regulations appropriately serve to maximize the public's gain. For example, if state regulations narrowly act against religious concerns, such as requiring the equal hiring/admission of employees/students apart from the faith concerns of schools, the joint venture system will be undermined with a zero net gain for the state. Either broad sectors of religious schools will fail to participate in the joint venture plan, or if they participate through a compromise of their faiths, their strongly believing families will leave to attend healthy religious schools outside the joint venture system. This latter result would leave the public with a school that was religious in name only. Hence, the state must regulate religious schools minimally if these schools are to remain the vitally nurturing sources that I have described them to be. Thus, if my arguments regarding the public value of religious schooling move the state toward a plural public education system, they must also move the state to regulate with a minimum of intrusion and offense. In short, public education leaders should not "kill the goose that lays the golden eggs."

Not only are burdensome and narrow regulations destructive to the religious health of schools, but also they invite court challenge. Court rulings tend to give religious schools broad protection regarding their religious missions. For example, the Ohio Supreme Court ruled in *Ohio v. Whisner* (1976) that the state could not require such detailed accreditation standards of private religious schools to interfere with their mission. With a similar concern that the state not interfere with the missions of religious schools, Supreme Court Justice Souter wrote in his dissent in *Zelman* that vouchers might pose a

> risk of "corrosive secularism" to religious schools, and the specific threat is to the primacy of the schools' mission to educate the children of the faithful according to the unaltered precepts of their faith. Even "the favored religion may be compromised as political figures reshape the religion's beliefs for their own purposes; it may be reformed as government largesse brings government regulation." (*Zelman v. Simmons-Harris*, 2002, p. 712)

Though *Zelman* affirmed the legality of vouchers, the regulatory warning is well taken. Following the religion clauses of the First Amendment, the courts understand that a concern for the protection of conscience creates an obligation for the state to regulate religious schools minimally.

Finally, liberal democratic philosophy speaks to the issue of school regulation. It favors "treating adults as self-governing persons entitled to choose and pursue their own conceptions of the good life" (Gilles, 1996, p. 946), and the educational expression of this high regard for individual adults allows communities broad discretion regarding the formation of meaningful schools. Thus, from a liberal democratic viewpoint, regulation that polices the extremes is more suitable than regulation that narrowly attempts to control religious school programs.

Since the historic trajectory of public endeavors is toward increasing regulation, plural public education systems must begin with a binding commitment toward minimal regulation. Though freedoms are often abused, the public must not reflexively respond to every abuse as a need for tighter controls. "Parent regulators" can inflict their own consequences by leaving the schools they disapprove of or reshaping it from within. Light regulation will prove to support the public's education interests by supporting a healthy religious school sector, avoiding legal challenges, and modeling liberal democratic trust.

Funding

How might joint-venture schools be funded? Without attempting to explore the details, I suggest that joint-venture schools be funded through a voucher system. The amount of these vouchers should be set equivalent to the per-pupil spending level of local public secular schools in accordance with the needs of the individual student. In other words, evaluative teams would designate students in need of special education services to receive a higher voucher amount than a student without special needs. Since religious schools would likely include religion classes, some might argue that this should reduce voucher amounts below secular-school levels. Their arguments might be grounded in either church-state concerns or merely in a pragmatic concern that the state should pay only for what it deems necessary. However, neither of these arguments gains traction in a plural public education system. Joint-venture schools are not merely acceptable *alternatives* to public schools, they *are* public schools. The extracurricular components of the religious schools are the "value added" components that the public intends to benefit from through its move to a plural public education system.

Thus, the opportunity for the public to promote civic concerns through the inclusion of democratically supportive religious schools may progress in a relatively straightforward manner. Though, under a plural public education system, parents will carry out many of the responsibilities previously delegated to the state, many state education leaders will remain to oversee state-run common schools and to provide broad oversight of other educational concerns, thus, these leaders must be chosen carefully. While emerging from a century in which the secular education ideal has reigned with little challenge, leaders must specifically value the distinctive educational opportunities religious schools provide for the public. This latter concern is key. It provides the motivation to persevere through the difficulties of transition, to protect religious schools from public secular encroachments, and to preserve religious education as a vital source of civic nurture.

Dealing With Opposition

It is apparent that the transition from a common to a plural public education system might be difficult if a large percentage of families desire to shift common schools to religious schools. In Australia, it is found that people increasingly move from secular public schools to religious schools to the degree that public money is made available to do so (Engelhardt, 2012). I predict the response of America's families would be similar due to the vitality of American religious communities. My key concern is not the difficulty of transition (for I believe it is driven by public necessity) but *public response* to the difficulties. As the public attempts to downsize the schools it operates while providing funding for students to attend religious schools, there will be inefficiencies and budgetary problems that many will leverage against a forward trajectory.

Since few within our secular culture currently seem to understand the particular value of religious schooling, many will erringly claim (as in the case of charter schools) that "true" public schools are being hurt for the sake of "private" religious schools. The temptation will be to limit the expansion of religious schools. While limiting the *rate* of transition may prove necessary to insure education quality in all areas, the ultimate point of equilibrium between the number of government-run common schools and the number of religious schools must remain a function of parental choice. Here, "choice" as a "right" is not the guiding value, but the educationally relevant concerns that parents become more engaged in the education of their children and that education become more ideologically engaging. "Choice" to enroll their children in schools that align with their ideological commitments ignites this academic engagement, and choice of religious schools provides public education with this ideological dimension. Thus, whereas latent concerns might continue to preference secular public education, a plural public education ideal should be given every opportunity to flourish.

Self-Interest Groups

In previous chapters, I addressed the primary philosophic concerns of scholars the who stand in the way of the implementation of a plural system of public education. Perhaps the future of my proposal would meet less resistance if public education's controlling interests battled primarily in ideological territory, but they do not. Arguably, over half of the "conservative" force opposing the changes I propose reflect not the best interest of either the public or children but the market players who have gained secure footholds within the current system of public education and draw their livelihoods from it.

The most notable of these players are found in teachers' unions, education colleges, and the public education bureaucracy. Though public school principals and teachers are currently in this group, I believe many will gladly exchange the bureaucracy, impersonality, and union benefits of the common education system for the greater freedoms, community, and meaningful student engagement expected under a plural public education system. At the local level, public school teachers and administrators are frequently frustrated by the lack of decision-making power that they are given, yet they take the brunt of the blame for poor educational outcomes. In an attempt to improve teacher performance, many education leaders are focusing on merit pay, and though the idea is not all bad, few teachers entered the profession to merely "make money." They entered, by and large, out of a concern to pour their lives into the next generation. Though a larger paycheck provides some incentive, it is likely that most teachers would feel greater personal reward with being given a greater degree of trust, which translates into freedom in the classroom. Currently, the church-state barriers inherent in our common school setting prevent teachers from truly giving their "best"—the "best" that inspires *them* and undergirds *their* efforts and curriculum with meaning—to their students. Within the model I propose, teachers and administrators would be free to seek employment within joint-venture schools where they would have greater freedom to help children grow and learn holistically in environments conducive to community relationships.

However, the benefits of a plural public education system may be lost on self-interested opponents. To them, maintaining the status quo of public education often merely implies job security, continued professional accomplishment, and ideological power. Surely core opponents share some concern for children and the public, but they often face pressures to support common education for personal rather than public interests.

The most obvious conflict is apparent in the case of teachers unions. Their most basic commitments are toward the educators they are committed to supporting, not necessarily to the public or to children. Their positive vision, mission, values, and *salaries* are predicated upon the survival and growth of their unions. Plural public education moves away from unionization and directly undermines the ideological and financial power base of the organizations. Though unionization may find a place within a plural system of public education, America's private religious schools are not unionized, and for reasons of community, they may never become unionized. Thus, although most school personnel will likely support the transition to a plural system, unions, secular colleges, and an entrenched bureaucracy will likely oppose change. I do not offer a particular solution to this opposition, but add my warning to proponents of educational change to wisely prepare for this expected resistance.

Centuries of Failed Analysis

As a review of key points of this book, I present what I believe are the key questions and issues America's education leadership has either failed to comprehend or failed to address adequately.

America's *19th* century leaders failed to adequately address these questions:

- If a national church was deemed unnecessary or even counter to the concerns of religious rights and public unity, would not a common public school system either tread upon the same religious liberties or prove to be so ideologically shallow as to be

incapable of reproducing the moral and civic qualities deemed
necessary for American liberty?

- Was ideologically based diversity as great a threat to public unity
  as presupposed?
- Would/could Catholics think for themselves and become good
  American citizens? Or more broadly, is human nature reasonable
  enough to challenge and even modify traditional religious beliefs
  according to new experience and understanding?
- To what degree are a state's educational interests indebted to
  religious educational settings to communicate meaningfully and
  inspire commitment?
- Which educational paradigm best allows the liberal state to
  conscientiously fulfill its education mission: private, common,
  or plural?

Education leaders of the 19th century answered these questions wrongly or inadequately. As a result, they failed to trust minority families and
implemented a quasi-Protestant system of common education. However,
the guilt of 19th-century education leaders *can be excused* due to their lack
of experience (or rather their negative experience) with extreme cultural
diversity. They were treading upon new ground in which both the resil-
ience of the American experiment and the adaptive capacity of religious
"others" were unknown. Both historical conflicts associated with the "wars
of religion" and the writings of John Locke (1824), the "philosopher of
the American Revolution," predisposed education leaders (and the general
Protestant public) to reasonably distrust the civic influence of Catholicism.
Additionally, in spite of the American ideal of human equality, many ethnic and religious minorities reflected cultural extremes that cast doubt not
only upon their civic capacities but also upon their very humanity. These
were days of slavery and "Indian" wars. At the expense of some degree of
religious liberty, all these observations seemed to support a benevolent yet
singularly authoritative public education system reflective of the Protestant
beliefs and values considered vital to liberty and public order.

Education leaders of the *20th* century faced similar questions with the
addition of the following:

- To what degree is human nature innately good vs. willful?
- To what degree is positive civic behavior indebted to youthful
  training, authoritative teaching, religious commitments, religious
  reasoning, and exercises in moral reasoning?
- In a diverse society, is it possible for *any* concept of common education to be both a meaningful preparation for life and nonreligious?

- Can concepts of truth and value that have vast social implications reasonably be separated from the school day in which social studies, art, language, economics, and such are taught to prepare children for meaningful personal and social life?
- To what degree is the public good indebted to the religious beliefs and values of its citizens?

Education leaders of the 20th century also answered these questions wrongly or inadequately. Similarly, their guilt *can be excused*; in this case, due to their lack of experience with secular ideology. At a time when long-held Protestant beliefs were being challenged by scientific discovery, public schools were growing in importance, religious diversity was increasing, and court rulings were mandating that public schools not align with any religion; education leaders were forced toward the secular educational ideal. Since rational and scientific methods appeared to provide successful and uncontroversial foundations for academic and technological development, could not these same foundations support the public's educational goals while replacing the controversial religious attachments still found in public schools?

Though the pressures and presumptions of the 19th and 20th centuries seemed to support common/secular public education as the best means to accomplish the public's educational goals, I have argued that this decision was wrong. Rather than proving the public necessity of common education or the vitality of secular education, public education leaders inadvertently demonstrated the religious nature of the public's education interests by educating consecutive generations of children largely apart from the influence of traditional religion. Whereas previous generations may claim ignorance regarding the dynamics of cultural diversity and the shortcomings of secular education philosophy, *we of the 21st century are without excuse.*

The answers of history seem to be clear:

- The concerns of public education are dependent upon deep ideological soil for their nourishment, empowerment, and stability. In spite of the public's best secularized efforts, public schools have not fulfilled their commitment to adequately nurture the morality, civic attachments, academic prowess, or intellectual understanding of past or present generations.
- The fears used to justify common education were exaggerated. Catholics became good American citizens *outside* the public schools long before they were accepted by the popular culture. It seems reasonable that members of all faiths that have not set

themselves in opposition to general American ideals can be expected to engage the issues of American liberty, democracy, and unity from within their faiths in a manner that might provide constructive insight for public discussion even as this engagement shapes their faith tradition from within.

- Though human nature has a strong rational component, that rationality must draw from some framework of truth and value. Superficial frameworks tend to lack sufficient depth of meaning to overcome the irrationality of human willfulness.

- Though the public can articulate diverse educational programs and ideals, unless these ideals take root in the life-shaping beliefs of the people, the public's efforts will be hindered by a lack of meaning and motivation. Worse, those who perceive the state to be an ideological opponent that unjustly supports secularism may oppose the state and/or its ideals.

- The moral and ideological dimensions of the education day are too vast to be severed from religious frameworks of truth and value. Unless we first begin with a secular definition of education, a "good education" encompasses concerns beyond the "common."

Final Conclusion: Revisiting Claims and Presumptions

It seems that human limitations may destine every generation to be acutely perceptive of some concerns and blind to others. The 19th century clearly saw that morality and citizenship are religious in nature, but it was blind to the degree to which the claims and appeals of democratic liberty could find support within diverse faiths. Modernity clearly saw that secular academic methodology provided a stable source of discovery, but it was blind to the degree to which the vast realms of value, philosophic understanding, and motivation, though vital to public life, were only weakly accessible to its presumptions and secular methodologies. Lastly, from the late 20th century to the present, the American public has clearly seen that a concern for conscience demands that the liberal state be unaligned with any comprehensive view, but is only beginning to see the degree to which healthy democracies rely upon supportive religious communities and their schools to nurture the qualities of good citizenship.

The problem of finding an educational source to nurture strong moral and civic development that is both *nonoffensive* and *effective* is central to the health of the nation. Though our present secular education system is the result of this enduring pursuit, most Americans would likely agree that it is more nonoffensive than it is effective. In spite of the integrity, skill, and effort of its teachers, our education system fails to address some of the public's educational concerns while addressing others only inadequately.

For nearly a century-and-a-half, numerous rationales and legal forces have mutually supported of *secular-only* public education. However, the 2003 *Zelman* decision brought division to this unified front. As the "secular-only" paradigm of public education continues to lose legal preeminence, researchers are obligated to investigate both the qualities of a religious education and the claim that the secular paradigm of public education best serves the "public interests."

I have argued that the public must grow to view religion as a resource of civic value rather than of fear. Religion is a motivator, a source of personal and public meaning, and a framework for knowledge, value, and reason. Religion has not diminished with scientific discovery. To overlook it is to neglect a historic source of moral and civic nurture; to oppose it as publicly destructive is to encourage its opposition; but to engage it respectfully opens the possibility of winning its strong support. The educational interests of the public are best served not by common education alone but by a public educational system in which parents choose the best schools for their children according to their view of the good.

Does this book imply that the implementation of a plural model of public education will remedy all education problems? Or does it imply that every citizen will fully accept the religious base of every school or that the public will readily agree upon the minimal acceptable curricular and policy standards of joint venture schools? No. But it does argue that a religious educational paradigm provides for richer, more coherent, more inspirational, and more personal education for the good of individuals and the public.

Whereas early common school proponents chose to endorse a nonsectarian Protestant system of beliefs as the unifying and effective ground of moral and civic nurture, the 21st century must actively engage a plurality of faiths toward the support of our liberal democratic society. There are areas in which public schools can engage religion by promoting religious discussions and reflections, but a joint venture with the private school sector promises the greatest opportunity for the public to benefit from the meaning, understanding, motivation, and order that religions provide. I have confronted the "secular ideal," and it has failed to provide a sufficient ground for the public's educational interests. It is time for a plural public education reform.

References

Abington Township v. Schempp, 364 U.S. 298 (1963).

Adams, C. F. (Ed.). (1854). *The works of John Adams, second president of the United States* (Vol. 9). Boston, MA: Little Brown.

Adler, J. (2004). Reconciling open-mindedness and belief. *Theory and Research in Education, 2*(2), 127–142.

Allman, D. D., & Beaty, M. D. (Eds.). (2002). *Cultivating citizens: Soulcraft and citizenship in contemporary America.* Lanham, MD: Lexington.

Anthony, M. J., & Benson, W. S. (2003). *Exploring the history and philosophy of Christian education: Principles for the 21st century.* Grand Rapids, MI: Kregel.

Arons, S. (1983). *Compelling belief: The culture of American schooling.* New York, NY: McGraw-Hill.

Arons, S. (1997). *Short route to chaos: Conscience, community, and the re-constitution of American schooling.* Amherst: University of Massachusetts Press.

Arthur, J. (2003). *Education with character: The moral economy of schooling.* New York, NY: Routledge Falmer.

Audi, R. (1993). The place of religious argument in a free and democratic society. *San Diego Law Review, 30,* 677–702.

Audi, R. (1997). *Moral knowledge and ethical character.* New York, NY: Oxford University Press.

Audi, R. (2000). *Religious commitment and secular reason.* Cambridge, UK; New York, NY: Cambridge University Press.

Audi, R. (2001). *The architecture of reason: The structure and substance of rationality.* Oxford, UK; New York, NY: Oxford University Press.

Audi, R., & Wolterstorff, N. (1997). *Religion in the public square: The place of religious convictions in political debate.* Lanham, MD: Rowman & Littlefield.

Education Reform, pages 209–222
Copyright © 2013 by Information Age Publishing
All rights of reproduction in any form reserved.

Bailey, C. (1984). *Beyond the present and the particular: A theory of liberal education.* London, UK: Routledge & Kegan Paul.

Barber, B. R. (1996). Constitutional faith. In J. Cohen (Ed.), *For love of country: Debating the limits of patriotism.* Boston, MA: Beacon.

Barber, B. R. (1997). Public schooling: Education for democracy. In J. I. Goodlad & T. J. McMannon (Eds.), *The public purpose of education and schooling* (pp. 21–32). San Francisco, CA: Jossey-Bass.

Barber, B. R. (2003). *Strong democracy: Participatory politics for a new age.* Berkeley: University of California Press.

Barnard, H. (Ed.). (1846). Ninth annual report of the secretary of the board. *Journal of the Rhode Island Institute of Instruction, 1.*

Barton, P. E., & Coley, R. J. (2010). *The Black-White achievement gap: When progress stopped* (Policy Information Report) (p. 42). Princeton, NJ: Educational Testing Services.

Beem, C. (1999). *The necessity of politics. Reclaiming American public life.* Chicago, IL: University of Chicago Press.

Bell, B. I. (1952). *Crowd culture: An examination of the American way of life.* New York, NY: Harper.

Bellah, R. N. (1985). *Habits of the heart: Individualism and commitment in American life.* Berkeley: University of California Press.

Bennett, W. J., & Nunn, S. (1998). A nation of spectators: How civil disengagement weakens America and what we can do about it: Final report. *The National Commission on Civic Renewal.* Retrieved from http://www.puaf. umd.edu/civicrenewal

Benson, P. L. et al. (1984). Study assesses quality of Catholic high schools. *Momentum, 15*(3), 4–9.

Berger, P. L. (1992). *A far glory: The quest for faith in an age of credulity.* New York, NY: Free Press; Toronto; Maxwell Macmillan Canada, Maxwell Macmillan International.

Berger, P. L. (1999). *The desecularization of the world: Resurgent religion and world politics.* Washington, DC: W.B. Eerdmans.

Berkowitz, P. (2003). *Never a matter of indifference: Sustaining virtue in a free republic.* Stanford, CA: Hoover Institution.

Bishaw, A. (2012). *Poverty: 2010 and 2011* (No. ACSBR/11-01) (p. 8). Washington, DC: Department of Commerce.

Boom, C. T. (1971). *The hiding place.* Toronto, Canada: New York, NY: Bantam.

Brandon, A. L. (2006). *Is competition a rising tide that lifts all boats? The effect of school competition on those that are left behind* (Dissertation).

Brighouse, H. (1998). Civic education and liberal legitimacy. *Ethics, 108*(4), 719–745.

Brighouse, H. (2004a). Funding religious schools. *Philosophy of Education Yearbook,* 72–75.

Brighouse, H. (2004b). What's wrong with privatising schools? *Journal of Philosophy of Education, 38*(4), 617–631.

Brighouse, H. (2006). Educational values must play role in school reform. *Curriculum Review, 46.*

Brighouse, H., & Swift, A. (2006). Parents' rights and the value of the family. *Ethics, 117,* 80–108.

Brown v. Board of Education, 521 U.S. 203 (1954).

Bryk, A. S., Lee, V. E., & Holland, P. B. (1993). *Catholic schools and the common good.* Cambridge, MA: Harvard University Press.

Bryk, A. S., & Schneider, B. L. (2002). *Trust in schools: A core resource for improvement.* New York, NY: Russell Sage.

Budziszewski, J. (1992). *True tolerance: Liberalism and the necessity of judgment.* New Brunswick, NJ: Transaction.

Butler. (1925) Butler Act, Pub. L. No. H.B. 185 § Chapter 27.

Cain, B. J. (2006). *Competition among high school principals of charter schools, public schools, and voucher-receiving private schools in the District of Columbia* (Dissertation). Retrieved from http://proquest.umi.com/pqdweb?did=1147 184381&Fmt=7&clientId=65345&RQT=309&VName=PQD

Callan, E. (1997). *Creating citizens: Political education and liberal democracy.* Oxford, UK; New York, NY: Clarendon Press; Oxford University Press.

Campbell, D. (2008). The civic side of school choice: An empirical analysis of civc education in public and private schools. *Brigham Young University Law Review, 2,* 487–524.

Carper, J. C., & Hunt, T. C. (2007). *The dissenting tradition in American education.* New York, NY: P. Lang.

Carter, S. L. (1994). *The culture of disbelief: How American law and politics trivialize religious devotion.* New York, NY: Anchor.

Carter, S. L. (2000). *God's name in vain: The wrongs and rights of religion in politics.* New York, NY: Basic.

Chakrabarti, R. (2004). *Impact of voucher design on public school performance and student sorting: Theory and evidence* (Dissertation). Retrieved from http:// proquest.umi.com/pqdweb?did=813761521&Fmt=7&clientId=65345&R QT=309&VName=PQD

Chubb, J. E., & Moe, T. M. (1990). *Politics, markets, and America's schools.* Washington, DC: Brookings Institution.

Chubb, J. E., & Moe, T. M. (1991). Schools in a marketplace: Chubb and Moe argue their bold proposal. *School Administrator, 48*(1), 18–25.

Code of Canon Law: 795. (2007). *IntraText CT.* Retrieved August 15, 2012, from http://www.intratext.com/ixt/ENG0017/_P2L.HTM

Coleman, J. (1998). Civic pedagogies and liberal-democratic curricula. *Ethics, 108*(July), 746–761.

Coleman, J. S. (1991). *Changes in family and implications for the common school* (No. 1991) (p. 153). Universtiy of Chicago Legal Forum.

Coleman, J. S. (1992). Some points on choice in education. *Sociology of Education, 65*(4), 260–262.

Coleman, J. S., & Hoffer, T. (1987). *Public and private high schools: The impact of communities.* New York, NY: Basic.

Cooper, B. S., McSween, R. B., & Murphy, P. (2012). Finding a golden mean in education policy. *Peabody Journal of Education, 87*(3), 368–382.

Cornelius, R. M., (Ed.) (1996). *Selected orations of William Jennings Bryan: The cross of gold centennial edition.* Dayton, TN: William Jennings Bryan College.

Costa, M. V. (2004). Rawlsian civic education: Political not minimal. *Journal of Applied Philosophy, 21*(1), 1–14.

Crittenden, B. S. (1988). *Parents, the state and the right to educate.* Carlton, Victoria, Australia: Melbourne University Press.

Curran, F. X. (1954). *The churches and the schools: American Protestantism and popular elementary education.* Chicago, IL: Loyola University Press.

DeRoche, E. F., & Williams, M. M. (2001). *Character education: A guide for school administrators.* Lanham, MD: Scarecrow Education.

Dewey, J. (1903). *Ethical principles underlying education.* Chicago, IL: University of Chicago Press.

Dewey, J. (1909). *Moral principles in education.* New York, NY: Houghton Mifflin.

Doyle, D. P. (1997). Education and character: A conservative view. *Phi Delta Kappan, 78*(6), 440–443.

Dunn, W. K. (1958). *What happened to religious education? The decline of religious teaching in the public elementary school, 1776–1861.* Baltimore, MD: Johns Hopkins Press.

Dwyer, J. G. (1998). *Religious schools v. children's rights.* Ithaca, NY: Cornell University Press.

Eberle, C. J. (2002). *Religious conviction in liberal politics.* Cambridge, UK; New York, NY: Cambridge University Press.

Edelmann, T. B. (1997). Schools and neighborhoods: Stabilizing partners. *Momentum, 28*(4), 54–56.

Ellwood, R. S. (1994). *The sixties spiritual awakening: American religion moving from modern to postmodern.* New Brunswick, NJ: Rutgers University Press.

Ellwood, R. S. (1997). *The fifties spiritual marketplace: American religion in a decade of conflict.* New Brunswick, NJ: Rutgers University Press.

Elson, R. M. (1964). *Guardians of tradition: American schoolbooks of the nineteenth century.* Lincoln: University of Nebraska Press.

Emerson, R. W. (1883). Education. In *Emerson's complete works, lectures and biographical sketches* (Vol. 10, p. 463). Boston: Houghton Mifflin.

Engel v. Vitale, 370 U.S. 421 (1962).

Engelhardt, C. S. (2009). The necessary role of religion in civic education. In S. P. Jones & E. Sheffield (Eds.), *The role of religion in 21st century public schools* (1st ed., Vol. 374, pp. 163–186). New York, NY: Peter Lang.

Engelhardt, C. S. (2012). Protestant education in Australia: A public asset. In W. H. Jeynes & D. W. Robinson (Eds.), *International handbook of Protestant education* (Vol. 6, pp. 481–506). New York, NY: Springer.

Epperson v. Arkansas, 393 U.S. 97 (1968).

Everson v. Board of Education, 330 U.S. 1 (1947).

Feinberg, W. (2006). *For goodness sake: Religious schools and education of democratic citizenry.* New York, NY: Routledge.

Finn, C. E. (2005). Character education and the challenge of raising a moral generation. In N. Garfinkle & D. Yankelovich (Eds.), *Uniting America: Restoring the vital center to American democracy.* New Haven, CT: Yale University Press.

Forster, G., & Thompson, C. B. (Eds.). (2011). *Freedom and school choice in American education* (1st ed.). New York, NY: Palgrave Macmillan.

Fraser, J. W. (1999). *Between church and state: Religion and public education in a multicultural America.* New York, NY: St. Martin's.

Fraser, J. W. (2001). *The school in the United States: A documentary history.* Boston, MA: McGraw-Hill.

Friedman, M. (1955). The role of government in education. In R. A. Solo (Ed.), (Vol. Economics and the Public Interest). New Brunswick, NJ: Rutgers University Press.

Friedman, M. (1962). *Capitalism and freedom.* Chicago, IL: Chicago University Press.

Fritch, W. S. (1999). Large or small? Public or private? What matters most in the formation of social capital (pp. 1–31). (ERIC Document Reproduction Services No. ED430293)

Fritch, W. S. (2001). The value of religion in uniting a school community capable of forming social capital (pp. 1–26). (ERIC Document Reproduction Services No. ED453303)

Galston, W. A. (1991). *Liberal purposes: Goods, virtues, and diversity in the liberal state.* Cambridge, MA; New York, NY: Cambridge University Press.

Galston, W. A. (2002). *Liberal pluralism: The implications of value pluralism for political theory and practice.* Cambridge, UK; New York, NY: Cambridge University Press.

Galston, W. A. (2004). Liberal pluralism and constitutional democracy: The case of freedom of conscience. *Philosophy of Public Policy Quarterly, 24*(3), 21–27.

Garfinkle, N., & Yankelovich, D. (2006). *Uniting America: Restoring the vital center to American democracy.* New Haven, CT; Yale University Press.

Gaus, G. F. (2003). *Contemporary theories of liberalism: Public reason as a post-Enlightenment project.* London, UK; Thousand Oaks, CA: Sage.

Geertz, C. (1973). *The interpretation of cultures: Selected essays.* New York, NY: Basic.

Gibbons, J. (1916). *A retrospect of fifty years.* Baltimore, MD; New York, NY: John Murphy.

Gilles, S. G. (1996). On educating children: A parentalist manifesto. *The University of Chicago Law Review, 63*(3), 937–1034.

Gimpel, J. G., Lay, J. C., & Schuknecht, J. E. (2003). *Cultivating democracy: Civic environments and political socialization in America.* Washington, DC: Brookings Institution.

Giordano, G. (2003). *Twentieth-century textbook wars: A history of advocacy and opposition* (Vol. 17). New York, NY: Peter Lang.

Glanzer, P. L. (2003). Did the moral education establishment kill character? An autopsy of the death of character. *Journal of Moral Education, 32*(3), 291–306.

Glendon, M. A. (2006). *Traditions in turmoil.* Ann Arbor, MI: Sapientia Press of Ave Maria University.

Glendon, M. A., & Blankenhorn, D. (1995). *Seedbeds of virtue: Sources of competence, character, and citizenship.* Lanham, MD: Madison.

Glenn, C. L. (1987). The new common school. *Phi Delta Kappan, 69*(4), 290–294.

Glenn, C. L. (1988). *The myth of the common school.* Amherst: University of Massachusetts Press.

Glenn, C. L. (1989). *Choice of schools in six nations: France, Netherlands, Belgium, Britain, Canada, West Germany.* Washington, DC: Department of Education, Office of Educational Research and Improvement.

Glenn, C. L. (2000). *The ambiguous embrace: Government and faith-based schools and social agencies.* Princeton, NJ: Princeton University Press.

Glenn, C. L. (2005). The challenge of diversity and choice. *Educational Horizons, 83*(2), 101–109.

Glenn, C. L. (2011). Contrasting models of state and school: A comparative historical study of parental choice and state control. New York, NY: Continuum.

Glenn, C. L., & Cook (2004). Vouchers choice & controversy. *American School Board Journal, 191*(1), 1–6.

Glenn, C. L., & de Groof, J. (2002). *Finding the right balance: Freedom, autonomy and accountability in education* (Vol. 1). Utrecht, The Netherlands: Lemma; Lafayette, IN: Purdue University Press.

Glenn, M., & Gininger, M. (2012). School choice now: The year of school choice–School Choice yearbook 2011–12 (p. 80). *Alliance for School Choice.* Retrieved from http://www.allianceforschoolchoice.org/yearbook

Goodlad, J. I., & McMannon, T. J. (Eds.). (1997). *The public purpose of education and schooling.* San Francisco, CA: Jossey-Bass.

Grant, U. S. (1898). General Grant's Des Moines speech: The circumstances of remarkable utterances. In *The Century* (Vol. 55). New York, NY: Century Company.

Greenawalt, K. (1995). *Private consciences and public reasons.* New York, NY: Oxford University Press.

Greene, J. P. (2005). *Education myths: What special interest groups want you to believe about our schools—And why it isn't so.* Lanham, MD: Rowman & Littlefield.

Greene, J. P., & Mellow, N. (1998, September 3–6). *Integration where it counts: A study of racial integration in public and private school lunchrooms* (p. 30). Paper presented at the meeting of the American Political Science Association, Boston, MA.

Greil, A. L., & Bromley, D. G. (Eds.). (2003). *Defining religion: Investigating the boundaries between the sacred and secular* (Vol. 10). Amsterdam, The Netherlands; Boston, MA: JAI.

Griffin v. County School Board of Prince Edward County, 377 U.S. 218 (1964).

Griffin v. State Board of Education, 296 F. Supp. 11789 (1969).

Gutmann, A. (1999). *Democratic education.* Princeton, NJ: Princeton University Press.

Gutmann, A. (2002). Civic minimalism, cosmopolitanism, and patriotism: Where does democratic education stand in relation to each? In S. Macedo & Y. Tamir (Eds.), *Moral and political education* (pp. 23–57). New York: New York University Press.

Gutmann, A., & Thompson, D. F. (1996). *Democracy and disagreement.* Cambridge, MA: Belknap.

Gutmann, A., & Thompson, D. F. (2004). *Why deliberative democracy?* Princeton, NJ: Princeton University Press.

Hamilton, A., Madison, J., & Jay, J. (1818). *The Federalist, on the new constitution.* Philadelphia, PA: Benjamin Warner.

Hand, M. (2004). The problem with faith schools: A reply to my critics. *Theory and Research in Education, 2*(3), 343–353.

Handy, R. T. (1991). *Undermined establishment: Church-state relations in America, 1880–1920.* Princeton, NJ: Princeton University Press.

Hauerwas, S. (1991). *After Christendom? How the church is to behave if freedom, justice, and a Christian nation are bad ideas.* Nashville, TN: Abingdon.

Hauerwas, S., & Westerhoff, J. H. (1992). *Schooling Christians: "Holy experiments" in American education.* Grand Rapids, MI: W.B. Eerdmans.

Haydon, G. (1995). Thick or thin? The cognitive content of moral education in a plural democracy. *Journal of Moral Education, 24*(1), 53–64.

Healey, R. M. (1962). *Jefferson on religion in public education* (Vol. 3). New Haven, CT: Yale University Press.

Hening, W. W. (Ed.). (1823). *The statutes at large: Being a collection of all the laws of Virginia from the first session of the legislature, in the year 1619* (Vol. 12). Richmond, VA: George Cochan.

Herberg, W. (1960). *Protestant, Catholic, Jew: An essay in American religious sociology.* Garden City, NY: Anchor.

Howard, R. W., Berkowitz, M. W., & Schaeffer, E. F. (2004). Politics of character education. *Educational Policy, 18*(1), 188–215.

Hunt, T. C., & Carper, J. C. (1997). *Religion and schooling in contemporary America: Confronting our cultural pluralism* (Vol. 50). New York, NY: Garland.

Hunt, T. C., & Mullins, M. (2005). *Moral education in America's schools: The continuing challenge.* Greenwich, CT: Information Age.

Hunter, J. D. (1991). *Culture wars: The struggle to define America.* New York, NY: Basic.

Hunter, J. D. (2000). *The death of character: Moral education in an age without good or evil.* New York, NY: Basic.

Huntington, S. P. (1996). *The clash of civilizations and the remaking of world order.* New York, NY: Simon & Schuster.

Isin, E. F., & Wood, P. K. (1999). *Citizenship and identity.* London, UK; Thousand Oaks, CA: Sage.

Jefferson, T. (1816). Quotations on education. *The Jefferson Monticello*. Retrieved August 8, 2012, from http://www.monticello.org/site/jefferson/quotations-education

Jeynes, W. H. (2003). *Religion, education, and academic success*. Greenwich, CT: Information Age.

Jeynes, W. H. (2005). The relationship between urban students attending religious revival services and academic and social outcomes. *Education & Urban Society, 38*(1), 3–20.

Jeynes, W. H. (2007a). Religion, intact families, and the achievement gap. *Interdisciplinary Journal of Research on Religion, 3*, 2–24.

Jeynes, W. H. (2007b). *American educational history: School, society, and the common good*. Thousand Oaks, CA: Sage.

Jeynes, W. H. (2008). The academic contributions of faith-based schools. *White House Summit on Inner-City Children and Faith-Based Schools Proceedings*.

Jeynes, W. H. (2009). *A call for character education and prayer in the schools*. Westport, CT: Praeger.

Jeynes, W. H., & Robinson, D. W. (Eds.). (2012). *International handbook of Protestant education* (Vol. 6). New York, NY; London, UK: Springer.

Ji, C-H. C. (2010). *Religiosity, cultural capital, and parochial schooling: Psychological empirical research*. Charlotte, N.C: Information Age.

Jones, S. L. (Ed.). (2008). *Religious schooling in America: Private education and public life*. Westport, CT: Praeger.

Jorgenson, L. P. (1987). *The state and the non-public school, 1825–1925*. Columbia: University of Missouri Press.

Kaestle, C. F. (1983). *Pillars of the republic: Common schools and American society, 1780–1860*. New York, NY: Hill and Wang.

Kaestle, C. F. (1984). Moral education and common schools in America: A historians view. *Journal of Moral Education, 13*, 101–111.

Kant, I. (1785). *Groundwork of the metaphysics of morals*.

Kilpatrick, W. (1992). *Why Johnny can't tell right from wrong*. New York, NY: Touchstone.

Kimball, B. A. (1995). *Orators & philosophers: A history of the idea of liberal education*. New York, NY: College Board.

Kleitz, B. R. (2005). *Civic education: A comparison of public and private schools in their ability to transmit democratic values*. (Dissertation, University of Houston) Retrieved from http://proquest.umi.com/pqdweb?did=913514661&Fmt=7&clientId=65345&RQT=309&VName=PQD

Kohlberg, L. (1981). *The philosophy of moral development: Moral stages and the idea of justice* (Vol. 1). San Francisco, CA: Harper & Row.

Kohlberg, L. (1984). *The psychology of moral development: The nature and validity of moral stages* (Vol. 2). San Francisco, CA: Harper & Row.

Kunzman, R. (2006). *Grappling with the good: Talking about religion and morality in public schools*. Albany: State University of New York Press.

Kymlicka, W. (2001). *Politics in the vernacular: Nationalism, multiculturalism, and citizenship.* Oxford, UK; New York, NY: Oxford University Press.

Kymlicka, W., & Norman, W. J. (2000). *Citizenship in diverse societies.* Oxford, UK; New York, NY: Oxford University Press.

Larson, E. J. (2006). *Summer for the gods: The Scopes trial and America's continuing debate over science and religion.* New York, NY; London, UK: Basic.

Leming, J. S. (1993). Synthesis of research: In search of effective character education. *Character Education, 51*(3), 63–71.

Leming, J. S. (1997). *Values and character education in public schools: Should the schools teach moral and civic virtue?* Carbondale: Southern Illinois University.

Leming, J. S. (2001). Historical and ideological perspectives on teaching moral and civic virtue. *International Journal of Social Education, 16*(1), 62–76.

Levinson, M. (1999). *The demands of liberal education.* New York, NY: Oxford University Press.

Levinson, M. (2002). Dilemmas of deliberative civic education. *Philosophy of Education,* 262–270.

Levinson, M. (2003). Challenging deliberation. *Theory and Research in Social Education, 1*(1), 23–49.

Levinson, M. (2004). Is autonomy imposing education too demanding? A response to Dr. De Ruyter. *Studies in Philosophy and Education, 23,* 223–233.

Levy, L. W. (1963). *Jefferson & civil liberties: The darker side.* Chicago, IL: I.R. Dee, 1989.

Lickona, T. (1991). *Educating for character: How our schools can teach respect and responsibility.* New York, NY: Bantam.

Lieberman, M. (2007). *The educational morass: Overcoming the stalemate in American education.* Lanham, MD: Rowman & Littlefield Education.

Linder, R. D., & Pierard, R. V. (1978). *Twilight of the saints: Biblical Christianity & civil religion in America.* Downers Grove, IL: InterVarsity Press.

Locke, J. (1824). *The works of John Locke in nine volumes* (12th ed., Vols. 1–9, Vol. 4). London, UK: Rivington. Retrieved from http://oll.libertyfund.org/title/763

Lynn, R. W. (1964). *Protestant strategies in education.* New York, NY: Association.

Macedo, S. (1991). *Liberal virtues: Citizenship, virtue, and community in liberal constitutionalism.* Oxford, UK; New York, NY: Clarendon Press; Oxford University Press.

Macedo, S. (1995). Liberal civic education and its limits. *Canadian Journal of Education, 20*(3), 304–314.

Macedo, S. (2000). *Diversity and distrust: Civic education in a multicultural democracy.* Cambridge, MA: Harvard University Press.

Macedo, S. (2005). *Democracy at risk: How political choices undermine citizen participation and what we can do about it.* Washington, DC: Brookings Institution.

Macedo, S., & Tamir, Y. (2002). *Moral and political education.* New York: New York University Press.

MacIntyre, A. (1999). How to seem virtuous without actually being so. In J. M. Halstead & T. McLaughlin (Eds.), *Education in morality* (Vol. 8). London, UK; New York, NY: Routledge.

MacMullen, I. (2004). Education for autonomy: The role of religious elementary schools. *Journal of Philosophy of Education, 38*(4), 601–615.

MacMullen, I. (2007). *Faith in schools?: Autonomy, citizenship, and religious education in the liberal state.* Princeton, NJ: Princeton University Press.

Madison, J. (2012). Speeches in the Virginia convention. 1–The Writings, vol. 5 (1787–1790). *Online Library of Liberty.* Retrieved August 9, 2012, from http://oll.libertyfund.org/?option=com_staticxt&staticfile=show.php%3Ftitle=1937&chapter=118812&layout=html&Itemid=27#a_2400442

Mann, H. (1838). Untitled editorial. *The Common School Journal, 1*(November), 14.

Mann, H. (1848). *Twelfth annual report.* Massachusetts State Board of Education.

Mann, H. (1891). *Annual reports of the secretary of the Board of Education of Massachusetts for the years 1845–1848.* New York, NY: Lee and Shepard.

Marsden, G. M. (1990). *Religion and American culture.* San Diego, CA: Harcourt Brace Jovanovich.

Marsden, G. M. (1994). *The soul of the American university: From protestant establishment to established nonbelief.* New York, NY: Oxford University Press.

Marsden, G. M. (1997). *The outrageous idea of Christian scholarship.* New York, NY: Oxford University Press.

Martin, W. C. (1996). *With God on our side: The rise of the religious right in America.* New York, NY: Broadway.

Marty, M. E. (2010). *Building cultures of trust.* Grand Rapids, MI: W.B. Eerdmans.

Marty, M. E., & Moore, J. (2000). *Politics, religion, and the common good: Advancing a distinctly American conversation about religion's role in our shared life.* San Francisco, CA: Jossey-Bass.

Maton, K. I., & Wells, E. A. (1995). Religion as a community resource for well-being: prevention, healing, and empowerment pathways. *Journal of Social Issues, 51*(2), 177–193. doi:10.1111/j.1540-4560.1995.tb01330.x

McClellan, B. (1992). *Schools and the shaping of character: Moral education in America, 1607–present.* Bloomington: Social Studies Development Center, Indiana University.

McClellan, B. (1999). *Moral education in America: Schools and the shaping of character from colonial times to the present.* New York, NY: Teachers College Press.

McCluskey, N. G. (1958). *Public schools and moral education: The influence of Horace Mann, William Torrey Harris, and John Dewey.* New York, NY: Columbia University Press.

McCluskey, N. G. (2007). *Why we fight: How public schools cause social conflict* (Policy Analysis #587.). Washington, DC: Cato Institute.

McConnell, M. W. (1996). Don't neglect the little platoons. In *For love of country: Debating the limits of patriotism.* Boston, MA: Beacon.

McConnell, M. W. (2002). Education disestablishment: Why democratic values are ill-served by democratic control of schooling. In S. Macedo & Y. Tamir (Eds.), *Moral and political education*. New York: New York University Press.

McConnell, M. W., Cochran, R. F., & Carmella, A. C. (2001). *Christian perspectives on legal thought*. New Haven, CT: Yale University Press.

McGreevy, J. T. (2003). *Catholicism and American freedom: A history*. New York, NY: W.W. Norton.

McKown, H. C. (1935). *Character education*. New York, NY; London, UK: McGraw-Hill.

McLaughlin, T. (1984). Parental rights and the religious upbringing of children. *Journal of Philosophy of Education, 19*(1), 119–127.

Mead, S. E. (1963). *The lively experiment: The shaping of Christianity in America*. New York, NY: Harper & Row.

Merry, M. S. (2005). Cultural coherence and the schooling for identity maintenance. *Journal of Philosophy of Education, 39*(3), 477–497.

Miller, D. L. (2012). *Emancipating the world: A Christian response to radical Islam and fundamentalist atheism*. Seattle, WA: YWAM.

Milson, A. J., Bohan, C. H., Glanzer, P. L., & Null, J. W. (Eds.). (2004). *Readings in American educational thought: From puritanism to progressivism*. Greenwich, CT: Information Age.

Moe, T. (2001). Teachers unions and the public school. In T. M. Moe (Ed.), *A primer on America's schools* (pp. 151–184). Stanford, CS: Hoover Institution Press, Stanford University.

Molnar, A. (1997). *The construction of children's character* (Vol. 2). Chicago, IL: National Society for the Study of Education.

Nash, R. J. (1997). *Answering the "virtuecrats": A moral conversation on character education* (Vol. 21). New York, NY: Teachers College Press.

National Education Association, D. of S. (1952). *Tenth yearbook: Character education*. Washington, DC: National Education Association.

Neuhaus, R. J. (1995). *The naked public square: Religion and democracy in America*. Grand Rapids, MI: W.B. Eerdmans.

New York Bill on History Textbooks. (1923, March). *School and Society*, (17), 349.

Noddings, N. (2007). *When school reform goes wrong*. New York, NY: Teachers College Press.

Nolen, E. W. (1942). The colored child in contemporary literature. *Hornbook, 18*, 348–355.

Noll, M. A. (1992). *A history of Christianity in the United States and Canada*. Grand Rapids, MI: William B. Eerdmans.

Nord, W. A. (1995). *Religion & American education: Rethinking a national dilemma*. Chapel Hill: University of North Carolina Press.

Null, J. W. (2011). *Curriculum: From theory to practice*. Lanham, MD: Rowman & Littlefield.

Nussbaum, M. C. (1996). *For love of country: Debating the limits of patriotism*. (J. Cohen, Ed.). Boston, MA: Beacon Press.

Ohio v. Whisner , 351 N.E.2d 750 (Ohio 1976) (N.E. 2d 1976).

Paquette, J. (2005). Public funding for "private" education: The equity challenge of enhanced choice. *American Journal of Education, 111*(4), 568–595.

Parker, W. C. (2005). Teaching against idiocy. *Phi Delta Kappan, 86*(5), 344–351.

Pierce v. Society of Sisters of the Holy Names of Jesus and Mary, 268 U.S. 510 (1925).

Pierce, B. L. (1934). The school and the spirit of nationalism. *Annals of the American Academy of Political and Social Science, 175*, 117–122.

Putnam, R. D. (2000). *Bowling alone: The collapse and revival of American community.* New York, NY: Simon & Schuster.

Putnam, R. D., & Feldstein, L. M. (2003). *Better together: Restoring the American community.* New York, NY: Simon & Schuster.

Ravitch, D. (2010). *The death and life of the great American school system: How testing and choice are undermining education.* New York, NY: Basic.

Rawls, J. (1971). *A theory of justice.* Cambridge, MA: Belknap Press of Harvard University Press.

Rawls, J. (1996). *Political liberalism.* New York, NY: Columbia University Press.

Rawls, J. (1999). *Collected papers: John Rawls* (S. R. Freeman, Ed.). Cambridge, MA: Harvard University Press.

Rawls, J. (2001). *Justice as fairness: A restatement* (E. Kelly, Ed.). Cambridge, MA: Harvard University Press.

Ray, B. (2011). Homeschool population report 2010. *National Home Education Research Institute.* Retrieved from http://www.nheri.org/research/nheri-news/homeschool-population-report-2010.html

Reich, R. (2002). *Bridging liberalism and multiculturalism in American education.* Chicago, IL: University of Chicago Press.

Reich, R. (2003). Liberal pluralism? *Philosophy of Education,* 74–75.

Rippa, S. A. (1992). *Education in a free society: An American history.* New York, NY: Longman.

Rorty, R. (1991). *Objectivity, relativism, and truth* (Vol. 1). Cambridge, UK; New York, NY: Cambridge University Press.

Rosenblum, N. L. (2003). Separating the Siamese twins: "Pluralism" and "school choice." In A. Wolfe (Ed.), *School choice: The moral debate* (pp. 79–103). Princeton, NJ: Princeton University Press.

Rousseau, J. J. (1762). *Emile, or on education.*

Rud, A. G. (2011). *Albert Schweitzer's legacy for education: Reverence for life.* New York, NY: Palgrave Macmillan.

Ryan, K., & Bohlin, K. E. (1999). *Building character in schools: Practical ways to bring moral instruction to life.* San Francisco, CA: Jossey-Bass.

Salisbury, D. F., & Lartigue, C. (2004). *Educational freedom in urban America: Brown v. Board after half a century.* Washington, DC: Cato Institute.

Salomone, R. C. (2000). *Visions of schooling: Conscience, community, and common education.* New Haven, CT: Yale University Press.

Sandel, M. J. (2002). Liberalism, consumerism, and citizenship. In D. D. Allman & M. D. Beaty (Eds.), *Cultivating citizens: Soulcraft and citizenship in contemporary America* (pp. 139–149). Lanham, MD: Lexington.

School District of Abington Township v. Schempp, 364 U.S. 298 (1963).

Schuck, P. H. (2006). Diversity, community, and government. In N. Garfinkle & D. Yankelovich (Eds.), *Uniting America: Restoring the vital center to American democracy* (pp. 109–123). New Haven, CT: Yale University Press.

Scopes, J. T. (n.d.). Reflections on the Scopes trial. *Reflections: Forty Years After.* Retrieved August 13, 2012, from http://law2.umkc.edu/faculty/projects/ftrials/scopes/scopesreflections.html

Scopes v. State of Tennessee, 278 S.W. 57 (1925).

Scorza, J. A. (2001). Teaching citizenship: The liberal dilemma (p. 48). (ERIC Document Reproduction Services No. ED474562) Retrieved from http://www.eric.ed.gov/ERICWebPortal/detail?accno=ED474562

Shapiro, T. M., & Johnson, H. B. (2005). Race, assets, and choosing schools. In J. Petrovich & A. S. Wells (Eds.), *Bringing equity back: Research for a new era in American educational policy* (pp. 244–262). New York, NY: Teachers College Press.

Simon, S. B., Howe, L. W., & Kirschenbaum, H. (1972). *Values clarification: A handbook of practical strategies for teachers and students.* New York, NY: Hart.

Skillen, J. W. (1994). *Recharging the American experiment: Principled pluralism for genuine civic community.* Grand Rapids, MI: Baker.

Smith, S. D. (1995). *Foreordained failure: The quest for a constitutional principle of religious freedom.* New York, NY: Oxford University Press.

Spilka, B., Hood, R. W. Jr, Hunsberger, B., & Gorsuch, R. (2003). *The psychology of religion: An empirical approach* (3rd ed.). New York, NY: Guilford.

Stark, R. (2004). *Exploring the religious life.* Baltimore, MD: Johns Hopkins University Press.

Stevens, M. L. (2001). *Kingdom of children: Culture and controversy in the homeschooling movement.* Princeton, NJ: Princeton University Press.

Strike, K. A. (2003). Toward a liberal conception of school communities: Community and the autonomy argument. *Theory and Research in Education, 1*(2), 171–193.

Taylor, C. (1989). *Sources of the self: The making of the modern identity.* Cambridge, MA: Harvard University Press.

Thiessen, E. J. (1993). *Teaching for commitment: Liberal education, indoctrination, and Christian nurture.* Montreal, Canada: McGill-Queen's University Press.

Thiessen, E. J. (1995). Liberal education, public schools, and the embarrassment of teaching for commitment. *Philosophy of Education,* 473–481.

Thiessen, E. J. (2001). *In defence of religious schools and colleges.* Montreal, Canada: McGill-Queen's University Press.

Thiessen, E. J. (2007). Religious education and committed openness. In M. C. Felderhof, D. Torevell, & P. Thompson (Eds.), *Inspiring faith in schools: Studies in religious education.* Aldershot, UK; Burlington, VT: Ashgate.

Turner, J. (1985). *Without God, without creed: The origins of unbelief in America.* Baltimore, MD: Johns Hopkins University Press.

Viteritti, J. P. (1999). *Choosing equality: School Choice, the Constitution, and civil society.* Washington, DC: Brookings Institution.

Viteritti, J. P. (2007). *The last freedom: Religion from the public school to the public square.* Princeton, NJ: Princeton University Press.

Vryhof, S. C. (2004). *Between memory and vision: The case for faith-based schooling.* Grand Rapids, MI: W.B. Eerdmans.

Vryhof, S. C. (2005). A system where everyone wins: The legitimacy of faith-based schools in a system of choice. *Educational Horizons, 83*(2), 125–142.

Vryhof, S. C. (2012). Between memory and vision: Schools as communities of meaning. In H. A. Alexander & A. K. Agbaria (Eds.), *Commitment, character, and citizenship: Religious education in liberal democracy* (p. 280). New York, NY: Routledge.

Walzer, M. (1996). Spheres of affection. In *For love of country: Debating the limits of patriotism.* Boston, MA: Beacon.

Washington, G. (2008, July 24). *Washington's farewell address (1796).*

Weinberg, L. D. (2007). *Religious charter schools: Legalities and practicalities.* Charlotte, NC: Information Age.

Weithman, P. J. (2002). *Religion and the obligations of citizenship.* Cambridge, UK; New York, NY: Cambridge University Press.

West Virginia State Board of Education v. Barnette, 319 U.S. 624 (1943).

Westbrook, R. B. (1991). *John Dewey and American democracy.* Ithaca, NY: Cornell University Press.

Winch, C. (2002). Strong autonomy and education. *Educational Theory, 52*(1), 27–41.

Witte, J. (2000). *Religion and the American constitutional experiment: Essential rights and liberties.* Boulder, CO: Westview.

Wolf, P. J. (2005). School choice and civic values. In J. R. Betts & T. Loveless (Eds.), *Getting choice right: Ensuring equity and efficiency in education policy.* Washington, DC: Brookings Institution.

Wolfe, A. (2005). Religion as unifier and divider. In N. Garfinkle & D. Yankelovich (Eds.), *Uniting America: Restoring the vital center to American democracy.* New Haven, CT: Yale University Press.

Wolterstorff, N. (1980). *Educating for responsible action.* Grand Rapids, MI: CSI; Eerdmans.

Woolcock, M. (2001). The place of social capital in understanding social and economic outcomes. *Isuma: Canadian Journal of Policy Research, 2*(1), 1–17.

Wuthnow, R. (1991). *Acts of compassion: Caring for others and helping ourselves.* Princeton, NJ: Princeton University Press.

Zelman v. Simmons-Harris, 536 U.S. 639 (2002).

About the Author

Craig S. Engelhardt is the director of the Society for the Advancement of Christian Education (SACE). A former teacher and administrator, he holds a BS in history and political science, an MA in educational administration, and a PhD from Baylor University in Religion, Politics, and Society. He is a writer and consultant on issues of public education and religious schooling. He is married with two children and lives in Waco, Texas.

Education Reform, page 223
Copyright © 2013 by Information Age Publishing

CPSIA information can be obtained at www.ICGtesting.com
Printed in the USA
LVOW102106120513

333313LV00002B/3/P